C-4978 CAREER EXAMINATION

This is your
PASSBOOK for...

Court Clerical Assistant

Test Preparation Study Guide
Questions & Answers

NLC®

NATIONAL LEARNING CORPORATION®

COPYRIGHT NOTICE

This book is SOLELY intended for, is sold ONLY to, and its use is RESTRICTED to individual, bona fide applicants or candidates who qualify by virtue of having seriously filed applications for appropriate license, certificate, professional and/or promotional advancement, higher school matriculation, scholarship, or other legitimate requirements of education and/or governmental authorities.

This book is NOT intended for use, class instruction, tutoring, training, duplication, copying, reprinting, excerption, or adaptation, etc., by:

1) Other publishers
2) Proprietors and/or Instructors of "Coaching" and/or Preparatory Courses
3) Personnel and/or Training Divisions of commercial, industrial, and governmental organizations
4) Schools, colleges, or universities and/or their departments and staffs, including teachers and other personnel
5) Testing Agencies or Bureaus
6) Study groups which seek by the purchase of a single volume to copy and/or duplicate and/or adapt this material for use by the group as a whole without having purchased individual volumes for each of the members of the group
7) Et al.

Such persons would be in violation of appropriate Federal and State statutes.

PROVISION OF LICENSING AGREEMENTS – Recognized educational, commercial, industrial, and governmental institutions and organizations, and others legitimately engaged in educational pursuits, including training, testing, and measurement activities, may address request for a licensing agreement to the copyright owners, who will determine whether, and under what conditions, including fees and charges, the materials in this book may be used them. In other words, a licensing facility exists for the legitimate use of the material in this book on other than an individual basis. However, it is asseverated and affirmed here that the material in this book CANNOT be used without the receipt of the express permission of such a licensing agreement from the Publishers. Inquiries re licensing should be addressed to the company, attention rights and permissions department.

All rights reserved, including the right of reproduction in whole or in part, in any form or by any means, electronic or mechanical, including photocopying, recording, or by any information storage and retrieval system, without permission in writing from the Publisher.

Copyright © 2024 by
National Learning Corporation

212 Michael Drive, Syosset, NY 11791
(516) 921-8888 • www.passbooks.com
E-mail: info@passbooks.com

PUBLISHED IN THE UNITED STATES OF AMERICA

PASSBOOK® SERIES

THE *PASSBOOK® SERIES* has been created to prepare applicants and candidates for the ultimate academic battlefield – the examination room.

At some time in our lives, each and every one of us may be required to take an examination – for validation, matriculation, admission, qualification, registration, certification, or licensure.

Based on the assumption that every applicant or candidate has met the basic formal educational standards, has taken the required number of courses, and read the necessary texts, the *PASSBOOK® SERIES* furnishes the one special preparation which may assure passing with confidence, instead of failing with insecurity. Examination questions – together with answers – are furnished as the basic vehicle for study so that the mysteries of the examination and its compounding difficulties may be eliminated or diminished by a sure method.

This book is meant to help you pass your examination provided that you qualify and are serious in your objective.

The entire field is reviewed through the huge store of content information which is succinctly presented through a provocative and challenging approach – the question-and-answer method.

A climate of success is established by furnishing the correct answers at the end of each test.

You soon learn to recognize types of questions, forms of questions, and patterns of questioning. You may even begin to anticipate expected outcomes.

You perceive that many questions are repeated or adapted so that you can gain acute insights, which may enable you to score many sure points.

You learn how to confront new questions, or types of questions, and to attack them confidently and work out the correct answers.

You note objectives and emphases, and recognize pitfalls and dangers, so that you may make positive educational adjustments.

Moreover, you are kept fully informed in relation to new concepts, methods, practices, and directions in the field.

You discover that you are actually taking the examination all the time: you are preparing for the examination by "taking" an examination, not by reading extraneous and/or supererogatory textbooks.

In short, this PASSBOOK®, used directedly, should be an important factor in helping you to pass your test.

COURT CLERICAL ASSISTANT

DUTIES

Under supervision, Clerical Assistants work with a limited degree of independence on a variety of office support and clerical tasks such as checking, sorting, filing, scanning, and retrieving court papers, keyboarding and data entering information, and responding to customer inquiries. Clerical Assistants may work at public counters as information clerks, may work in courts of every jurisdiction as part clerks in those parts that operate on less than a full-time basis, and perform other related duties. Clerical Assistants are located in courts of every jurisdiction, County Clerks' and Commissioners of Jurors' Offices, law libraries, and administrative offices and auxiliary agencies in the Unified Court System.

SUBJECT OF EXAMINATION

The written exam is designed to cover knowledge, skills and abilities in such areas as:

1. **Clerical checking** - These questions assess applicants' ability to distinguish between sets of names, numbers, letters and/or codes which are almost exactly alike. There are three sets of information which may appear in different fonts. Applicants will be asked to compare the information in the three sets and identify whether the sets differ. Applicants must use the directions provided to determine the correct answer.
2. **Coding and decoding** - These questions assess applicants' ability to use written sets of directions to encode information and use coded information for keeping records. Applicants will be presented with a table of coded information and then be asked to apply a set of coding rules to encode information accurately.
3. **Filing** - These questions assess applicants' ability to arrange information into files according to categories specified by the directions in alphabetical, numerical and chronological order. Questions are based on the completed files.
4. **Reading, understanding and interpreting written material** - These questions assess applicants' ability to understand brief written passages. Applicants will be provided with short written passages from which words or phrases have been removed. Applicants will be required to select from four alternatives the word or phrase that logically completes the sentence within the passage when inserted for the missing word or phrase.
5. **Number facility** - These questions assess applicants' ability to perform basic calculations involving addition, subtraction, multiplication, division, and percentages. These questions do not require the use of a calculator, and calculators will not be permitted at the test center.
6. **Preparing written material** - These questions assess applicants' ability to apply the rules of English grammar and usage, punctuation, and sentence structure. Applicants will be presented with a series of sentences and must select the sentence that best conforms to standard English grammar and usage, punctuation, and sentence structure.
7. **Applying facts and information to given situations** - These questions assess applicants' ability to use the information provided and apply it to a specific situation defined by a given set of facts. Applicants are presented with a regulation, policy or procedure similar to what a Clerical Assistant may encounter on the job. Applicants must use this information to answer questions about specific situations. All of the information required to answer the questions is contained in the passages and in the description of the situation.
8. **Court record keeping** - These questions assess applicants' ability to read, combine, and manipulate written information organized from several sources. Applicants will be presented with different types of tables, which contain names, numbers, codes and other information, and must combine and reorganize the information to answer specific questions.

HOW TO TAKE A TEST

I. YOU MUST PASS AN EXAMINATION

A. WHAT EVERY CANDIDATE SHOULD KNOW

Examination applicants often ask us for help in preparing for the written test. What can I study in advance? What kinds of questions will be asked? How will the test be given? How will the papers be graded?

As an applicant for a civil service examination, you may be wondering about some of these things. Our purpose here is to suggest effective methods of advance study and to describe civil service examinations.

Your chances for success on this examination can be increased if you know how to prepare. Those "pre-examination jitters" can be reduced if you know what to expect. You can even experience an adventure in good citizenship if you know why civil service exams are given.

B. WHY ARE CIVIL SERVICE EXAMINATIONS GIVEN?

Civil service examinations are important to you in two ways. As a citizen, you want public jobs filled by employees who know how to do their work. As a job seeker, you want a fair chance to compete for that job on an equal footing with other candidates. The best-known means of accomplishing this two-fold goal is the competitive examination.

Exams are widely publicized throughout the nation. They may be administered for jobs in federal, state, city, municipal, town or village governments or agencies.

Any citizen may apply, with some limitations, such as the age or residence of applicants. Your experience and education may be reviewed to see whether you meet the requirements for the particular examination. When these requirements exist, they are reasonable and applied consistently to all applicants. Thus, a competitive examination may cause you some uneasiness now, but it is your privilege and safeguard.

C. HOW ARE CIVIL SERVICE EXAMS DEVELOPED?

Examinations are carefully written by trained technicians who are specialists in the field known as "psychological measurement," in consultation with recognized authorities in the field of work that the test will cover. These experts recommend the subject matter areas or skills to be tested; only those knowledges or skills important to your success on the job are included. The most reliable books and source materials available are used as references. Together, the experts and technicians judge the difficulty level of the questions.

Test technicians know how to phrase questions so that the problem is clearly stated. Their ethics do not permit "trick" or "catch" questions. Questions may have been tried out on sample groups, or subjected to statistical analysis, to determine their usefulness.

Written tests are often used in combination with performance tests, ratings of training and experience, and oral interviews. All of these measures combine to form the best-known means of finding the right person for the right job.

II. HOW TO PASS THE WRITTEN TEST

A. NATURE OF THE EXAMINATION

To prepare intelligently for civil service examinations, you should know how they differ from school examinations you have taken. In school you were assigned certain definite pages to read or subjects to cover. The examination questions were quite detailed and usually emphasized memory. Civil service exams, on the other hand, try to discover your present ability to perform the duties of a position, plus your potentiality to learn these duties. In other words, a civil service exam attempts to predict how successful you will be. Questions cover such a broad area that they cannot be as minute and detailed as school exam questions.

In the public service similar kinds of work, or positions, are grouped together in one "class." This process is known as *position-classification*. All the positions in a class are paid according to the salary range for that class. One class title covers all of these positions, and they are all tested by the same examination.

B. FOUR BASIC STEPS

1) Study the announcement

How, then, can you know what subjects to study? Our best answer is: "Learn as much as possible about the class of positions for which you've applied." The exam will test the knowledge, skills and abilities needed to do the work.

Your most valuable source of information about the position you want is the official exam announcement. This announcement lists the training and experience qualifications. Check these standards and apply only if you come reasonably close to meeting them.

The brief description of the position in the examination announcement offers some clues to the subjects which will be tested. Think about the job itself. Review the duties in your mind. Can you perform them, or are there some in which you are rusty? Fill in the blank spots in your preparation.

Many jurisdictions preview the written test in the exam announcement by including a section called "Knowledge and Abilities Required," "Scope of the Examination," or some similar heading. Here you will find out specifically what fields will be tested.

2) Review your own background

Once you learn in general what the position is all about, and what you need to know to do the work, ask yourself which subjects you already know fairly well and which need improvement. You may wonder whether to concentrate on improving your strong areas or on building some background in your fields of weakness. When the announcement has specified "some knowledge" or "considerable knowledge," or has used adjectives like "beginning principles of..." or "advanced ... methods," you can get a clue as to the number and difficulty of questions to be asked in any given field. More questions, and hence broader coverage, would be included for those subjects which are more important in the work. Now weigh your strengths and weaknesses against the job requirements and prepare accordingly.

3) Determine the level of the position

Another way to tell how intensively you should prepare is to understand the level of the job for which you are applying. Is it the entering level? In other words, is this the position in which beginners in a field of work are hired? Or is it an intermediate or advanced level? Sometimes this is indicated by such words as "Junior" or "Senior" in the class title. Other jurisdictions use Roman numerals to designate the level – Clerk I, Clerk II, for example. The word "Supervisor" sometimes appears in the title. If the level is not indicated by the title, check the description of duties. Will you be working under very close supervision, or will you have responsibility for independent decisions in this work?

4) Choose appropriate study materials

Now that you know the subjects to be examined and the relative amount of each subject to be covered, you can choose suitable study materials. For beginning level jobs, or even advanced ones, if you have a pronounced weakness in some aspect of your training, read a modern, standard textbook in that field. Be sure it is up to date and has general coverage. Such books are normally available at your library, and the librarian will be glad to help you locate one. For entry-level positions, questions of appropriate difficulty are chosen – neither highly advanced questions, nor those too simple. Such questions require careful thought but not advanced training.

If the position for which you are applying is technical or advanced, you will read more advanced, specialized material. If you are already familiar with the basic principles of your field, elementary textbooks would waste your time. Concentrate on advanced textbooks and technical periodicals. Think through the concepts and review difficult problems in your field.

These are all general sources. You can get more ideas on your own initiative, following these leads. For example, training manuals and publications of the government agency which employs workers in your field can be useful, particularly for technical and professional positions. A letter or visit to the government department involved may result in more specific study suggestions, and certainly will provide you with a more definite idea of the exact nature of the position you are seeking.

III. KINDS OF TESTS

Tests are used for purposes other than measuring knowledge and ability to perform specified duties. For some positions, it is equally important to test ability to make adjustments to new situations or to profit from training. In others, basic mental abilities not dependent on information are essential. Questions which test these things may not appear as pertinent to the duties of the position as those which test for knowledge and information. Yet they are often highly important parts of a fair examination. For very general questions, it is almost impossible to help you direct your study efforts. What we can do is to point out some of the more common of these general abilities needed in public service positions and describe some typical questions.

1) General information

Broad, general information has been found useful for predicting job success in some kinds of work. This is tested in a variety of ways, from vocabulary lists to questions about current events. Basic background in some field of work, such as sociology or economics, may be sampled in a group of questions. Often these are principles which have become familiar to most persons through exposure rather than through formal training. It is difficult to advise you how to study for these questions; being alert to the world around you is our best suggestion.

2) Verbal ability

An example of an ability needed in many positions is verbal or language ability. Verbal ability is, in brief, the ability to use and understand words. Vocabulary and grammar tests are typical measures of this ability. Reading comprehension or paragraph interpretation questions are common in many kinds of civil service tests. You are given a paragraph of written material and asked to find its central meaning.

3) Numerical ability

Number skills can be tested by the familiar arithmetic problem, by checking paired lists of numbers to see which are alike and which are different, or by interpreting charts and graphs. In the latter test, a graph may be printed in the test booklet which you are asked to use as the basis for answering questions.

4) Observation

A popular test for law-enforcement positions is the observation test. A picture is shown to you for several minutes, then taken away. Questions about the picture test your ability to observe both details and larger elements.

5) Following directions

In many positions in the public service, the employee must be able to carry out written instructions dependably and accurately. You may be given a chart with several columns, each column listing a variety of information. The questions require you to carry out directions involving the information given in the chart.

6) Skills and aptitudes

Performance tests effectively measure some manual skills and aptitudes. When the skill is one in which you are trained, such as typing or shorthand, you can practice. These tests are often very much like those given in business school or high school courses. For many of the other skills and aptitudes, however, no short-time preparation can be made. Skills and abilities natural to you or that you have developed throughout your lifetime are being tested.

Many of the general questions just described provide all the data needed to answer the questions and ask you to use your reasoning ability to find the answers. Your best preparation for these tests, as well as for tests of facts and ideas, is to be at your physical and mental best. You, no doubt, have your own methods of getting into an exam-taking mood and keeping "in shape." The next section lists some ideas on this subject.

IV. KINDS OF QUESTIONS

Only rarely is the "essay" question, which you answer in narrative form, used in civil service tests. Civil service tests are usually of the short-answer type. Full instructions for answering these questions will be given to you at the examination. But in case this is your first experience with short-answer questions and separate answer sheets, here is what you need to know:

1) Multiple-choice Questions

Most popular of the short-answer questions is the "multiple choice" or "best answer" question. It can be used, for example, to test for factual knowledge, ability to solve problems or judgment in meeting situations found at work.

A multiple-choice question is normally one of three types—
- It can begin with an incomplete statement followed by several possible endings. You are to find the one ending which *best* completes the statement, although some of the others may not be entirely wrong.
- It can also be a complete statement in the form of a question which is answered by choosing one of the statements listed.

- It can be in the form of a problem – again you select the best answer.

Here is an example of a multiple-choice question with a discussion which should give you some clues as to the method for choosing the right answer:

When an employee has a complaint about his assignment, the action which will *best* help him overcome his difficulty is to
  A. discuss his difficulty with his coworkers
  B. take the problem to the head of the organization
  C. take the problem to the person who gave him the assignment
  D. say nothing to anyone about his complaint

In answering this question, you should study each of the choices to find which is best. Consider choice "A" – Certainly an employee may discuss his complaint with fellow employees, but no change or improvement can result, and the complaint remains unresolved. Choice "B" is a poor choice since the head of the organization probably does not know what assignment you have been given, and taking your problem to him is known as "going over the head" of the supervisor. The supervisor, or person who made the assignment, is the person who can clarify it or correct any injustice. Choice "C" is, therefore, correct. To say nothing, as in choice "D," is unwise. Supervisors have and interest in knowing the problems employees are facing, and the employee is seeking a solution to his problem.

2) True/False Questions

The "true/false" or "right/wrong" form of question is sometimes used. Here a complete statement is given. Your job is to decide whether the statement is right or wrong.

SAMPLE: A roaming cell-phone call to a nearby city costs less than a non-roaming call to a distant city.

This statement is wrong, or false, since roaming calls are more expensive.

This is not a complete list of all possible question forms, although most of the others are variations of these common types. You will always get complete directions for answering questions. Be sure you understand *how* to mark your answers – ask questions until you do.

V. RECORDING YOUR ANSWERS

Computer terminals are used more and more today for many different kinds of exams.

For an examination with very few applicants, you may be told to record your answers in the test booklet itself. Separate answer sheets are much more common. If this separate answer sheet is to be scored by machine – and this is often the case – it is highly important that you mark your answers correctly in order to get credit.

An electronic scoring machine is often used in civil service offices because of the speed with which papers can be scored. Machine-scored answer sheets must be marked with a pencil, which will be given to you. This pencil has a high graphite content which responds to the electronic scoring machine. As a matter of fact, stray dots may register as answers, so do not let your pencil rest on the answer sheet while you are pondering the correct answer. Also, if your pencil lead breaks or is otherwise defective, ask for another.

Since the answer sheet will be dropped in a slot in the scoring machine, be careful not to bend the corners or get the paper crumpled.

The answer sheet normally has five vertical columns of numbers, with 30 numbers to a column. These numbers correspond to the question numbers in your test booklet. After each number, going across the page are four or five pairs of dotted lines. These short dotted lines have small letters or numbers above them. The first two pairs may also have a "T" or "F" above the letters. This indicates that the first two pairs only are to be used if the questions are of the true-false type. If the questions are multiple choice, disregard the "T" and "F" and pay attention only to the small letters or numbers.

Answer your questions in the manner of the sample that follows:

32. The largest city in the United States is
    A. Washington, D.C.
    B. New York City
    C. Chicago
    D. Detroit
    E. San Francisco

1) Choose the answer you think is best. (New York City is the largest, so "B" is correct.)
2) Find the row of dotted lines numbered the same as the question you are answering. (Find row number 32)
3) Find the pair of dotted lines corresponding to the answer. (Find the pair of lines under the mark "B.")
4) Make a solid black mark between the dotted lines.

VI. BEFORE THE TEST

Common sense will help you find procedures to follow to get ready for an examination. Too many of us, however, overlook these sensible measures. Indeed, nervousness and fatigue have been found to be the most serious reasons why applicants fail to do their best on civil service tests. Here is a list of reminders:

- Begin your preparation early – Don't wait until the last minute to go scurrying around for books and materials or to find out what the position is all about.
- Prepare continuously – An hour a night for a week is better than an all-night cram session. This has been definitely established. What is more, a night a week for a month will return better dividends than crowding your study into a shorter period of time.
- Locate the place of the exam – You have been sent a notice telling you when and where to report for the examination. If the location is in a different town or otherwise unfamiliar to you, it would be well to inquire the best route and learn something about the building.
- Relax the night before the test – Allow your mind to rest. Do not study at all that night. Plan some mild recreation or diversion; then go to bed early and get a good night's sleep.
- Get up early enough to make a leisurely trip to the place for the test – This way unforeseen events, traffic snarls, unfamiliar buildings, etc. will not upset you.
- Dress comfortably – A written test is not a fashion show. You will be known by number and not by name, so wear something comfortable.

- Leave excess paraphernalia at home – Shopping bags and odd bundles will get in your way. You need bring only the items mentioned in the official notice you received; usually everything you need is provided. Do not bring reference books to the exam. They will only confuse those last minutes and be taken away from you when in the test room.
- Arrive somewhat ahead of time – If because of transportation schedules you must get there very early, bring a newspaper or magazine to take your mind off yourself while waiting.
- Locate the examination room – When you have found the proper room, you will be directed to the seat or part of the room where you will sit. Sometimes you are given a sheet of instructions to read while you are waiting. Do not fill out any forms until you are told to do so; just read them and be prepared.
- Relax and prepare to listen to the instructions
- If you have any physical problem that may keep you from doing your best, be sure to tell the test administrator. If you are sick or in poor health, you really cannot do your best on the exam. You can come back and take the test some other time.

VII. AT THE TEST

The day of the test is here and you have the test booklet in your hand. The temptation to get going is very strong. Caution! There is more to success than knowing the right answers. You must know how to identify your papers and understand variations in the type of short-answer question used in this particular examination. Follow these suggestions for maximum results from your efforts:

1) Cooperate with the monitor

The test administrator has a duty to create a situation in which you can be as much at ease as possible. He will give instructions, tell you when to begin, check to see that you are marking your answer sheet correctly, and so on. He is not there to guard you, although he will see that your competitors do not take unfair advantage. He wants to help you do your best.

2) Listen to all instructions

Don't jump the gun! Wait until you understand all directions. In most civil service tests you get more time than you need to answer the questions. So don't be in a hurry. Read each word of instructions until you clearly understand the meaning. Study the examples, listen to all announcements and follow directions. Ask questions if you do not understand what to do.

3) Identify your papers

Civil service exams are usually identified by number only. You will be assigned a number; you must not put your name on your test papers. Be sure to copy your number correctly. Since more than one exam may be given, copy your exact examination title.

4) Plan your time

Unless you are told that a test is a "speed" or "rate of work" test, speed itself is usually not important. Time enough to answer all the questions will be provided, but this does not mean that you have all day. An overall time limit has been set. Divide the total time (in minutes) by the number of questions to determine the approximate time you have for each question.

5) Do not linger over difficult questions

If you come across a difficult question, mark it with a paper clip (useful to have along) and come back to it when you have been through the booklet. One caution if you do this – be sure to skip a number on your answer sheet as well. Check often to be sure that you have not lost your place and that you are marking in the row numbered the same as the question you are answering.

6) Read the questions

Be sure you know what the question asks! Many capable people are unsuccessful because they failed to *read* the questions correctly.

7) Answer all questions

Unless you have been instructed that a penalty will be deducted for incorrect answers, it is better to guess than to omit a question.

8) Speed tests

It is often better NOT to guess on speed tests. It has been found that on timed tests people are tempted to spend the last few seconds before time is called in marking answers at random – without even reading them – in the hope of picking up a few extra points. To discourage this practice, the instructions may warn you that your score will be "corrected" for guessing. That is, a penalty will be applied. The incorrect answers will be deducted from the correct ones, or some other penalty formula will be used.

9) Review your answers

If you finish before time is called, go back to the questions you guessed or omitted to give them further thought. Review other answers if you have time.

10) Return your test materials

If you are ready to leave before others have finished or time is called, take ALL your materials to the monitor and leave quietly. Never take any test material with you. The monitor can discover whose papers are not complete, and taking a test booklet may be grounds for disqualification.

VIII. EXAMINATION TECHNIQUES

1) Read the general instructions carefully. These are usually printed on the first page of the exam booklet. As a rule, these instructions refer to the timing of the examination; the fact that you should not start work until the signal and must stop work at a signal, etc. If there are any *special* instructions, such as a choice of questions to be answered, make sure that you note this instruction carefully.

2) When you are ready to start work on the examination, that is as soon as the signal has been given, read the instructions to each question booklet, underline any key words or phrases, such as *least, best, outline, describe* and the like. In this way you will tend to answer as requested rather than discover on reviewing your paper that you *listed without describing*, that you selected the *worst* choice rather than the *best* choice, etc.

3) If the examination is of the objective or multiple-choice type – that is, each question will also give a series of possible answers: A, B, C or D, and you are called upon to select the best answer and write the letter next to that answer on your answer paper – it is advisable to start answering each question in turn. There may be anywhere from 50 to 100 such questions in the three or four hours allotted and you can see how much time would be taken if you read through all the questions before beginning to answer any. Furthermore, if you come across a question or group of questions which you know would be difficult to answer, it would undoubtedly affect your handling of all the other questions.

4) If the examination is of the essay type and contains but a few questions, it is a moot point as to whether you should read all the questions before starting to answer any one. Of course, if you are given a choice – say five out of seven and the like – then it is essential to read all the questions so you can eliminate the two that are most difficult. If, however, you are asked to answer all the questions, there may be danger in trying to answer the easiest one first because you may find that you will spend too much time on it. The best technique is to answer the first question, then proceed to the second, etc.

5) Time your answers. Before the exam begins, write down the time it started, then add the time allowed for the examination and write down the time it must be completed, then divide the time available somewhat as follows:
   - If 3-1/2 hours are allowed, that would be 210 minutes. If you have 80 objective-type questions, that would be an average of 2-1/2 minutes per question. Allow yourself no more than 2 minutes per question, or a total of 160 minutes, which will permit about 50 minutes to review.
   - If for the time allotment of 210 minutes there are 7 essay questions to answer, that would average about 30 minutes a question. Give yourself only 25 minutes per question so that you have about 35 minutes to review.

6) The most important instruction is to *read each question* and make sure you know what is wanted. The second most important instruction is to *time yourself properly* so that you answer every question. The third most important instruction is to *answer every question*. Guess if you have to but include something for each question. Remember that you will receive no credit for a blank and will probably receive some credit if you write something in answer to an essay question. If you guess a letter – say "B" for a multiple-choice question – you may have guessed right. If you leave a blank as an answer to a multiple-choice question, the examiners may respect your feelings but it will not add a point to your score. Some exams may penalize you for wrong answers, so in such cases *only*, you may not want to guess unless you have some basis for your answer.

7) Suggestions
   a. Objective-type questions
      1. Examine the question booklet for proper sequence of pages and questions
      2. Read all instructions carefully
      3. Skip any question which seems too difficult; return to it after all other questions have been answered
      4. Apportion your time properly; do not spend too much time on any single question or group of questions

5. Note and underline key words – *all, most, fewest, least, best, worst, same, opposite*, etc.
6. Pay particular attention to negatives
7. Note unusual option, e.g., unduly long, short, complex, different or similar in content to the body of the question
8. Observe the use of "hedging" words – *probably, may, most likely*, etc.
9. Make sure that your answer is put next to the same number as the question
10. Do not second-guess unless you have good reason to believe the second answer is definitely more correct
11. Cross out original answer if you decide another answer is more accurate; do not erase until you are ready to hand your paper in
12. Answer all questions; guess unless instructed otherwise
13. Leave time for review

b. Essay questions
  1. Read each question carefully
  2. Determine exactly what is wanted. Underline key words or phrases.
  3. Decide on outline or paragraph answer
  4. Include many different points and elements unless asked to develop any one or two points or elements
  5. Show impartiality by giving pros and cons unless directed to select one side only
  6. Make and write down any assumptions you find necessary to answer the questions
  7. Watch your English, grammar, punctuation and choice of words
  8. Time your answers; don't crowd material

8) Answering the essay question

Most essay questions can be answered by framing the specific response around several key words or ideas. Here are a few such key words or ideas:

M's: manpower, materials, methods, money, management
P's: purpose, program, policy, plan, procedure, practice, problems, pitfalls, personnel, public relations

  a. Six basic steps in handling problems:
     1. Preliminary plan and background development
     2. Collect information, data and facts
     3. Analyze and interpret information, data and facts
     4. Analyze and develop solutions as well as make recommendations
     5. Prepare report and sell recommendations
     6. Install recommendations and follow up effectiveness

  b. Pitfalls to avoid
     1. *Taking things for granted* – A statement of the situation does not necessarily imply that each of the elements is necessarily true; for example, a complaint may be invalid and biased so that all that can be taken for granted is that a complaint has been registered

2. *Considering only one side of a situation* – Wherever possible, indicate several alternatives and then point out the reasons you selected the best one
3. *Failing to indicate follow up* – Whenever your answer indicates action on your part, make certain that you will take proper follow-up action to see how successful your recommendations, procedures or actions turn out to be
4. *Taking too long in answering any single question* – Remember to time your answers properly

IX. AFTER THE TEST

Scoring procedures differ in detail among civil service jurisdictions although the general principles are the same. Whether the papers are hand-scored or graded by machine we have described, they are nearly always graded by number. That is, the person who marks the paper knows only the number – never the name – of the applicant. Not until all the papers have been graded will they be matched with names. If other tests, such as training and experience or oral interview ratings have been given, scores will be combined. Different parts of the examination usually have different weights. For example, the written test might count 60 percent of the final grade, and a rating of training and experience 40 percent. In many jurisdictions, veterans will have a certain number of points added to their grades.

After the final grade has been determined, the names are placed in grade order and an eligible list is established. There are various methods for resolving ties between those who get the same final grade – probably the most common is to place first the name of the person whose application was received first. Job offers are made from the eligible list in the order the names appear on it. You will be notified of your grade and your rank as soon as all these computations have been made. This will be done as rapidly as possible.

People who are found to meet the requirements in the announcement are called "eligibles." Their names are put on a list of eligible candidates. An eligible's chances of getting a job depend on how high he stands on this list and how fast agencies are filling jobs from the list.

When a job is to be filled from a list of eligibles, the agency asks for the names of people on the list of eligibles for that job. When the civil service commission receives this request, it sends to the agency the names of the three people highest on this list. Or, if the job to be filled has specialized requirements, the office sends the agency the names of the top three persons who meet these requirements from the general list.

The appointing officer makes a choice from among the three people whose names were sent to him. If the selected person accepts the appointment, the names of the others are put back on the list to be considered for future openings.

That is the rule in hiring from all kinds of eligible lists, whether they are for typist, carpenter, chemist, or something else. For every vacancy, the appointing officer has his choice of any one of the top three eligibles on the list. This explains why the person whose name is on top of the list sometimes does not get an appointment when some of the persons lower on the list do. If the appointing officer chooses the second or third eligible, the No. 1 eligible does not get a job at once, but stays on the list until he is appointed or the list is terminated.

X. HOW TO PASS THE INTERVIEW TEST

The examination for which you applied requires an oral interview test. You have already taken the written test and you are now being called for the interview test – the final part of the formal examination.

You may think that it is not possible to prepare for an interview test and that there are no procedures to follow during an interview. Our purpose is to point out some things you can do in advance that will help you and some good rules to follow and pitfalls to avoid while you are being interviewed.

What is an interview supposed to test?

The written examination is designed to test the technical knowledge and competence of the candidate; the oral is designed to evaluate intangible qualities, not readily measured otherwise, and to establish a list showing the relative fitness of each candidate – as measured against his competitors – for the position sought. Scoring is not on the basis of "right" and "wrong," but on a sliding scale of values ranging from "not passable" to "outstanding." As a matter of fact, it is possible to achieve a relatively low score without a single "incorrect" answer because of evident weakness in the qualities being measured.

Occasionally, an examination may consist entirely of an oral test – either an individual or a group oral. In such cases, information is sought concerning the technical knowledges and abilities of the candidate, since there has been no written examination for this purpose. More commonly, however, an oral test is used to supplement a written examination.

Who conducts interviews?

The composition of oral boards varies among different jurisdictions. In nearly all, a representative of the personnel department serves as chairman. One of the members of the board may be a representative of the department in which the candidate would work. In some cases, "outside experts" are used, and, frequently, a businessman or some other representative of the general public is asked to serve. Labor and management or other special groups may be represented. The aim is to secure the services of experts in the appropriate field.

However the board is composed, it is a good idea (and not at all improper or unethical) to ascertain in advance of the interview who the members are and what groups they represent. When you are introduced to them, you will have some idea of their backgrounds and interests, and at least you will not stutter and stammer over their names.

What should be done before the interview?

While knowledge about the board members is useful and takes some of the surprise element out of the interview, there is other preparation which is more substantive. It *is* possible to prepare for an oral interview – in several ways:

1) Keep a copy of your application and review it carefully before the interview

This may be the only document before the oral board, and the starting point of the interview. Know what education and experience you have listed there, and the sequence and dates of all of it. Sometimes the board will ask you to review the highlights of your experience for them; you should not have to hem and haw doing it.

2) Study the class specification and the examination announcement

Usually, the oral board has one or both of these to guide them. The qualities, characteristics or knowledges required by the position sought are stated in these documents. They offer valuable clues as to the nature of the oral interview. For example, if the job involves supervisory responsibilities, the announcement will usually indicate that knowledge of modern supervisory methods and the qualifications of the candidate as a supervisor will be tested. If so, you can expect such questions, frequently in the form of a hypothetical situation which you are expected to solve. NEVER go into an oral without knowledge of the duties and responsibilities of the job you seek.

3) Think through each qualification required

Try to visualize the kind of questions you would ask if you were a board member. How well could you answer them? Try especially to appraise your own knowledge and background in each area, *measured against the job sought*, and identify any areas in which you are weak. Be critical and realistic – do not flatter yourself.

4) Do some general reading in areas in which you feel you may be weak

For example, if the job involves supervision and your past experience has NOT, some general reading in supervisory methods and practices, particularly in the field of human relations, might be useful. Do NOT study agency procedures or detailed manuals. The oral board will be testing your understanding and capacity, not your memory.

5) Get a good night's sleep and watch your general health and mental attitude

You will want a clear head at the interview. Take care of a cold or any other minor ailment, and of course, no hangovers.

What should be done on the day of the interview?

Now comes the day of the interview itself. Give yourself plenty of time to get there. Plan to arrive somewhat ahead of the scheduled time, particularly if your appointment is in the fore part of the day. If a previous candidate fails to appear, the board might be ready for you a bit early. By early afternoon an oral board is almost invariably behind schedule if there are many candidates, and you may have to wait. Take along a book or magazine to read, or your application to review, but leave any extraneous material in the waiting room when you go in for your interview. In any event, relax and compose yourself.

The matter of dress is important. The board is forming impressions about you – from your experience, your manners, your attitude, and your appearance. Give your personal appearance careful attention. Dress your best, but not your flashiest. Choose conservative, appropriate clothing, and be sure it is immaculate. This is a business interview, and your appearance should indicate that you regard it as such. Besides, being well groomed and properly dressed will help boost your confidence.

Sooner or later, someone will call your name and escort you into the interview room. *This is it.* From here on you are on your own. It is too late for any more preparation. But remember, you asked for this opportunity to prove your fitness, and you are here because your request was granted.

What happens when you go in?

The usual sequence of events will be as follows: The clerk (who is often the board stenographer) will introduce you to the chairman of the oral board, who will introduce you to the other members of the board. Acknowledge the introductions before you sit down. Do not be surprised if you find a microphone facing you or a stenotypist sitting by. Oral interviews are usually recorded in the event of an appeal or other review.

Usually the chairman of the board will open the interview by reviewing the highlights of your education and work experience from your application – primarily for the benefit of the other members of the board, as well as to get the material into the record. Do not interrupt or comment unless there is an error or significant misinterpretation; if that is the case, do not hesitate. But do not quibble about insignificant matters. Also, he will usually ask you some question about your education, experience or your present job – partly to get you to start talking and to establish the interviewing "rapport." He may start the actual questioning, or turn it over to one of the other members. Frequently, each member undertakes the questioning on a particular area, one in which he is perhaps most competent, so you can expect each member to participate in the examination. Because time is limited, you may also expect some rather abrupt switches in the direction the questioning takes, so do not be upset by it. Normally, a board member will not pursue a single line of questioning unless he discovers a particular strength or weakness.

After each member has participated, the chairman will usually ask whether any member has any further questions, then will ask you if you have anything you wish to add. Unless you are expecting this question, it may floor you. Worse, it may start you off on an extended, extemporaneous speech. The board is not usually seeking more information. The question is principally to offer you a last opportunity to present further qualifications or to indicate that you have nothing to add. So, if you feel that a significant qualification or characteristic has been overlooked, it is proper to point it out in a sentence or so. Do not compliment the board on the thoroughness of their examination – they have been sketchy, and you know it. If you wish, merely say, "No thank you, I have nothing further to add." This is a point where you can "talk yourself out" of a good impression or fail to present an important bit of information. Remember, *you close the interview yourself.*

The chairman will then say, "That is all, Mr. _____, thank you." Do not be startled; the interview is over, and quicker than you think. Thank him, gather your belongings and take your leave. Save your sigh of relief for the other side of the door.

How to put your best foot forward
Throughout this entire process, you may feel that the board individually and collectively is trying to pierce your defenses, seek out your hidden weaknesses and embarrass and confuse you. Actually, this is not true. They are obliged to make an appraisal of your qualifications for the job you are seeking, and they want to see you in your best light. Remember, they must interview all candidates and a non-cooperative candidate may become a failure in spite of their best efforts to bring out his qualifications. Here are 15 suggestions that will help you:

1) Be natural – Keep your attitude confident, not cocky
If you are not confident that you can do the job, do not expect the board to be. Do not apologize for your weaknesses, try to bring out your strong points. The board is interested in a positive, not negative, presentation. Cockiness will antagonize any board member and make him wonder if you are covering up a weakness by a false show of strength.

2) Get comfortable, but don't lounge or sprawl
Sit erectly but not stiffly. A careless posture may lead the board to conclude that you are careless in other things, or at least that you are not impressed by the importance of the occasion. Either conclusion is natural, even if incorrect. Do not fuss with your clothing, a pencil or an ashtray. Your hands may occasionally be useful to emphasize a point; do not let them become a point of distraction.

3) Do not wisecrack or make small talk
This is a serious situation, and your attitude should show that you consider it as such. Further, the time of the board is limited – they do not want to waste it, and neither should you.

4) Do not exaggerate your experience or abilities

In the first place, from information in the application or other interviews and sources, the board may know more about you than you think. Secondly, you probably will not get away with it. An experienced board is rather adept at spotting such a situation, so do not take the chance.

5) If you know a board member, do not make a point of it, yet do not hide it

Certainly you are not fooling him, and probably not the other members of the board. Do not try to take advantage of your acquaintanceship – it will probably do you little good.

6) Do not dominate the interview

Let the board do that. They will give you the clues – do not assume that you have to do all the talking. Realize that the board has a number of questions to ask you, and do not try to take up all the interview time by showing off your extensive knowledge of the answer to the first one.

7) Be attentive

You only have 20 minutes or so, and you should keep your attention at its sharpest throughout. When a member is addressing a problem or question to you, give him your undivided attention. Address your reply principally to him, but do not exclude the other board members.

8) Do not interrupt

A board member may be stating a problem for you to analyze. He will ask you a question when the time comes. Let him state the problem, and wait for the question.

9) Make sure you understand the question

Do not try to answer until you are sure what the question is. If it is not clear, restate it in your own words or ask the board member to clarify it for you. However, do not haggle about minor elements.

10) Reply promptly but not hastily

A common entry on oral board rating sheets is "candidate responded readily," or "candidate hesitated in replies." Respond as promptly and quickly as you can, but do not jump to a hasty, ill-considered answer.

11) Do not be peremptory in your answers

A brief answer is proper – but do not fire your answer back. That is a losing game from your point of view. The board member can probably ask questions much faster than you can answer them.

12) Do not try to create the answer you think the board member wants

He is interested in what kind of mind you have and how it works – not in playing games. Furthermore, he can usually spot this practice and will actually grade you down on it.

13) Do not switch sides in your reply merely to agree with a board member

Frequently, a member will take a contrary position merely to draw you out and to see if you are willing and able to defend your point of view. Do not start a debate, yet do not surrender a good position. If a position is worth taking, it is worth defending.

14) Do not be afraid to admit an error in judgment if you are shown to be wrong

The board knows that you are forced to reply without any opportunity for careful consideration. Your answer may be demonstrably wrong. If so, admit it and get on with the interview.

15) Do not dwell at length on your present job

The opening question may relate to your present assignment. Answer the question but do not go into an extended discussion. You are being examined for a *new* job, not your present one. As a matter of fact, try to phrase ALL your answers in terms of the job for which you are being examined.

Basis of Rating

Probably you will forget most of these "do's" and "don'ts" when you walk into the oral interview room. Even remembering them all will not ensure you a passing grade. Perhaps you did not have the qualifications in the first place. But remembering them will help you to put your best foot forward, without treading on the toes of the board members.

Rumor and popular opinion to the contrary notwithstanding, an oral board wants you to make the best appearance possible. They know you are under pressure – but they also want to see how you respond to it as a guide to what your reaction would be under the pressures of the job you seek. They will be influenced by the degree of poise you display, the personal traits you show and the manner in which you respond.

ABOUT THIS BOOK

This book contains tests divided into Examination Sections. Go through each test, answering every question in the margin. We have also attached a sample answer sheet at the back of the book that can be removed and used. At the end of each test look at the answer key and check your answers. On the ones you got wrong, look at the right answer choice and learn. Do not fill in the answers first. Do not memorize the questions and answers, but understand the answer and principles involved. On your test, the questions will likely be different from the samples. Questions are changed and new ones added. If you understand these past questions you should have success with any changes that arise. Tests may consist of several types of questions. We have additional books on each subject should more study be advisable or necessary for you. Finally, the more you study, the better prepared you will be. This book is intended to be the last thing you study before you walk into the examination room. Prior study of relevant texts is also recommended. NLC publishes some of these in our Fundamental Series. Knowledge and good sense are important factors in passing your exam. Good luck also helps. So now study this Passbook, absorb the material contained within and take that knowledge into the examination. Then do your best to pass that exam.

EXAMINATION SECTION

EXAMINATION SECTION
TEST 1

DIRECTIONS: Each question or incomplete statement is followed by several suggested answers or completions. Select the one that BEST answers the question or completes the statement. *PRINT THE LETTER OF THE CORRECT ANSWER IN THE SPACE AT THE RIGHT.*

Questions 1-9.

DIRECTIONS: Questions 1 through 9 consist of sentences which may or may not be examples of good English usage. Consider grammar, punctuation, spelling, capitalization, awkwardness, etc. Examine each sentence, and then choose the correct statement about it from the four choices below it. If the English usage in the sentence given is better than it would be with any of the changes suggested in options B, C, and D, choose option A. Do not choose an option that will change the meaning of the sentence.

1. According to Judge Frank, the grocer's sons found guilty of assault and sentenced last Thursday.   1.____

    A. This is an example of acceptable writing.
    B. A comma should be placed after the word *sentenced*.
    C. The word *were* should be placed after *sons*
    D. The apostrophe in *grocer's* should be placed after the *s*.

2. The department heads assistant said that the stenographers should type duplicate copies of all contracts, leases, and bills.   2.____

    A. This is an example of acceptable writing.
    B. A comma should be placed before the word *contracts*.
    C. An apostrophe should be placed before the *s* in *heads*.
    D. Quotation marks should be placed before *the stenographers* and after *bills*.

3. The lawyers questioned the men to determine who was the true property owner?   3.____

    A. This is an example of acceptable writing.
    B. The phrase *questioned the men* should be changed to *asked the men questions*.
    C. The word *was* should be changed to *were*.
    D. The question mark should be changed to a period.

4. The terms stated in the present contract are more specific than those stated in the previous contract.   4.____

    A. This is an example of acceptable writing.
    B. The word *are* should be changed to *is*.
    C. The word *than* should be changed to *then*.
    D. The word *specific* should be changed to *specified*.

5. Of the lawyers considered, the one who argued more skillful was chosen for the job.   5.____

    A. This is an example of acceptable writing.
    B. The word *more* should be replaced by the word *most*.
    C. The word *skillful* should be replaced by the word *skillfully,*
    D. The word *chosen* should be replaced by the word *selected*.

1

6. Each of the states has a court of appeals; some states have circuit courts.   6._____

    A. This is an example of acceptable writing.
    B. The semi-colon should be changed to a comma.
    C. The word *has* should be changed to *have*.
    D. The word *some* should be capitalized.

7. The court trial has greatly effected the child's mental condition.   7._____

    A. This is an example of acceptable writing.
    B. The word *effected* should be changed to *affected*.
    C. The word *greatly* should be placed after *effected*.
    D. The apostrophe in *child's* should be placed after the *s*.

8. Last week, the petition signed by all the officers was sent to the Better Business Bureau.   8._____

    A. This is an example of acceptable writing.
    B. The phrase *last week* should be placed after *officers*.
    C. A comma should be placed after *petition*.
    D. The word *was* should be changed to *were*.

9. Mr. Farrell claims that he requested form A-12, and three booklets describing court procedures.   9._____

    A. This is an example of acceptable writing.
    B. The word *that* should be eliminated.
    C. A colon should be placed after *requested*.
    D. The comma after *A-12* should be eliminated.

Questions 10-21.

DIRECTIONS: Questions 10 through 21 contain a word in capital letters followed by four suggested meanings of the word. For each question, choose the BEST meaning for the word in capital letters.

10. SIGNATORY - A   10._____

    A. lawyer who draws up a legal document
    B. document that must be signed by a judge
    C. person who signs a document
    D. true copy of a signature

11. RETAINER - A   11._____

    A. fee paid to a lawyer for his services
    B. document held by a third party
    C. court decision to send a prisoner back to custody pending trial
    D. legal requirement to keep certain types of files

12. BEQUEATH - To   12._____

    A. receive assistance from a charitable organization
    B. give personal property by will to another
    C. transfer real property from one person to another
    D. receive an inheritance upon the death of a relative

13. RATIFY - To

    A. approve and sanction
    B. forego
    C. produce evidence
    D. summarize

14. CODICIL - A

    A. document introduced in evidence in a civil action
    B. subsection of a law
    C. type of legal action that can be brought by a plaintiff
    D. supplement or an addition to a will

15. ALIAS

    A. Assumed name
    B. In favor of
    C. Against
    D. A writ

16. PROXY - A(n)

    A. phony document in a real estate transaction
    B. opinion by a judge of a civil court
    C. document containing appointment of an agent
    D. summons in a lawsuit

17. ALLEGED

    A. Innocent
    B. Asserted
    C. Guilty
    D. Called upon

18. EXECUTE - To

    A. complete a legal document by signing it
    B. set requirements
    C. render services to a duly elected executive of a municipality
    D. initiate legal action such as a lawsuit

19. NOTARY PUBLIC - A

    A. lawyer who is running for public office
    B. judge who hears minor cases
    C. public officer, one of whose functions is to administer oaths
    D. lawyer who gives free legal services to persons unable to pay

20. WAIVE - To

    A. disturb a calm state of affairs
    B. knowingly renounce a right or claim
    C. pardon someone for a minor fault
    D. purposely mislead a person during an investigation

21. ARRAIGN - To

    A. prevent an escape
    B. defend a prisoner
    C. verify a document
    D. accuse in a court of law

Questions 22-40.

DIRECTIONS: Questions 22 through 40 each consist of four words which may or may not be spelled correctly. If you find an error in
only one word, mark your answer A;
any two words, mark your answer B;
any three words, mark your answer C;
none of these words, mark your answer D.

22.	occurrence	Febuary	privilege	similiar	22._____
23.	separate	transferring	analyze	column	23._____
24.	develop	license	bankrupcy	abreviate	24._____
25.	subpoena	arguement	dissolution	foreclosure	25._____
26.	exaggerate	fundamental	significance	warrant	26._____
27.	citizen	endorsed	marraige	appraissal	27._____
28.	precedant	univercity	observence	preliminary	28._____
29.	stipulate	negligence	judgment	prominent	29._____
30.	judisial	whereas	release	guardian	30._____
31.	appeal	larcenny	transcrip	jurist	31._____
32.	petition	tenancy	agenda	insurance	32._____
33.	superfical	premise	morgaged	maintainance	33._____
34.	testamony	publically	installment	possessed	34._____
35.	escrow	decree	eviction	miscelaneous	35._____
36.	securitys	abeyance	adhere	corporate	36._____
37.	kaleidoscope	anesthesia	vermilion	tafetta	37._____
38.	congruant	barrenness	plebescite	vigilance	38._____
39.	picnicing	promisory	resevoir	omission	39._____
40.	supersede	banister	wholly	seize	40._____

KEY (CORRECT ANSWERS)

1.	C	11.	A	21.	D	31.	B
2.	C	12.	B	22.	B	32.	D
3.	D	13.	A	23.	D	33.	C
4.	A	14.	D	24.	B	34.	B
5.	C	15.	A	25.	A	35.	A
6.	A	16.	C	26.	D	36.	A
7.	B	17.	B	27.	B	37.	A
8.	A	18.	A	28.	C	38.	B
9.	D	19.	C	29.	D	39.	C
10.	C	20.	B	30.	A	40.	D

EXAMINATION SECTION
TEST 1

DIRECTIONS: Each question or incomplete statement is followed by several suggested answers or completions. Select the one that BEST answers the question or completes the statement. *PRINT THE LETTER OF THE CORRECT ANSWER IN THE SPACE AT THE RIGHT.*

Questions 1-6.

DIRECTIONS: Questions 1 through 6 consist of descriptions of material to which a filing designation must be assigned.

Assume that the matters and cases described in the questions were referred for handling to a government legal office which has its files set up according to these file designations. The file designation consists of a number of characters and punctuation marks as described below.

The first character refers to agencies whose legal work is handled by this office. These agencies are numbered consecutively in the order in which they first submit a matter for attention, and are identified in an alphabetical card index. To date numbers have been assigned to agencies as follows:

Department of Correction	1
Police Department	2
Department of Traffic	3
Department of Consumer Affairs	4
Commission on Human Rights	5
Board of Elections	6
Department of Personnel	7
Board of Estimate	8

The second character is separated from the first character by a dash. The second character is the last digit of the year in which a particular lawsuit or matter is referred to the legal office.

The third character is separated from the second character by a colon and may consist of either of the following:

I. *A sub-number assigned to each lawsuit to which the agency is a party. Lawsuits are numbered consecutively regardless of year. (Lawsuits are brought by or against agency heads rather than agencies themselves, but references are made to agencies for the purpose of simplification.)*

or II. *A capital letter assigned to each matter other than a lawsuit according to subject, the subject being identified in an alphabetical index. To date, letters have been assigned to subjects as follows:*

Citizenship	A	Housing	E
Discrimination	B	Gambling	F
Residence Requirements	C	Freedom of Religion	G
Civil Service Examinations	D		

These referrals are numbered consecutively regardless of year. The first referral by a particular agency on citizenship, for example, would be designated A1, followed by A2, A3, etc.

If no reference is made in a question as to how many letters involving a certain subject or how many lawsuits have been referred by an agency, assume that it is the first.

For each question, choose the file designation which is MOST appropriate for filing the material described in the question.

1. In January 2010, two candidates in a 2009 civil service examination for positions with the Department of Correction filed a suit against the Department of Personnel seeking to set aside an educational requirement for the title.
   The Department of Personnel immediately referred the lawsuit to the legal office for handling.

   A. 1-9:1   B. 1-0:D1   C. 7-9:D1   D. 7-0:1

2. In 2014, the Police Department made its sixth request for an opinion on whether an employee assignment proposed for 2015 could be considered discriminatory.

   A. 2-5:1-B6   B. 2-4:6   C. 2-4:1-B6   D. 2-4:B6

3. In 2015, a lawsuit was brought by the Bay Island Action Committee against the Board of Estimate in which the plaintiff sought withdrawal of approval of housing for the elderly in the Bay Island area given by the Board in 2015.

   A. 8-3:1   B. 8-5:1   C. 8-3:B1   D. 8-5:E1

4. In December 2014, community leaders asked the Police Department to ban outdoor meetings of a religious group on the grounds that the meetings were disrupting the area. Such meetings had been held from time to time during 2014. On January 31, 2015, the Police Department asked the government legal office for an opinion on whether granting this request would violate the worshippers' right to freedom of religion.

   A. 2-4:G-1   B. 2-5:G1   C. 2-5:B-1   D. 2-4:B1

5. In 2014, a woman filed suit against the Board of Elections. She alleged that she had not been permitted to vote at her usual polling place in the 2013 election and had been told she was not registered there. She claimed that she had always voted there and that her record card had been lost. This was the fourth case of its type for this agency.

   A. 6-4:4   B. 6-3:C4   C. 3-4:6   D. 6-3:4

6. A lawsuit was brought in 2011 by the Ace Pinball Machine Company against the Commissioner of Consumer Affairs. The lawsuit contested an ordinance which banned the use of pinball machines on the ground that they are gambling devices.
   This was the third lawsuit to which the Department of Consumer Affairs was a party.

   A. 4-1:1   B. 4-3:F1   C. 4-1:3   D. 3F-4:1

7. You are instructed by your supervisor to type a statement that must be signed by the person making the statement and by three witnesses to the signature. The typed statement will take two pages and will leave no room for signatures if the normal margin is maintained at the bottom of the second page.
In this situation, the PREFERRED method is to type

   A. the signature lines below the normal margin on the second page
   B. nothing further and have the witnesses sign without a typed signature line
   C. the signature lines on a third page
   D. some of the text and the signature lines on a third page

8. Certain legal documents always begin with a statement of venue - that is, the county and state in which the document is executed. This is usually boxed with a parentheses or colons.
The one of the following documents that ALWAYS bears a statement of venue in a prominent position at its head is a(n)

   A. affidavit   B. memorandum of law
   C. contract of sale   D. will

9. A court stenographer is to take stenographic notes and transcribe the statements of a person under oath. The person has a heavy accent and speaks in ungrammatical and broken English.
When he or she is transcribing the testimony, of the following, the BEST thing for them to do is to

   A. transcribe the testimony exactly as spoken, making no grammatical changes
   B. make only the grammatical changes which would clarify the client's statements
   C. make all grammatical changes so that the testimony is in standard English form
   D. ask the client's permission before making any grammatical changes

10. When the material typed on a printed form does not fill the space provided, a Z-ruling is frequently drawn to fill up the unused space.
The MAIN purpose of this practice is to

    A. make the document more pleasing to the eye
    B. indicate that the preceding material is correct
    C. insure that the document is not altered
    D. show that the lawyer has read it

11. After you had typed an original and five copies of a certain document, some changes were made in ink on the original and were initialed by all the parties. The original was signed by all the parties, and the signatures were notarized.
Which of the following should *generally* be typed on the copies BEFORE filing the original and the copies? The inked changes

    A. but not the signatures, initials, or notarial data
    B. the signatures and the initials but not the notarial data
    C. and the notarial data but not the signatures or initials
    D. the signatures, the initials, and the notarial data

12. The first paragraph of a noncourt agreement *generally* contains all of the following EXCEPT the

   A. specific terms of the agreement
   B. date of the agreement
   C. purpose of the agreement
   D. names of the parties involved

13. When typing an answer in a court proceeding, the place where the word ANSWER should be typed on the first page of the document is

   A. at the upper left-hand corner
   B. below the index number and to the right of the box containing the names of the parties to the action
   C. above the index number and to the right of the box containing the names of the parties to the action
   D. to the left of the names of the attorneys for the defendant

14. Which one of the following statements BEST describes the legal document called an acknowledgment?
    It is

   A. an answer to an affidavit
   B. a receipt issued by the court when a document is filed
   C. proof of service of a summons
   D. a declaration that a signature is valid

15. Suppose you typed the original and three copies of a legal document which was dictated by an attorney in your office. He has already signed the original copy, and corrections have been made on all copies.
    Regarding the copies, which one of the following procedures is the PROPER one to follow?

   A. Leave the signature line blank on the copies
   B. Ask the attorney to sign the copies
   C. Print or type the attorney's name on the signature line on the copies
   D. Sign your name to the copies followed by the attorney's initials

16. Suppose your office is defending a particular person in a court action. This person comes to the office and asks to see some of the lawyer's working papers in his file. The lawyer assigned to the case is out of the office at the time.
    You SHOULD

   A. permit him to examine his entire file as long as he does not remove any materials from it
   B. make an appointment for the caller to come back later when the lawyer will be there
   C. ask him what working papers he wants to see and show him only those papers
   D. tell him that he needs written permission from the lawyer in order to see any records

17. Suppose that you receive a phone call from an official who is annoyed about a letter from your office which she just received. The lawyer who dictated the letter is not in the office at the moment.
Of the following, the BEST action for you to take is to

   A. explain that the lawyer is out but that you will ask the lawyer to return her call when he returns
   B. take down all of the details of her complaint and tell her that you will get back to her with an explanation
   C. refer to the proper file so that you can give her an explanation of the reasons for the letter over the phone
   D. make an appointment for her to stop by the office to speak with the lawyer

18. Suppose that you have taken dictation for an interoffice memorandum. You are asked to prepare it for distribution to four lawyers in your department whose names are given to you. You will type an original and make four copies. Which one of the following is CORRECT with regard to the typing of the lawyers' names?
The names of all of the lawyers should appear

   A. *only* on the original
   B. on the original and each copy should have the name of one lawyer
   C. on each of the copies but not on the original
   D. on the original and on all of the copies

19. Regarding the correct typing of punctuation, the GENERALLY accepted practice is that there should be

   A. two spaces after a semi-colon
   B. one space before an apostrophe used in the body of a word
   C. no space between parentheses and the matter enclosed
   D. one space before and after a hyphen

20. Suppose you have just completed typing an original and two copies of a letter requesting information. The original is to be signed by a lawyer in your office. The first copy is for the files, and the second is to be used as a reminder to follow up.
The PROPER time to file the file copy of the letter is

   A. after the letter has been signed and corrections have been made on the copies
   B. before you take the letter to the lawyer for his signature
   C. after a follow-up letter has been sent
   D. after a response to the letter has been received

21. A secretary in a legal office has just typed a letter. She has typed the copy distribution notation on the copies to indicate *blind copy distribution*. This *blind copy* notation shows that

   A. copies of the letter are being sent to persons that the addressee does not know
   B. copies of the letter are being sent to other persons without the addressee's knowledge
   C. a copy of the letter will be enlarged for a legally blind person
   D. a copy of the letter is being given as an extra copy to the addressee

22. Suppose that one of the attorneys in your office dictates material to you without indicating punctuation. He has asked that you give him, as soon as possible, a single copy of a rough draft to be triple-spaced so that he can make corrections.
Of the following, what is the BEST thing for you to do in this situation?

   A. Assume that no punctuation is desired in the material
   B. Insert the punctuation as you type the rough draft
   C. Transcribe the material exactly as dictated, but attach a note to the attorney stating your suggested changes
   D. Before you start to type the draft, tell the attorney you want to read back your notes so that he can indicate punctuation

22.____

23. When it is necessary to type a mailing notation such as CERTIFIED, REGISTERED, or FEDEX on an envelope, the GENERALLY accepted place to type it is

   A. directly above the address
   B. in the area below where the stamp will be affixed
   C. in the lower left-hand corner
   D. in the upper left-hand corner

23.____

24. When taking a citation of a case in shorthand, which of the following should you write FIRST if you are having difficulty keeping up with the dictation?

   A. Volume and page number
   B. Title of volume
   C. Name of plaintiff
   D. Name of defendant

24.____

25. All of the following abbreviations and their meanings are correctly paired EXCEPT

   A. viz. - namely
   B. ibid. - refer
   C. n.b. - note well
   D. q.v. - which see

25.____

KEY (CORRECT ANSWERS)

1.	D	11.	D
2.	D	12.	A
3.	B	13.	B
4.	B	14.	D
5.	A	15.	C
6.	C	16.	B
7.	D	17.	A
8.	A	18.	D
9.	A	19.	C
10.	C	20.	A

21. B
22. B
23. B
24. A
25. B

EXAMINATION SECTION
TEST 1

DIRECTIONS: Each question or incomplete statement is followed by several suggested answers or completions. Select the one that BEST answers the question or completes the statement. *PRINT THE LETTER OF THE CORRECT ANSWER IN THE SPACE AT THE RIGHT.*

Questions 1-4.

DIRECTIONS: Questions 1 through 4 consist of sentences concerning criminal law. Some of the sentences contain errors in English grammar or usage, punctuation, spelling or capitalization. A sentence does not contain an error simply because it could be written in a different manner. Choose answer
- A. if the sentence contains an error in English grammar or usage
- B. if the sentence contains an error in punctuation
- C. if the sentence contains an error in spelling or capitalization
- D. if the sentence does not contain any errors

1. The severity of the sentence prescribed by contemporary statutes - including both the former and the revised New York Penal Laws - do not depend on what crime was intended by the offender.

2. It is generally recognized that two defects in the early law of attempt played a part in the birth of burglary: (1) immunity from prosecution for conduct short of the last act before completion of the crime, and (2) the relatively minor penalty imposed for an attempt (it being a common law misdemeanor) vis-a-vis the completed offense.

3. The first sentence of the statute is applicable to employees who enter their place of employment, invited guests, and all other persons who have an express or implied license or privilege to enter the premises.

4. Contemporary criminal codes in the United States generally divide burglary into various degrees, differentiating the categories according to place, time and other attendent circumstances.

Questions 5-8.

DIRECTIONS: Questions 5 through 8 are to be answered SOLELY on the basis of the following passage.

The difficulty experienced in determining which party has the burden of proving payment or non-payment is due largely to a tack of consistency between the rules of pleading and the rules of proof. In some cases, a plaintiff is obligated by a rule of pleading to allege non-payment on his complaint, yet is not obligated to prove non-payment on the trial. An action upon a contract for the payment of money will serve as an illustration. In such a case, the plaintiff must allege non-payment in his complaint, but the burden of proving payment on the trial is upon the defendant. An important and frequently cited case on this problem is Conkling v. Weatherwax. In that case, the action was brought to establish and enforce a legacy as a lien upon real property. The defendant alleged in her answer that the legacy had been paid. There was no witness competent to testify for the plaintiff to show that the legacy had not been paid. Therefore, the question of the burden of proof became of primary importance since, if the plaintiff had the burden of proving non-payment, she must fail in her action; whereas, if the burden of proof was on the defendant to prove payment, the plaintiff might win. The Court of Appeals held that the burden of proof was on the plaintiff. In the course of his opinion, Judge Vann attempted to harmonize the conflicting cases on this subject, and for that purpose formulated three rules. These rules have been construed and applied to numerous subsequent cases. As so construed and applied, these may be summarized as follows:

Rule 1: In an action upon a contract for the payment of money only, where the complaint does not allege a balance due over and above all payments made, the plaintiff must allege nonpayment in his complaint, but the burden of proving payment is upon the defendant. In such a case, payment is an affirmative defense which the defendant must plead in his answer. If the defendant fails to plead payment, but pleads a general denial instead, he will not be permitted to introduce evidence of payment.

Rule 2: Where the complaint sets forth a balance in excess of all payments, owing to the structure of the pleading, burden is upon the plaintiff to prove his allegation. In this case, the defendant is not required to plead payment as a defense in his answer but may introduce evidence of payment under a general denial.

Rule 3: When the action is not upon contract for the payment of money, but is upon an obligation created by operation of law, or is for the enforcement of a lien where non-payment of the amount secured is part of the cause of action, it is necessary both to allege and prove the fact of nonpayment.

5. In the above passage, the case of Conkling v. Weatherwax was cited PRIMARILY to illustrate

   A. a case where the burden of proof was on the defendant to prove payment
   B. how the question of the burden of proof can affect the outcome of a case
   C. the effect of a legacy as a lien upon real property
   D. how conflicting cases concerning the burden of proof were harmonized

6. According to the above passage, the pleading of payment is a defense in

   A. Rule 1, but not Rules 2 and 3
   B. Rule 2, but not Rules 1 and 3
   C. Rules 1 and 3, but not Rule 2
   D. Rules 2 and 3, but not Rule 1

7. The facts in Conkling v. Weatherwax closely resemble the conditions described in Rule

   A. 1   B. 2
   C. 3   D. none of the rules

8. The major topic of the above passage may BEST be described as

   A. determining the ownership of property
   B. providing a legal definition
   C. placing the burden of proof
   D. formulating rules for deciding cases

Questions 9-12.

DIRECTIONS: Questions 9 through 12 consist of six sentences which can be arranged in a logical sequence. For each question, select the choice which places the numbered sentences in the MOST logical sequence.

9. I. The burden of proof as to each issue is determined before trial and remains upon the same party throughout the trial.
    II. The jury is at liberty to believe one witness testimony as against a number of contradictory witnesses.
    III. In a civil case, the party bearing the burden of proof is required to prove his contention by a fair preponderance of the evidence.
    IV. However, it must be noted that a fair preponderance of evidence does not necessarily mean a greater number of witnesses.
    V. The burden of proof is the burden which rests upon one of the parties to an action to persuade the trier of the facts, generally the jury, that a proposition he asserts is true.
    VI. If the evidence is equally balanced, or if it leaves the jury in such doubt as to be unable to decide the controversy either way, judgment must be given against the party upon whom the burden of proof rests.

    The CORRECT sequence is:

    A. III, II, V, IV, I, VI
    B. I, II, VI, V, III, IV
    C. III, IV, V, I, II, VI
    D. V, I, III, VI, IV, II

10. I. If a parent is without assets and is unemployed, he cannot be convicted of the crime of non-support of a child.
    II. The term *sufficient ability* has been held to mean sufficient financial ability.
    III. It does not matter if his unemployment is by choice or unavoidable circumstances.
    IV. If he fails to take any steps at all, he may be liable to prosecution for endangering the welfare of a child.
    V. Under the penal law, a parent is responsible for the support of his minor child only if the parent is of sufficient ability.
    VI. An indigent parent may meet his obligation by borrowing money or by seeking aid under the provisions of the Social Welfare Law.

    The CORRECT sequence is:

    A. VI, I, V, III, II, IV
    B. I, III, V, II, IV, VI
    C. V, II, I, III, VI, IV
    D. I, VI, IV, V, II, III

11.
   I. Consider, for example, the case of a rabble rouser who urges a group of twenty people to go out and break the windows of a nearby factory.
   II. Therefore, the law fills the indicated gap with the crime of *inciting to riot*.
   III. A person is considered guilty of inciting to riot when he urges ten or more persons to engage in tumultuous and violent conduct of a kind likely to create public alarm.
   IV. However, if he has not obtained the cooperation of at least four people, he cannot be charged with unlawful assembly.
   V. The charge of inciting to riot was added to the law to cover types of conduct which cannot be classified as either the crime of *riot* or the crime of *unlawful* assembly.
   VI. If he acquires the acquiescence of at least four of them, he is guilty of unlawful assembly even if the project does not materialize.

   The CORRECT sequence is:
   A. III, V, I, VI, IV, II
   B. V, I, IV, VI, II, III
   C. III, IV, I, V, II, VI
   D. V, I, IV, VI, III, II

12.
   I. If, however, the rebuttal evidence presents an issue of credibility, it is for the jury to determine whether the presumption has, in fact, been destroyed.
   II. Once sufficient evidence to the contrary is introduced, the presumption disappears from the trial.
   III. The effect of a presumption is to place the burden upon the adversary to come forward with evidence to rebut the presumption.
   IV. When a presumption is overcome and ceases to exist in the case, the fact or facts which gave rise to the presumption still remain.
   V. Whether a presumption has been overcome is ordinarily a question for the court.
   VI. Such information may furnish a basis for a logical inference.

   The CORRECT sequence is:
   A. IV, VI, II, V, I, III
   B. III, II, V, I, IV, VI
   C. V, III, VI, IV, II, I
   D. V, IV, I, II, VI, III

13. In order to obtain an accurate statement from a person who has witnessed a crime, it is BEST to question the witness

   A. as soon as possible after the crime was committed
   B. after the witness has discussed the crime with other witnesses
   C. after the witness has had sufficient time to reflect on events and formulate a logical statement
   D. after the witness has been advised that he is obligated to tell the whole truth

14. A young woman was stabbed in the hand in her home by her estranged boyfriend. Her mother and two sisters were at home at the time.
   Of the following, it would generally be BEST to interview the young woman in the presence of

   A. her mother only
   B. all members of her immediate family
   C. members of the family who actually observed the crime
   D. the official authorities

15. The one of the following which is NOT effective in obtaining complete testimony from a witness during an interview is to   15._____

    A. ask questions in chronological order
    B. permit the witness to structure the interview
    C. make sure you fully understand the response to each question
    D. review questions to be asked beforehand

KEY (CORRECT ANSWERS)

1.	A	6.	A
2.	D	7.	C
3.	D	8.	C
4.	C	9.	D
5.	B	10.	C

11. A
12. B
13. A
14. D
15. B

TEST 2

DIRECTIONS: Each question or incomplete statement is followed by several suggested answers or completions. Select the one that BEST answers the question or completes the statement. *PRINT THE LETTER OF THE CORRECT ANSWER IN THE SPACE AT THE RIGHT.*

1. You are conducting an initial interview with a witness who expresses reluctance, even hostility, to being questioned. You feel it would be helpful to take some notes during the interview.
   In this situation, it would be BEST to

   A. put off note-taking until a follow-up interview and concentrate on establishing rapport with the witness
   B. explain the necessity of note-taking and proceed to take notes during the interview
   C. make notes from memory after the witness has left
   D. take notes, but as unobtrusively as possible

   1._____

2. An assistant is starting an interview with an elderly man who was the victim of a robbery. The man begins by mentioning his minor aches and pains. The aide immediately changes the subject to the robbery.
   This action by the aide should GENERALLY be considered

   A. *proper* chiefly because it speeds up the interviewing process
   B. *improper* chiefly because the man is likely to become confused as to what information is really important
   C. *proper* chiefly because the man is likely to be impressed with the aide's interest in the crime
   D. *improper* chiefly because an opportunity for gaining pertinent information may be lost

   2._____

3. You are interviewing the owner of a stolen car about facts relating to the robbery. After completing his statement, the car owner suddenly states that some of the details he has just related are not correct. You realize that this change might be significant.
   Of the following, it would be BEST for you to

   A. ask the owner what other details he may have given incorrectly
   B. make a note of the discrepancy for discussion at a later date
   C. repeat your questioning on the details that were misstated until you have covered that area completely
   D. explain to the owner that because of his change of testimony, you will have to repeat the entire interview

   3._____

4. You are interviewing a client who has just been assaulted. He has trouble collecting his thoughts and telling his story coherently.
   Which of the following represents the MOST effective method of questioning under these circumstances?

   A. Ask questions which structure the client's story chronologically into units, each with a beginning, middle, and end.
   B. Ask several questions at a time to structure the interview.

   4._____

C. Ask open-ended questions which allow the client to respond in a variety of ways.
D. Begin the interview with several detailed questions in order to focus the client's attention on the situation.

5. Following are two statements that might be correct concerning the relationship with clients:

    I. When practical the client should be encouraged to take some steps on his own behalf to aid the office in handling his case
    II. The client should be told what steps the office proposes to take on his behalf

    Which of the following CORRECTLY classifies the above statements?

    A. Statement I is generally correct, but Statement II is not.
    B. Statement II is generally correct, but Statement I is not.
    C. Both statements are generally correct.
    D. Neither statement is generally correct.

6. You are in the District Attorney's office interviewing an elderly female victim of an assault in order to prepare a list of charges.
    The one of the following which would be MOST important in determining all the facts is

    A. creating a close, cooperative working relationship with the victim
    B. establishing your authority at the beginning of the interview
    C. maintaining a relaxed atmosphere during the interview
    D. having access to the particular statutes which might apply to this case

7. A client is critical of the way he has been treated by government agencies in the past. A paralegal aide interviewing him defends the overall performance of government employees.
    This reaction by the aide is GENERALLY

    A. *appropriate;* the aide has an obligation to defend fellow workers in government service when such defense is justified
    B. *inappropriate;* the aide should remain neutral rather than volunteer his personal opinions
    C. *appropriate;* the aide should honestly express his personal opinions in such circumstances unless it is likely to provoke antagonism
    D. *inappropriate;* the aide should agree with the client's comments to help establish a greater rapport with him

Questions 8-11.

DIRECTIONS: Questions 8 through 11 are to be answered SOLELY on the basis of the following passage.

A person may use physical force upon another person when and to the extent he reasonably believes such to be necessary to defend himself or a third person from what he reasonably believes to be the use or imminent use of unlawful physical force by such other person, unless (a) the latter's conduct was provoked by the actor himself with intent to cause physical injury to another person, or (b) the actor was the initial aggressor; or (c) the physical force involved is the product of a combat by agreement not specifically authorized by law.

A person may not use deadly physical force upon another person under the circumstances specified above unless: (a) he reasonably believes that such other person is using or is about to use deadly physical force. Even in such case, however, the actor may not use deadly physical force if he knows he can with complete safety as to himself and others avoid the necessity of doing so by retreating, except that he is under no duty to retreat if he is in his dwelling and is not the initial aggressor; or (b) he reasonably believes that such other person is committing or attempting to commit a kidnapping, forcible rape, or forcible sodomy.

8. Jones and Smith, who have not met before, get into an argument in a tavern. Smith takes a punch at Jones but misses. Jones then hits Smith on the chin with his fist. Smith falls to the floor and suffers minor injuries. According to the above passage, it would be CORRECT to state that

   A. *only* Smith was justified in using physical force
   B. *only* Jones was justified in using physical force
   C. both Smith and Jones were justified in using physical force
   D. neither Smith nor Jones was justified in using physical force

8.____

9. While walking down the street, Brady observes Miller striking Mrs. Adams on the head with his fist in an attempt to steal her purse.
   According to the above passage, it would be CORRECT to state that Brady would

   A. not be justified in using deadly physical force against Miller since Brady can safety retreat
   B. be justified in using physical force against Miller, but not deadly physical force
   C. not be justified in using physical force against Miller since Brady himself is not being attacked
   D. be justified in using deadly physical force

9.____

10. Winters is attacked from behind by Sharp, who attempts to beat up Winters with a blackjack. Winters disarms Sharp and succeeds in subduing him with a series of blows to the head. Sharp stops fighting and explains that he thought Winters was the person who had robbed his apartment a few minutes before, but now realizes his mistake. According to the above passage, it would be CORRECT to state that

    A. Winters was justified in using physical force on Sharp only to the extent necessary to defend himself
    B. Winters was not justified in using physical force on Sharp since Sharp's attack was provoked by what he believed to be Winters' behavior
    C. Sharp was justified in using physical force on Winters since he reasonably believed that Winters had unlawfully robbed him
    D. Winters was justified in using physical force on Sharp only because Sharp was acting mistakenly in attacking him

10.____

11. Roberts hears a noise in the cellar of his home and, upon investigation, discovers an intruder, Welch. Welch moves towards Roberts in a threatening manner, thrusts his hand into a bulging pocket, and withdraws what appears to be a gun. Roberts thereupon strikes Welch over the head with a golf club. He then sees that the *gun* is a toy. Welch later dies of head injuries.
    According to the above passage, it would be CORRECT to state that Roberts

11.____

A. *was justified* in using deadly physical force because he reasonably believed Welch was about to use deadly physical force
B. *was not justified* in using deadly physical force
C. *was justified* in using deadly physical force only because he did not provoke Welch's conduct
D. *was justified* in using deadly physical force only because he was not the initial aggressor

Questions 12-15.

DIRECTIONS: Questions 12 through 15 are to be answered SOLELY on the basis of the following passage.

From the beginning, the Supreme Court has supervised the fairness of trials conducted by the Federal government. But the Constitution, as originally drafted, gave the court no such general authority in state oases. The court's power to deal with state cases comes from the Fourteenth Amendment, which became part of the Constitution in 1868. The crucial provision forbids any state to "deprive any person of life, liberty or property without due process of law."

The guarantee of "due process" would seem, at the least, to require fair procedure in criminal trials. But curiously, the Supreme Court did not speak on the question for many decades. During that time, however, the due process clause was interpreted to bar "unreasonable" state economic regulations, such as minimum wage laws.

In 1915, there came the case of Leo M. Frank, a Georgian convicted of murder in a trial that he contended was dominated by mob hysteria. Historians now agree that there was such hysteria, with overtones of anti-semitism.

The Supreme Court held that it could not look past the findings of the Georgia courts that there had been no mob atmosphere at the trial. Justices Oliver Wendell Holmes and Charles Evans Hughes dissented, arguing that the constitutional guarantee would be "a barren one" if the Federal courts could not make their own inferences from the facts.

In 1923, the case of Moore v. Dempsey involved five Arkansas blacks convicted of murder and sentenced to death in a community so aroused against them that at one point they were saved from lynching only by Federal troops. Witnesses against them were said to have been beaten into testifying.

The court, though not actually setting aside the convictions, directed a lower Federal court to hold a habeas corpus hearing to find out whether the trial had been fair, or whether the whole proceeding had been "a mask — that counsel, jury, and judge were swept to the fatal end by an irresistible wave of public opinion."

12. According to the above passage, the Supreme Court's INITIAL interpretation of the Fourteenth Amendment

    A. protected state supremacy in economic matters
    B. increased the scope of Federal jurisdiction
    C. required fair procedures in criminal trials
    D. prohibited the enactment of minimum wage laws

13. According to the above passage, the Supreme Court in the Frank case   13._____

    A. denied that there had been mob hysteria at the trial
    B. decided that the guilty verdict was supported by the evidence
    C. declined to question the state court's determination of the facts
    D. found that Leo Frank had not received *due process*

14. According to the above passage, the dissenting judges in the Frank case maintained that   14._____

    A. due process was an empty promise in the circumstances of that case
    B. the Federal courts could not guarantee certain provisions of the Constitution
    C. the Federal courts should not make their own inferences from the facts in state cases
    D. the Supreme Court had rendered the Constitution *barren*

15. Of the following, the MOST appropriate title for the above passage is: 15._____

    A. THE CONDUCT OF FEDERAL TRIALS
    B. THE DEVELOPMENT OF STATES' RIGHTS: 1868-1923
    C. MOORE V. DEMPSEY: A CASE STUDY IN CRIMINAL JUSTICE
    D. DUE PROCESS - THE EVOLUTION OF A CONSTITUTIONAL CORNERSTONE

KEY (CORRECT ANSWERS)

1.	B		6.	A
2.	D		7.	B
3.	C		8.	B
4.	A		9.	B
5.	C		10.	A

11. A
12. D
13. C
14. A
15. D

READING COMPREHENSION
UNDERSTANDING AND INTERPRETING WRITTEN MATERIAL

EXAMINATION SECTION
TEST 1

DIRECTIONS: Each question or incomplete statement is followed by several suggested answers or completions. Select the one that BEST answers the question or completes the statement. *PRINT THE LETTER OF THE CORRECT ANSWER IN THE SPACE AT THE RIGHT.*

Questions 1-5.

DIRECTIONS: Questions 1 through 5 are to be answered on the basis of the following passage.

The laws with which criminal courts are concerned contain threats of punishment for infraction of specified rules. Consequently, the courts are organized primarily for implementation of the punitive societal reaction of crime. While the informal organization of most courts allows the judge to use discretion as to which guilty persons actually are to be punished, the threat of punishment for all guilty persons always is present. Also, in recent years a number of formal provisions for the use of non-punitive and treatment methods by the criminal courts have been made, but the threat of punishment remains, even for the recipients of the treatment and non-punitive measures. For example, it has become possible for courts to grant probation, which can be non-punitive, to some offenders, but the probationer is constantly under the threat of punishment, for, if he does not maintain the conditions of his probation, he may be imprisoned. As the treatment reaction to crime becomes more popular, the criminal courts may have as their sole function the determination of the guilt or innocence of the accused persons, leaving the problem of correcting criminals entirely to outsiders. Under such conditions, the organization of the court system, the duties and activities of court personnel, and the nature of the trial all would be decidedly different.

1. Which one of the following is the BEST description of the subject matter of the above passage?
The

   A. value of non-punitive measures for criminals
   B. effect of punishment on guilty individuals
   C. punitive functions of the criminal courts
   D. success of probation as a deterrent of crime

1.____

2. It may be INFERRED from the above passage that the present traditional organization of the criminal court system is a result of

   A. the nature of the laws with which these courts are concerned
   B. a shift from non-punitive to punitive measures for correctional purposes
   C. an informal arrangement between court personnel and the government
   D. a formal decision made by court personnel to increase efficiency

2.____

23

3. All persons guilty of breaking certain specified rules, according to the above passage, are subject to the threat of

   A. treatment
   B. punishment
   C. probation
   D. retrial

4. According to the above passage, the decision whether or not to punish a guilty person is a function USUALLY performed by

   A. the jury
   B. the criminal code
   C. the judge
   D. corrections personnel

5. According to the above passage, which one of the following is a possible effect of an increase in the *treatment reactions to crime?*

   A. A decrease in the number of court personnel
   B. An increase in the number of criminal trials
   C. Less reliance on probation as a non-punitive treatment measure
   D. A decrease in the functions of the court following determination of guilt

Questions 6-8.

DIRECTIONS: Questions 6 through 8 are to be answered on the basis of the following passage.

A glaring exception to the usual practice of the judicial trial as a means of conflict resolution is the utilization of administrative hearings. The growing tendency to create administrative bodies with rule-making and quasi-judicial powers has shattered many standard concepts. A comprehensive examination of the legal process cannot neglect these newer patterns.

In the administrative process, the legislative, executive, and judicial functions are mixed together, and many functions, such as investigating, advocating, negotiating, testifying, rule making, and adjudicating, are carried out by the same agency. The reason for the breakdown of the separation-of-powers formula is not hard to find. It was felt by Congress, and state and municipal legislatures, that certain regulatory tasks could not be performed efficiently, rapidly, expertly, and with due concern for the public interest by the traditional branches of government. Accordingly, regulatory agencies were delegated powers to consider disputes from the earliest stage of investigation to the final stages of adjudication entirely within each agency itself, subject only to limited review in the regular courts.

6. The above passage states that the usual means for conflict resolution is through the use of

   A. judicial trial
   B. administrative hearing
   C. legislation
   D. regulatory agencies

7. The above passage IMPLIES that the use of administrative hearing in resolving conflict is a(n) _____ approach.

   A. traditional
   B. new
   C. dangerous
   D. experimental

8. The above passage states that the reason for the breakdown of the separation-of-powers formula in the administrative process is that

A. Congress believed that certain regulatory tasks could be better performed by separate agencies
B. legislative and executive functions are incompatible in the same agency
C. investigative and regulatory functions are not normally reviewed by the courts
D. state and municipal legislatures are more concerned with efficiency than with legality

Questions 9-10.

DIRECTIONS: Questions 9 and 10 are to be answered SOLELY on the basis of the information given in the following paragraph.

An assumption commonly made in regard to the reliability of testimony is that when a number of persons report upon the same matter, those details upon which there is an agreement may, in general, be considered as substantiated. Experiments have shown, however, that there is a tendency for the same errors to appear in the testimony of different individuals, and that, quite apart from any collusion, agreement of testimony is no proof of dependability.

9. According to the above paragraph, it is commonly assumed that details of an event are substantiated when

   A. a number of persons report upon them
   B. a reliable person testifies to them
   C. no errors are apparent in the testimony of different individuals
   D. several witnesses are in agreement about them

10. According to the above paragraph, agreement in the testimony of different witnesses to the same event is

    A. evaluated more reliably when considered apart from collusion
    B. not the result of chance
    C. not a guarantee of the accuracy of the facts
    D. the result of a mass reaction of the witnesses

Questions 11-12.

DIRECTIONS: Questions 11 and 12 are to be answered SOLELY on the basis of the information given in the following paragraph.

The accuracy of the information about past occurrence obtainable in an interview is so low that one must take the stand that the best use to be made of the interview in this connection is a means of finding clues and avenues of access to more reliable sources of information. On the other hand, feelings and attitudes have been found to be clearly and correctly revealed in a properly conducted personal interview.

11. According to the above paragraph, information obtained in a personal interview

    A. can be corroborated by other clues and more reliable sources of information revealed at the interview
    B. can be used to develop leads to other sources of information about past events
    C. is not reliable
    D. is reliable if it relates to recent occurrences

12. According to the above paragraph, the personal interview is suitable for obtaining   12.____

    A. emotional reactions to a given situation
    B. fresh information on factors which may be forgotten
    C. revived recollection of previous events for later use as testimony
    D. specific information on material already reduced to writing

Questions 13-15.

DIRECTIONS: Questions 13 through 15 are to be answered on the basis of the following paragraph.

Admissibility of handwriting standards (samples of handwriting for the purpose of comparison) as a basis for expert testimony is frequently necessary when the authenticity of disputed documents may be at issue. Under the older rules of common law, only that writing relating to the issues in the case could be used as a basis for handwriting testimony by an expert. Today, most jurisdictions admit irrelevant writings as standards for comparison. However, their genuineness, in all instances, must be established to the satisfaction of the court. There are a number of types of documents, however, not ordinarily relevant to the issues which are seldom acceptable to the court as handwriting standards, such as bail bonds, signatures on affidavits, depositions, etc. These are usually already before the court as part of the record in a case. Exhibits written in the presence of a witness or prepared voluntarily for a law enforcement officer are readily admissible in most jurisdictions. Testimony of a witness who is considered familiar with the writing is admissible in some jurisdictions. In criminal cases, it is possible that the signature on the fingerprint card obtained in connection with the arrest of the defendant for the crime currently charged may be admitted as a handwriting standard. In order to give the defendant the fairest possible treatment, most jurisdictions do not admit the signatures on fingerprint cards pertaining to prior arrests. However, they are admitted sometimes. In such instances, the court usually requires that the signature be photographed or removed from the card and no reference be made to the origin of the signature.

13. Of the following, the types of handwriting standards MOST likely to be admitted in evidence by most jurisdictions are those   13.____

    A. appearing on depositions and bail bonds
    B. which were written in the presence of a witness or voluntarily given to a law enforcement officer
    C. identified by witnesses who claim to be familiar with the handwriting
    D. which are in conformity with the rules of common law only

14. The PRINCIPAL factor which generally determines the acceptance of handwriting standards by the courts is   14.____

    A. the relevance of the submitted documents to the issues of the case
    B. the number of witnesses who have knowledge of the submitted documents
    C. testimony that the writing has been examined by a handwriting expert
    D. acknowledgment by the court of the authenticity of the submitted documents

15. The MOST logical reason for requiring the removal of the signature of a defendant from fingerprint cards pertaining to prior arrests, before admitting the signature in court as a handwriting standard, is that   15.____

A. it simplifies the process of identification of the signature as a standard for comparison
B. the need for identifying the fingerprints is eliminated
C. mention of prior arrests may be prejudicial to the defendant
D. a handwriting expert does not need information pertaining to prior arrests in order to make his identification

Questions 16-20.

DIRECTIONS: Questions 16 through 20 are to be answered SOLELY on the basis of the information contained in the following paragraph.

A statement which is offered in an attempt to prove the truth of the matters therein stated, but which is not made by the author as a witness before the court at the particular trial in which it is so offered, is hearsay. This is so whether the statement consists of words (oral or written), of symbols used as a substitute for words, or of signs or other conduct offered as the equivalent of a statement. Subject to some well-established exceptions, hearsay is not generally acceptable as evidence, and it does not become competent evidence just because it is received by the court without objection. One basis for this rule is simply that a fact cannot be proved by showing that somebody stated it was a fact. Another basis for the rule is the fundamental principle that in a criminal prosecution the testimony of the witness shall be taken before the court, so that at the time he gives the testimony offered in evidence he will be sworn and subject to cross-examination, the scrutiny of the court, and confrontation by the accused.

16. Which of the following is hearsay? 16._____
    A(n)

    A. written statement by a person not present at the court hearing where the statement is submitted as proof of an occurrence
    B. oral statement in court by a witness of what he saw
    C. written statement of what he saw by a witness present in court
    D. re-enactment by a witness in court of what he saw

17. In a criminal case, a statement by a person not present in court is 17._____

    A. *acceptable* evidence if not objected to by the prosecutor
    B. *acceptable* evidence if not objected to by the defense lawyer
    C. *not acceptable* evidence except in certain well-settled circumstances
    D. *not acceptable* evidence under any circumstances

18. The rule on hearsay is founded on the belief that 18._____

    A. proving someone said an act occurred is not proof that the act did occur
    B. a person who has knowledge about a case should be willing to appear in court
    C. persons not present in court are likely to be unreliable witnesses
    D. permitting persons to testify without appearing in court will lead to a disrespect for law

19. One reason for the general rule that a witness in a criminal case must give his testimony in court is that

   A. a witness may be influenced by threats to make untrue statements
   B. the opposite side is then permitted to question him
   C. the court provides protection for a witness against unfair questioning
   D. the adversary system is designed to prevent a miscarriage of justice

20. Of the following, the MOST appropriate title for the above passage would be

   A. WHAT IS HEARSAY?
   B. RIGHTS OF DEFENDANTS
   C. TRIAL PROCEDURES
   D. TESTIMONY OF WITNESSES

21. A person's statements are independent of who he is or what he is. Statements made by a person are not proved true or false by questioning his character or his position. A statement should stand or fall on its merits, regardless of who makes the statement. Truth is determined by evidence only. A person's character or personality should not be the determining factor in logic. Discussions should not become incidents of name calling.
   According to the above, whether or not a statement is true depends on the

   A. recipient's conception of validity
   B. maker's reliability
   C. extent of support by facts
   D. degree of merit the discussion has

Question 22-25.

DIRECTIONS: Questions 22 through 25 are to be answered on the basis of the following passage.

The question, whether an act, repugnant to the Constitution, can become the law of the land, is a question deeply interesting to the United States; but, happily, not of an intricacy proportioned to its interest. It seems only necessary to recognize certain principles, supposed to have been long and well-established, to decide it. That the people have an original right to establish, for their future government, such principles as, in their opinion, shall most conduce to their own happiness, is the basis on which the whole American fabric has been erected. The exercise of this original right is a very great exertion; nor can it, nor ought it, to be frequently repeated. The principles, therefore, so established are deemed fundamental; and as the authority from which they proceed is supreme, and can seldom act, they are designed to be permanent.

22. The BEST title for the above passage would be

   A. PRINCIPLES OF THE CONSTITUTION
   B. THE ROOT OF CONSTITUTIONAL CHANGE
   C. ONLY PEOPLE CAN CHANGE THE CONSTITUTION
   D. METHODS OF CONSTITUTIONAL CHANGE

23. According to the above passage, original right is

   A. fundamental to the principle that the people may choose their own form of government
   B. established by the Constitution

C. the result of a very great exertion and should not often be repeated
D. supreme, can seldom act, and is designed to be permanent

24. Whether an act not in keeping with Constitutional principles can become law is, according to the above passage,

   A. an intricate problem requiring great thought and concentration
   B. determined by the proportionate interests of legislators
   C. determined by certain long established principles, fundamental to Constitutional Law
   D. an intricate problem, but less intricate than it would seem from the interest shown in it

24._____

25. According to the above passage, the phrase *and can seldom act* refers to the

   A. principle enacted early into law by Americans when they chose their future form of government
   B. original rights of the people as vested in the Constitution
   C. original framers of the Constitution
   D. established, fundamental principles of government

25._____

KEY (CORRECT ANSWERS)

1.	C	11.	B
2.	A	12.	A
3.	B	13.	B
4.	C	14.	D
5.	D	15.	C
6.	A	16.	A
7.	B	17.	C
8.	A	18.	A
9.	D	19.	B
10.	C	20.	A

21. C
22. B
23. A
24. D
25. A

TEST 2

DIRECTIONS: Each question or incomplete statement is followed by several suggested answers or completions. Select the one that BEST answers the question or completes the statement. *PRINT THE LETTER OF THE CORRECT ANSWER IN THE SPACE AT THE RIGHT.*

Questions 1-3.

DIRECTIONS: Questions 1 through 3 are to be answered SOLELY on the basis of the following paragraph.

The police laboratory performs a valuable service in crime investigation by assisting in the reconstruction of criminal action and by aiding in the identification of persons and things. When studied by a technician, physical things found at crime scenes often reveal facts useful in identifying the criminal and in determining what has occurred. The nature of substances to be examined and the character of the examination to be made vary so widely that the services of a large variety of skilled scientific persons are needed in crime investigations. To employ such a complete staff and to provide them with equipment and standards needed for all possible analysis and comparisons is beyond the means and the needs of any but the largest police departments. The search of crime scenes for physical evidence also calls for the services of specialists supplied with essential equipment and assigned to each tour of duty so as to provide service at any hour.

1. If a police department employs a large staff of technicians of various types in its laboratory, it will affect crime investigations to the extent that

    A. most crimes will be speedily solved
    B. identification of criminals will be aided
    C. search of crime scenes for physical evidence will become of less importance
    D. investigation by police officers will not usually be required

1._____

2. According to the above paragraph, the MOST complete study of objects found at the scenes of crimes is

    A. always done in all large police departments
    B. based on assigning one technician to each tour of duty
    C. probably done only in large police departments
    D. probably done in police departments of communities with low crime rates

2._____

3. According to the above paragraph, a large variety of skilled technicians is useful in criminal investigations because

    A. crimes cannot be solved without their assistance as part of the police team
    B. large police departments need large staffs
    C. many different kinds of tests on various substances can be made
    D. the police cannot predict what methods may be tried by wily criminals

3._____

Questions 4-6.

DIRECTIONS: Questions 4 through 6 are to be answered SOLELY on the basis of the following passage.

Probably the most important single mechanism for bringing the resources of science and technology to bear on the problems of crime would be the establishment of a major prestigious science and technology research program within a research institute. The program would create interdisciplinary teams of mathematicians, computer scientists, electronics engineers, physicists, biologists, and other natural scientists, psychologists, sociologists, economists, and lawyers. The institute and the program must be significant enough to attract the best scientists available, and, to this end, the director of this institute must himself have a background in science and technology and have the respect of scientists. Because it would be difficult to attract such a staff into the Federal government, the institute should be established by a university, a group of universities, or an independent nonprofit organization, and should be within a major metropolitan area. The institute would have to establish close ties with neighboring criminal justice agencies that would receive the benefit of serving as experimental laboratories for such an institute. In fact, the proposal for the institute might be jointly submitted with the criminal justice agencies. The research program would require, in order to bring together the necessary *critical mass* of competent staff, an annual budget which might reach 5 million dollars, funded with at least three years of lead time to assure continuity. Such a major scientific and technological research institute should be supported by the Federal government.

4. Of the following, the MOST appropriate title for the foregoing passage is

   A. RESEARCH - AN INTERDISCIPLINARY APPROACH TO FIGHTING CRIME
   B. A CURRICULUM FOR FIGHTING CRIME
   C. THE ROLE OF THE UNIVERSITY IN THE FIGHT AGAINST CRIME
   D. GOVERNMENTAL SUPPORT OF CRIMINAL RESEARCH PROGRAMS

5. According to the above passage, in order to attract the best scientists available, the research institute should

   A. provide psychologists and sociologists to counsel individual members of interdisciplinary teams
   B. encourage close ties with neighboring criminal justice agencies
   C. be led by a person who is respected in the scientific community
   D. be directly operated and funded by the Federal government

6. The term *critical mass,* as used in the above passage, refers MAINLY to

   A. a staff which would remain for three years of continuous service to the institute
   B. staff members necessary to carry out the research program of the institute successfully
   C. the staff necessary to establish relations with criminal justice agencies which will serve as experimental laboratories for the institute
   D. a staff which would be able to assist the institute in raising adequate funds

Questions 7-9.

DIRECTIONS: Questions 7 through 9 are to be answered SOLELY on the basis of the following paragraph.

The use of modern scientific methods in the examination of physical evidence often provides information to the investigator which he could not otherwise obtain. This applies particularly to small objects and materials present in minute quantities or trace evidence because the quantities here are such that they may be overlooked without methodical searching, and often special means of detection are needed. Whenever two objects come in contact with one another, there is a transfer of material, however slight. Usually, the softer object will transfer to the harder, but the transfer may be mutual. The quantity of material transferred differs with the type of material involved and the more violent the contact the greater the degree of transference. Through scientific methods of determining physical properties and chemical composition, we can add to the facts observable by the investigator's unaided senses, and thereby increase the chances of identification.

7. According to the above paragraph, the amount of material transferred whenever two objects come in contact with one another

   A. varies directly with the softness of the objects involved
   B. varies directly with the violence of the contact of the objects
   C. is greater when two soft, rather than hard, objects come into violent contact with each other
   D. is greater when coarse-grained, rather than smooth-grained, materials are involved

8. According to the above paragraph, the PRINCIPAL reason for employing scientific methods in obtaining trace evidence is that

   A. other methods do not involve a methodical search of the crime scene
   B. scientific methods of examination frequently reveal physical evidence which did not previously exist
   C. the amount of trace evidence may be so sparse that other methods are useless
   D. trace evidence cannot be properly identified unless special means of detection are employed

9. According to the above paragraph, the one of the following statements which BEST describes the manner in which scientific methods of analyzing physical evidence assists the investigator is that such methods

   A. add additional valuable information to the investigator's own knowledge of complex and rarely occurring materials found as evidence
   B. compensate for the lack of important evidential material through the use of physical and chemical analyses
   C. make possible an analysis of evidence which goes beyond the ordinary capacity of the investigator's senses
   D. identify precisely those physical characteristics of the individual which the untrained senses of the investigator are unable to discern

Questions 10-13.

DIRECTIONS: Questions 10 through 13 are to be answered SOLELY on the basis of the information contained in the following paragraph.

Under the provisions of the Bank Protection Act of 1968, enacted July 8, 1968, each Federal banking supervisory agency, as of January 7, 1969, had to issue rules establishing minimum standards with which financial institutions under their control must comply with respect to the installation, maintenance, and operation of security devices and procedures, reasonable in cost, to discourage robberies, burglaries, and larcenies, and to assist in the identification and apprehension of persons who commit such acts. The rules set the time limits within which the affected banks and savings and loan associations must comply with the standards, and the rules require the submission of periodic reports on the steps taken. A violator of a rule under this Act is subject to a civil penalty not to exceed $100 for each day of the violation. The enforcement of these regulations rests with the responsible banking supervisory agencies.

10. The Bank Protection Act of 1968 was designed to 10.____

    A. provide Federal police protection for banks covered by the Act
    B. have organizations covered by the Act take precautions against criminals
    C. set up a system for reporting all bank robberies to the FBI
    D. insure institutions covered by the Act from financial loss due to robberies, burglaries, and larcenies

11. Under the provisions of the Bank Protection Act of 1968, each Federal banking supervisory agency was required to set up rules for financial institutions covered by the Act governing the 11.____

    A. hiring of personnel
    B. punishment of burglars
    C. taking of protective measures
    D. penalties for violations

12. Financial institutions covered by the Bank Protection Act of 1968 were required to 12.____

    A. file reports at regular intervals on what they had done to prevent theft
    B. identify and apprehend persons who commit robberies, burglaries, and larcenies
    C. draw up a code of ethics for their employees
    D. have fingerprints of their employees filed with the FBI

13. Under the provisions of the Bank Protection Act of 1968, a bank which is subject to the rules established under the Act and which violates a rule is liable to a penalty of NOT _____ than $100 for each _____. 13.____

    A. more; violation   B. less; day of violation
    C. less; violation   D. more; day of violation

Questions 14-17.

DIRECTIONS: Questions 14 through 17 are to be answered SOLELY on the basis of the following passage.

Specific measures for prevention of pilferage will be based on careful analysis of the conditions at each agency. The most practical and effective method to control casual pilferage is the establishment of psychological deterrents.

One of the most common means of discouraging casual pilferage is to search individuals leaving the agency at unannounced times and places. These spot searches may occasionally detect attempts at theft, but greater value is realized by bringing to the attention of individuals the fact that they may be apprehended if they do attempt the illegal removal of property.

An aggressive security education program is an effective means of convincing employees that they have much more to lose than they do to gain by engaging in acts of theft. It is important for all employees to realize that pilferage is morally wrong no matter how insignificant the value of the item which is taken. In establishing any deterrent to casual pilferage, security officers must not lose sight of the fact that most employees are honest and disapprove of thievery. Mutual respect between security personnel and other employees of the agency must be maintained if the facility is to be protected from other more dangerous forms of human hazards. Any security measure which infringes on the human rights or dignity of others will jeopardize, rather than enhance, the overall protection of the agency.

14. The $100,000 yearly inventory of an agency revealed that $50 worth of goods had been stolen; the only individuals with access to the stolen materials were the employees. Of the following measures, which would the author of the above passage MOST likely recommend to a security officer?

    A. Conduct an intensive investigation of all employees to find the culprit.
    B. Make a record of the theft, but take no investigative or disciplinary action against any employee.
    C. Place a tight security check on all future movements of personnel.
    D. Remove the remainder of the material to an area with much greater security.

15. What does the passage imply is the percentage of employees whom a security officer should expect to be honest?

    A. No employee can be expected to be honest all of the time
    B. Just 50%
    C. Less than 50%
    D. More than 50%

16. According to the above passage, the security officer would use which of the following methods to minimize theft in buildings with many exits when his staff is very small?

    A. Conduct an inventory of all material and place a guard near that which is most likely to be pilfered
    B. Inform employees of the consequences of legal prosecution for pilfering
    C. Close off the unimportant exits and have all his men concentrate on a few exits
    D. Place a guard at each exit and conduct a casual search of individuals leaving the premises

17. Of the following, the title BEST suited for this passage is

    A. CONTROL MEASURES FOR CASUAL PILFERING
    B. DETECTING THE POTENTIAL PILFERER
    C. FINANCIAL LOSSES RESULTING FROM PILFERING
    D. THE USE OF MORAL PERSUASION IN PHYSICAL SECURITY

Questions 18-24.

DIRECTIONS: Questions 18 through 24 are to be answered SOLELY on the basis of the following passage.

Burglar alarms are designed to detect intrusion automatically. Robbery alarms enable a victim of a robbery or an attack to signal for help. Such devices can be located in elevators, hallways, homes and apartments, businesses and factories, and subways, as well as on the street in high-crime areas. Alarms could deter some potential criminals from attacking targets so protected. If alarms were prevalent and not visible, then they might serve to suppress crime generally. In addition, of course, the alarms can summon the police when they are needed.

All alarms must perform three functions: sensing or initiation of the signal, transmission of the signal and annunciation of the alarm. A burglar alarm needs a sensor to detect human presence or activity in an unoccupied enclosed area like a building or a room. A robbery victim would initiate the alarm by closing a foot or wall switch, or by triggering a portable transmitter which would send the alarm signal to a remote receiver. The signal can sound locally as a loud noise to frighten away a criminal, or it can be sent silently by wire to a central agency. A centralized annunciator requires either private lines from each alarmed point, or the transmission of some information on the location of the signal.

18. A conclusion which follows LOGICALLY from the above passage is that 18.____

    A. burglar alarms employ sensor devices; robbery alarms make use of initiation devices
    B. robbery alarms signal intrusion without the help of the victim; burglar alarms require the victim to trigger a switch
    C. robbery alarms sound locally; burglar alarms are transmitted to a central agency
    D. the mechanisms for a burglar alarm and a robbery alarm are alike

19. According to the above passage, alarms can be located 19.____

    A. in a wide variety of settings
    B. only in enclosed areas
    C. at low cost in high-crime areas
    D. only in places where potential criminals will be deterred

20. According to the above passage, which of the following is ESSENTIAL if a signal is to be received in a central office? 20.____

    A. A foot or wall switch
    B. A noise-producing mechanism
    C. A portable reception device
    D. Information regarding the location of the source

21. According to the above passage, an alarm system can function WITHOUT a 21.____

    A. centralized annunciating device
    B. device to stop the alarm
    C. sensing or initiating device
    D. transmission device

22. According to the above passage, the purpose of robbery alarms is to 22.____

    A. find out automatically whether a robbery has taken place
    B. lower the crime rate in high-crime areas
    C. make a loud noise to frighten away the criminal
    D. provide a victim with the means to signal for help

23. According to the above passage, alarms might aid in lessening crime if they were

    A. answered promptly by police
    B. completely automatic
    C. easily accessible to victims
    D. hidden and widespread

24. Of the following, the BEST title for the above passage is

    A. DETECTION OF CRIME BY ALARMS
    B. LOWERING THE CRIME RATE
    C. SUPPRESSION OF CRIME
    D. THE PREVENTION OF ROBBERY

25. Although the rural crime reporting area is much less developed than that for cities and towns, current data are collected in sufficient volume to justify the generalization that rural crime rates are lower than those or urban communities.
    According to this statement,

    A. better reporting of crime occurs in rural areas than in cities
    B. there appears to be a lower proportion of crime in rural areas than in cities
    C. cities have more crime than towns
    D. crime depends on the amount of reporting

KEY (CORRECT ANSWERS)

1.	B	11.	C
2.	C	12.	A
3.	C	13.	D
4.	A	14.	B
5.	C	15.	D
6.	B	16.	B
7.	B	17.	A
8.	C	18.	A
9.	C	19.	A
10.	B	20.	D

21. A
22. D
23. D
24. A
25. B

EXAMINATION SECTION
TEST 1

DIRECTIONS: Each question or incomplete statement is followed by several suggested answers or completions. Select the one that BEST answers the question or completes the statement. *PRINT THE LETTER OF THE CORRECT ANSWER IN THE SPACE AT THE RIGHT.*

Questions 1-5.

DIRECTIONS: Questions 1 through 5 are to be answered on the basis of the following passage.

The jury could not decide the verdict in the case of *The People of New York vs. Tim Jones*. One of the main reasons why the jury was deadlocked was because the jury found the presentation of the evidence by the prosecutor and the defense was quite confusing. One of the major focal points in the case was the __(1)__ of __(2)__ against the defendant, Tim Jones. When the jury initially came back to the courtroom and announced they could not come to a decision, the judge asked that the jury return to __(3)__. Three hours later, after still not arriving at a decision, the judge declared the jury to be a hung jury. Because it was a jury trial and not a __(4)__ trial, the court polled the jury.

1. The CORRECT word to fill in space number 1 is
   A. admissibility
   B. entertainment
   C. exclusion
   D. branding

   1.____

2. The CORRECT word to fill in space number 2 is
   A. documents
   B. testimony
   C. ex parte
   D. voir dire

   2.____

3. The CORRECT word to fill in space number 3 is
   A. deliberations
   B. group
   C. court
   D. bench

   3.____

4. The CORRECT word to fill in space number 4 is
   A. bench
   B. regular
   C. heightened
   D. closed

   4.____

5. A _____, unlike a hung jury, is an invalid trial caused by a fundamental error.
   A. erroneous trial
   B. deadlocked jury
   C. bilateral trial
   D. mistrial

   5.____

Questions 6-7.

DIRECTIONS: Questions 6 and 7 are to be answered on the basis of the following passage.

Two former friends are embattled in a legal dispute whereby one friend, James, accuses the other, Robin, of negligence and fraud. In addition to a complaint, James also submitted an __(6)__ accounting the events that led up to the lawsuit. James is not represented by counsel. Robin, however, is represented by an attorney. James is considered a __(7)__ litigant.

6. The CORRECT word to fill in space number 6 is
   A. motion   B. document   C. affidavit   D. complaint

7. The CORRECT word to fill in space number 7 is
   A. represented   B. pro se   C. individual   D. per diem

8. Testimony is a type of _____, which is more broadly defined as information presented and/or used to persuade the fact finder to decide the case in favor of one side or the other.
   A. evidence
   B. conference
   C. pre-hearing motion
   D. deposition

9. Erin is accused of following her former boss home, burglarizing his home and assaulting him. The crimes are serious, especially the charge of assault which is punishable by imprisonment for more than one year. Consequently, Erin will be charged with at least one _____.
   A. felony
   B. misdemeanor
   C. offense
   D. civil crime

10. A _____ is a body of 16-23 citizens who listen to evidence of criminal allegations, which is presented by the prosecutors, and determine whether there is probable cause to believe an individual committed an offense.
    A. jury
    B. alternate jury
    C. grand jury
    D. exculpatory hearing

11. The same body returns an _____ if there is probable cause to believe an individual committed an offense.
    A. indictment   B. information   C. conviction   D. acquittal

12. If the same is presented by a government body, the body returns an _____.
    A. information   B. verdict   C. ex-parte   D. ramification

Questions 13-16.

DIRECTIONS: Questions 13 through 16 are to be answered on the basis of the following passage.

Stacy appears at the Nassau County Courthouse to support her cousin, Dave, who is on trial for attempted robbery. While Stacy knows Dave is innocent, the testimony presented by the prosecutor is convincing. The prosecutor calls four different witnesses who testified they saw Dave point a gun at an elderly gentleman and demand that he turn over his wallet and cellphone. The defense __(13)__ and does not present any evidence. The prosecutor and defense then both presented their __(14)__ to the jury, which summarized their cases __(15)__.

13. The CORRECT word to fill in space number 13 is
    A. persists   B. re-examines   C. rests   D. repositions

14. The CORRECT word to fill in space number 14 is   14.____
    A. closing argument   B. opening arguments
    C. summaries   D. depositions

15. The CORRECT word to fill in space number 15 is   15.____
    A. in brief   B. in totality
    C. amicus   D. sua sponte

16. Which part of the trial did Stacy miss?   16.____
    A. Closing argument   B. Opening argument
    C. Evidence presentation   D. Direct examination

Questions 17-20.

DIRECTIONS: Questions 17 through 20 are to be answered on the basis of the following passage.

During jury deliberations, two jurors cannot seem to agree. Melissa feels strongly that the defendant is innocent and continues to argue with another juror, Jim, who strongly believes the defendant is guilty of a __(17)__ , which is a crime punishable by death. Melissa argues that much of the evidence presented during the trial was __(18)__ and should not be considered because it creates a __(19)__ against the defendant.

17. The CORRECT word to fill in space number 17 is   17.____
    A. capital offense   B. delinquency
    C. delinquent crime   D. obstructionist offense

18. The CORRECT word to fill in space number 18 is   18.____
    A. admissible   B. triable   C. presentable   D. inadmissible

19. The CORRECT word to fill in space number 19 is   19.____
    A. demands   B. bias   C. recant   D. confusion

20. What is the term used to described the outcome if Melissa, Jim, and the other   20.____
    jurors do not agree on a verdict?
    A. Suspended jury   B. Hung jury
    C. Dreaded jury   D. Misguided jury

Questions 21-25.

DIRECTIONS: Questions 21 through 25 are to be answered on the basis of the following passage.

The pre-trial process, like the actual trial, takes place in multiple __(21)__ . Hearings are scheduled by __(22)__ between the parties and the judge. If the factfinder is not a judge, the __(23)__ is selected in a separate process called voir dire. __(24)__ are argued in court before a trial begins, in which an issue relating to the case is decided. Finally, the trial begins once a __(25)__ has been set. Even then, the case may settle before the start of opening statements.

21. The CORRECT word to fill in space number 21 is 21._____
    A. parts B. pieces C. units D. slices

22. The CORRECT word to fill in space number 22 is 22._____
    A. schedules B. calendars C. conference D. telephone

23. The CORRECT word to fill in space number 23 is 23._____
    A. jury B. panel C. composition D. attorneys

24. The CORRECT word to fill in space number 24 is 24._____
    A. Motions   B. Witnesses
    C. Issue statements D. Stipulations

25. The CORRECT word to fill in space number 25 is 25._____
    A. trial date   B. defendant
    C. judge   D. final conference

KEY (CORRECT ANSWERS)

1. A	11. A
2. B	12. A
3. A	13. C
4. A	14. B
5. D	15. A
6. C	16. B
7. B	17. A
8. A	18. D
9. A	19. B
10. C	20. B

21. A
22. C
23. A
24. A
25. A

TEST 2

DIRECTIONS: Each question or incomplete statement is followed by several suggested answers or completions. Select the one that BEST answers the question or completes the statement. *PRINT THE LETTER OF THE CORRECT ANSWER IN THE SPACE AT THE RIGHT.*

Questions 1-3.

DIRECTIONS: Questions 1 through 3 are to be answered on the basis of the following passage.

In a divorce proceeding, Alice and Tom have each filed for __(1)__ of their son, Jack. Alice wants Jack to live with her full time, and Tom has asked the court for the same. In their petitions, each party has outlined why living with them would be in the __(2)__ of the child. The family court judge has taken account of all the evidence and is currently deliberating on the final __(3)__.

1. The CORRECT word to fill in space number 1 is
   A. physical custody
   B. alimony
   C. child support
   D. restraining order

2. The CORRECT word to fill in space number 2 is
   A. best interests
   B. sustaining interests
   C. limited interests
   D. maternal wishes

3. The CORRECT word to fill in space number 3 is
   A. issue
   B. order
   C. motion
   D. request

4. A _____ is a sworn statement containing facts about a child involved in a case, including the full name of the child, date of birth, current and past residences, and other information as may be required by law.
   A. surrogates certificate
   B. custody affidavit
   C. remembrance order
   D. restraining order

Questions 5-7.

DIRECTIONS: Questions 5 through 7 are to be answered on the basis of the following passage.

Bill is on the witness stand providing details on when he last saw Kevin. Bill and Kevin do not know one another. Bill believes that he saw Kevin in the bank two months ago, just before the bank was robbed. Kevin is accused of writing bad checks. Bill's attorney questions him on the stand, then Kevin's attorney questions Bill on the stand. Kevin does not take the stand in his own defense.

5. Kevin's attorney will _____ Bill.
   A. examine
   B. decipher
   C. impeach
   D. cross-examine

6. Bill is providing which of the following?
   A. Testimony
   B. Interrogatory
   C. Illustrative examination
   D. Demonstration

7. Kevin is exercising his right against
   A. self-inducement
   B. judgment
   C. self-incrimination
   D. perjury

8. In a criminal case, one of the major issues is whether the defendant had a guilty mind, or _____. Without it, the charge from second degree murder would drop to manslaughter, given the lack of premeditation.
   A. anger reduction
   B. mens rea
   C. exclusionary rule
   D. per diem application

Questions 9-11.

DIRECTIONS: Questions 9 through 11 are to be answered on the basis of the following passage.

Mary brought a wrongful death __(9)__ against a manufacturer of antibiotic ointment after her husband applied the ointment to an open wound on his knee and became fatally ill. In her lawsuit, Mary alleges that the manufacturer knew certain shipments of the ointment had been tainted and did not issue a recall to consumers. After a lengthy trial, the court awarded her punitive __(10)__. Assume that the manufacturer Mary sued was ABC, Inc. The manufacturer of the ointment Mary's husband used, however, is Ointment, Inc. The judge __(11)__ the case __(12)__, allowing Mary to bring the suit again after the correct manufacturer was identified.

9. The CORRECT word to fill in space number 9 is
   A. action   B. exercise   C. request   D. application

10. The CORRECT word to fill in space number 10 is
    A. funds
    B. null award
    C. compensatory
    D. damages

11. The CORRECT word to fill in space number 11 is
    A. dismissed   B. acquitted   C. relieved   D. excused

12. The CORRECT word to fill in space number 12 is
    A. without prejudice
    B. knowingly
    C. erroneously
    D. with prejudice

13. A tort action would most likely be filed and litigated in _____ court, rather than criminal court.
    A. Civil   B. Surrogate's   C. Supreme   D. District

14. Newlyweds Richard and Erica are in the process of closing on their new home in Bronx County. An examination of public records to determine the state of a title and confirm that the seller of a property is its legal owner is deemed a
    A. title search
    B. seizure
    C. lien in assets
    D. forfeiture

15. Ronnie was convicted of assault with a deadly weapon in Orange County Supreme Court and sentenced to eleven years imprisonment. The verdict in Ronnie's case was
    A. nolo contendere   B. moot   C. arraigned   D. guilty

16. Eric's hearing, stemming from an alleged petty larceny, was scheduled for Friday at 3 P.M. At noon, Eric's mother informed him that his grandmother had passed. Eric rushed to the hospital in disbelief, missing his hearing. Eric's attorney was not informed by Eric that he would not be able to attend the hearing. Eric's _____ will certainly be detrimental to his case.
    A. failure to appear
    B. failed deposition
    C. failed interrogatory
    D. failed hearing

17. During a break, one of the jurors in the *Tim James v. Alpha, Inc.* spots one of the courthouse judges speaking to a lawyer in the Tim James case. The juror has witnessed a possible
    A. ex-parte communication
    B. domiciled conversation
    C. un-docketed conversation
    D. delinquent conversation

Questions 18-20.

DIRECTIONS: Questions 18 through 20 are to be answered on the basis of the following passage.

In a __(18)__, the attorneys for the Estate of Abe Smith and Red Bank, Inc. are attempting to determine the scope of possible trial. The Estate of Abe Smith is suing the bank for mismanagement of the estate's funds.

18. The CORRECT word to fill in space number 18 is
    A. probationary hearing
    B. pretrial conference
    C. protective order hearing
    D. pleading

19. Red Bank, Inc. is identified as the _____ in the case.
    A. litigant   B. plaintiff   C. appellant   D. defendant

20. The case will MOST likely be heard in _____ Court.
    A. Criminal   B. Surrogate's   C. Bankruptcy   D. Family

21. To avoid trial, Benjamin agrees to a _____ which requires that he serve three years in jail, followed by five years of probation.
    A. dismissal
    B. reduced issue
    C. plea bargain
    D. unilateral contract

22. Jamal and Nicole want to legally separate. Jamal and Nicole are both represented by attorneys. Jamal's attorney, Sam, went to law school with Nicole's attorney, Barbara. Who are the litigants in this case?
   A. Jamal only
   B. Jamal and Nicole
   C. Nicole only
   D. Sam and Barbara

Questions 23-25.

DIRECTIONS: Questions 23 through 25 are to be answered on the basis of the following passage.

A jury is selected in a criminal trial in Suffolk County Supreme Court. Each __(23)__ as selected from a larger pool and subjected to __(24)__, or the process of questioning each prospective juror about their qualifications to serve on a panel. After the trial concludes, the judge delivers formal instructions, or the __(25)__ on the law before the jury can begin their official deliberations.

23. The CORRECT word to fill in space number 23 is
   A. party
   B. juror
   C. representative
   D. attorney

24. The CORRECT word to fill in space number 24 is
   A. voir dire
   B. peremptory challenge
   C. exclusionary rule
   D. exclusion-based bias

25. The CORRECT word to fill in space number 25 is
   A. jury charge
   B. mandate
   C. directive
   D. affirmative response

KEY (CORRECT ANSWERS)

1.	A		11.	A
2.	A		12.	A
3.	B		13.	C
4.	B		14.	A
5.	D		15.	D
6.	A		16.	A
7.	C		17.	A
8.	B		18.	B
9.	A		19.	D
10.	D		20.	B

21.	C
22.	B
23.	B
24.	A
25.	A

EXAMINATION SECTION

TEST 1

DIRECTIONS: Each question or incomplete statement is followed by several suggested answers or completions. Select the one that BEST answers the question or completes the statement. *PRINT THE LETTER OF THE CORRECT ANSWER IN THE SPACE AT THE RIGHT.*

Questions 1-3.

DIRECTIONS: Questions 1 through 3 are to be answered on the basis of the following passage.

Bryan accused his uncle, Jeremy, of petty larceny after he discovered $300 in cash was missing from his car's glove compartment. As a defense, Jeremy testified that he left the car windows rolled down while he ran errands and, therefore, it was possible that someone else stole the money. Bryan initiated the lawsuit against Jeremy after Jeremy refused to give Bryan $300.

1. The dispute is BEST deemed a(n)
   A. congenial dispute
   B. adversarial proceeding
   C. stipulated matter
   D. raised issue

2. Bryan and Jeremy would have recounted their respective statement of the facts in which of the following documents?
   A. Affidavit B. Notice C. Subpoena D. Warrant

3. Assume that Jeremy wants to change his accounting of the events that led to the theft from Bryan's car. Jeremy would need to _____ his statement of facts.
   A. relieve B. amend C. recount D. rename

4. Jared's mother is accused of child abuse. At her arraignment, Jared begins yelling obscenities at the judge. Jared is held in
   A. grievance
   B. collateral estoppel
   C. contempt of court
   D. recognizance

5. Attorneys in a libel and defamation lawsuit are not prepared for their pretrial conference. The attorneys, jointly, petition the court for a _____, which would allow for a postponement of the hearing and provide each side with more time to gather information for trial.
   A. hearing adjustment
   B. continuance
   C. leverage
   D. codicil

6. Given that Lindsay has been found guilty of mail fraud, a federal crime and felony, she is now considered a _____ felon.
   A. convicted B. contrived C. imperiled D. contracted

47

Questions 7-9.

DIRECTIONS: Questions 7 through 9 are to be answered on the basis of the following passage.

Tim and Lisa are in the midst of a contentious legal battle. Tim has accused Lisa, his former employer, of paying him less than minimum wage. Lisa, an owner of a local restaurant, maintains that Tim was paid in accordance with the laws of New York State. As part of __(7)__, Tim was asked by Lisa's attorney to turn copies of all paystubs during his employment at the restaurant. Tim never complied; instead he stopped responding to all requests from Lisa's attorney and the judge. Additionally, he stopped __(8)__ at court hearings. Consequently, the judge issued a __(9)__ in Lisa's favor.

7. The CORRECT word to fill in space number 7 is
   A. discovery
   B. investigation
   C. interrogatories
   D. motions

8. The CORRECT word to fill in space number 8 is
   A. recounting   B. revisiting   C. defending   D. appearing

9. The CORRECT word to fill in space number 9 is
   A. default judgment
   B. support judgment
   C. cause of action
   D. in rem motion

10. A subordinate employee to the clerk who is empowered to act in the place of the clerk in the official business of the court is also known as the
    A. regular clerk
    B. municipal judge
    C. supervisory magistrate
    D. deputy clerk

11. A divorce decree is equivalent to a(n)
    A. order of the court
    B. void certificate
    C. effective disclaimer
    D. dismissal order

Questions 12-13.

DIRECTIONS: Questions 12 and 13 are to be answered on the basis of the following passage.

Robert was ordered to pay child support three years ago. Since then, Robert has not missed any payments, as they are deducted automatically from his paycheck, but he has recently lost his job. Robert would like to petition the court for a downward __(12)__ of the child support law.

12. The CORRECT word to fill in space number 12 is
    A. modification   B. recipient   C. treatment   D. restitution

13. Robert is subject to
    A. garnishee   B. indictment   C. incarceration   D. garnishment

Questions 14-15.

DIRECTIONS: Questions 14 and 15 are to be answered on the basis of the following passage.

The judge in the Bronx County Criminal Court has asked her clerk to take notes during the trial of The People vs. Joe Smith. More specifically, the judge requested that the clerk record any factor that may reduce the severity of the crime raised by the defense. Mr. Smith is accused of armed robbery and attempted arson. The prosecutor asked Mr. Smith if he was of sound mind during the incident, whether he was at the scene of the crime during the night in question, and whether he was with anyone while the crime was being committed. Mr. Smith denied knowing anything about the robbery or the arson.

14. The judge has asked the clerk to identify 14.____
 A. mitigating factors
 B. letters testamentary
 C. litigant application(s)
 D. raison d'etre

15. Which of the following has Mr. Smith NOT provided in his testimony? 15.____
 A. Jurisdiction
 B. Alibi
 C. Plea bargain
 D. Indemnification

Questions 16-19.

DIRECTIONS: Questions 16 through 19 are to be answered on the basis of the following passage.

Lily and Dan Johnson are suing the landscaping company that used to mow their lawn. The landscaping company is owned by Richard. The Johnsons did not sign a contract for Richard's company to mow their lawn, but two of Richard's workers continued to mow the Johnson's lawn for the entire summer of 2016. Lily received a bill for $2,000 in May of 2016 and disputes the bill. Richard countersued, claiming the Johnson's did not honor the contract that was rightfully in place for mowing services. The Court estopped Richard's company from performing all landscaping activities for the Johnsons and their respective parties.

16. What is the cause of action for Richard's claim? 16.____
 A. Fraud
 B. Breach of contract
 C. Libel
 D. Negligence

17. Who are the cross-claimants in this case? 17.____
 A. Richard's company
 B. Lily and Dan
 C. Richard and Richard's contractors
 D. There are no cross-claimants in this matter

18. Which parties are consanguineous, or related by blood? 18.____
 A. Lily and Dan
 B. Lily and Richard
 C. Dan and Richard
 D. None of the parties

19. What did the court order Richard's company to do? 19._____
    A. Stop landscaping activities
    B. Stop mailing bills to the Johnsons
    C. Stop engaging the Johnsons in conversations about landscaping
    D. Continue landscaping activities

Questions 20-22.

DIRECTIONS: Questions 20 through 22 are to be answered on the basis of the following passage.

The Southern District Court of New York is a court of __(20)__ jurisdiction, meaning that the court only has jurisdiction over actions authorized by law. In a class action suit, heard at the District Court, there are more than one hundred plaintiffs that are suing a New York-based manufacturer of a particular drug. Some plaintiffs claim that the drug causes death while others claim the drug is illegally manufactured. All claims have been __(21)__ in the class action suit. One requirement in a class action suit is that the class be represented by the same __(22)__.

20. The CORRECT word to fill in space number 20 is 20._____
    A. limited   B. unlimited   C. timely   D. wholly

21. The CORRECT word to fill in space number 21 is 21._____
    A. consolidated   B. remarkable   C. accepted   D. stipulated

22. The CORRECT word to fill in space number 22 is 22._____
    A. litigants   B. judge   C. jury   D. counsel

Questions 23-25.

DIRECTIONS: Questions 23 through 25 are to be answered on the basis of the following passage.

During cross-examination by Jackson, Katie stated that she witnessed someone leaving the scene of an accident in a red car. The driver, she said, was a male with blond hair like the defendant, Adam. During the direct examination by Carl, Katie said the driver had blondish-reddish hair.

23. Who is Adam's attorney? 23._____
    A. Carl
    B. Jackson
    C. Katie
    D. Adam is not represented by counsel

24. In which court is this trial MOST likely to be held? 24._____
    A. Civil   B. Criminal   C. Surrogates   D. Family

25. Who is Katie's attorney?
    A. Jackson
    B. Carl
    C. Katie is not represented by counsel
    D. It is unclear if Katie has an attorney

25.____

KEY (CORRECT ANSWERS)

1.	B		11.	A
2.	A		12.	A
3.	B		13.	D
4.	C		14.	A
5.	B		15.	B
6.	A		16.	B
7.	A		17.	D
8.	D		18.	D
9.	A		19.	A
10.	D		20.	A

21. A
22. D
23. B
24. B
25. D

TEST 2

DIRECTIONS: Each question or incomplete statement is followed by several suggested answers or completions. Select the one that BEST answers the question or completes the statement. *PRINT THE LETTER OF THE CORRECT ANSWER IN THE SPACE AT THE RIGHT.*

1. A case that has been decided is declared _____ by the court. 1._____
   A. adjudicated
   B. annulled
   C. detrimental
   D. acknowledged

Questions 2-4.

DIRECTIONS: Questions 2 through 4 are to be answered on the basis of the following passage.

Three different individuals approach the clerk's desk at different times, each in need of assistance in filing their lawsuit. Amy wants to respond to a notice that she received in the mail that names her as a party in a lawsuit. Bill wants to start a lawsuit and name a party. Carl wants to respond to a lawsuit in which he has been named, and sue the person that sued him. Amy, Bill, and Carl each want to know what they would need to get started.

2. Amy needs to file a(n) 2._____
   A. letter   B. response   C. answer   D. reply

3. Bill needs to file a(n) 3._____
   A. immediate interrogatory
   B. complaint
   C. affiant
   D. codicil

4. Carl is MOST likely seeking to file a 4._____
   A. counterclaim
   B. restitution claim
   C. defamatory issuance
   D. interlocutory demand

5. If a jury finds that there is insufficient evidence to convict, the recorded verdict is not guilty and the case results in a(n) 5._____
   A. reversal   B. acquittal   C. recusal   D. repository

Questions 6-8.

DIRECTIONS: Questions 6 through 8 are to be answered on the basis of the following passage.

At the close of a bench trial, the defendant, John Ash, was found not guilty. The plaintiff in the case against Mr. Ash, Mr. Steel, wants to appeal the verdict. Mr. Steel's friend, Mr. Smith, wants to file a brief in support of her friend. Mr. Smith is an attorney and her brief would take the form of a memorandum of law.

6. Mr. Steel is which of the following in the appellate case? 6._____
   A. Appellate   B. Appellee   C. Appellant   D. Affirmation

7. If Mr. Ash was found guilty, could Mr. Steel file an appeal?
   A. Yes, any party can appeal any verdict.
   B. Yes, Mr. Steel has an affirmative right to appeal a verdict he is a party to.
   C. No, Mr. Steel can only appeal in federal court.
   D. No, Mr. Steel would not need to file an appeal if Mr. Ash was found guilty.

8. Mr. Smith is seeking to file a(n)
   A. amicus brief
   B. dissertation brief
   C. motion in limine
   D. motion of law

9. During arraignment, the defendant may choose to have one of two types of trials. A jury trial will consist of 6-12 jurors, with _____ while a _____ trial will be decided by a single judge.
   A. alternates; brief
   B. alternate jurors; bench
   C. alternative jurors; trustee
   D. alternate jurors; hearing

10. A _____ bankruptcy can occur in two circumstances; the debtor can be a business or an individual involved in business and the debts are for business purposes.
    A. liquidation
    B. reorganization
    C. business
    D. restitution

Questions 11-12.

DIRECTIONS: Questions 11 through 12 are to be answered on the basis of the following passage.

As is standard procedure in many divorce cases, the judge presiding over Brian and Kate's divorce has asked that the parties attempt to settle matters in __(11)__, or the dispute resolution process in which an impartial third party assists the parties to reach a mutually acceptable settlement. Both Brian and Kate request additional time to decide on whether to complete that process, which is granted by the judge.

11. The CORRECT word to fill in space number 11 is
    A. arbitration
    B. mediation
    C. dispute training
    D. mandamus

12. Which of the following was MOST likely granted by the judge?
    A. Adjournment
    B. Adjudication
    C. Allegation
    D. Acknowledgment

13. The clerk is responsible for calling the cases scheduled for the day, also termed a
    A. calendar call
    B. document review
    C. docketing
    D. case certification

Questions 14-16.

DIRECTIONS: Questions 14 through 16 are to be answered on the basis of the following passage.

In an effort to speed matters along in the courtroom, Judge Johnson would like the clerks to begin summarizing the hearings on the daily docket at the beginning of each day. Judge Johnson asks that pleadings submitted by pro se parties be given special attention. Specifically, the judge wants to know if any of the pleadings are defective on their face. If so, the judge would like the clerk to assist the litigants in correcting the pleadings before the hearing so as not to waste the court's time.

14. Pro se litigants are those
    A. who represent themselves in any kind of case
    B. that represent others on a pro bono basis
    C. that represent family members for a small fee or on a volunteer basis
    D. who represent themselves under anonymity

14.____

15. Which of the following are considered pleadings?
    A. Motion to dismiss   B. Answer
    C. Complaint   D. All of the above

15.____

16. A defective complaint would be one that
    A. listed the parties' names   B. did not state a cause of action
    C. did not list a location of the action   D. contains a notary public stamp

16.____

Questions 17-19.

DIRECTIONS: Questions 17 through 19 are to be answered on the basis of the following passage.

As documents are filed with the Court, they are stamped with a __(17)__ date which usually indicates the date a motion will be heard in court. Jamie is at the clerk's desk and wants to know if this date is picked and asks the clerk for guidance.

17. The CORRECT word to fill in space number 17 is
    A. blank   B. expedited   C. return   D. sealant

17.____

18. Which of the following should be considered in the selection of the above date?
    I. Notice to the other parties.
    II. Day of the week the proper court hears motions
    III. Convenience of the clerk
    IV. Will of the attorneys
    The CORRECT answer is:
    A. None of the above   B. I, II, III
    C. I, IV   D. I and II

18.____

4 (#2)

19. Motions to the court must include which of the following? 19.____
    A. Full address of the courthouse
    B. Relief sought
    C. Part, room, and time the motion will be heard
    D. All of the above

Questions 20-25.

DIRECTIONS: Questions 20 through 25 are to be answered on the basis of the following passage.

Harper hired Janelle to write articles for Harper's online magazine. Harper paid Janelle for two articles, then ceased paying Janelle. In Civil Court, Janelle sued Harper for fraud and breach of contract. In a countersuit, Harper sued Janelle for defamation. The clerk is asked to first confer with the parties about a date for __(20)__ or a conference with the judge to discuss discovery and possible settlement. Harper is representing herself at trial as she cannot afford an attorney, while Janelle is represented by Jane. Janelle submits an affidavit to the court, swearing to the events that led up to her filing a suit against Janelle.

20. The CORRECT word to fill in space number 20 is 20.____
    A. pretrial
    B. pre-sentence investigation
    C. restraining order hearing
    D. show cause hearing

21. Harper is _____ and considered a _____ litigant. 21.____
    A. incapable; pro se
    B. injunction; pro bono
    C. indigent; pro se
    D. incarcerated; per diem

22. If Harper were to prevail in her suit, which of the following is she MOST likely to recover? 22.____
    A. Janelle's imprisonment
    B. Janelle's probation
    C. Payment of fines
    D. Asset seizure and forfeiture

23. If Janelle were to prevail in her suit against Harper, which of the following is she LEAST likely to recover? 23.____
    A. Back-payment for the articles written
    B. Punitive damages for fraud and breach of contract
    C. Monetary damages for breach of contract
    D. Harper's imprisonment

24. Which of the following is likely to be entered into evidence? 24.____
    A. Employment contract(s)
    B. Paystubs
    C. Articles written and websites where the articles were published
    D. All of the above

25. Who is the affiant in Janelle's affidavit? 25.____
    A. Harper
    B. Harper's attorney
    C. Janelle
    D. Janelle's attorney

KEY (CORRECT ANSWERS)

1.	A		11.	B
2.	C		12.	A
3.	B		13.	A
4.	A		14.	A
5.	B		15.	D
6.	C		16.	B
7.	D		17.	C
8.	A		18.	D
9.	B		19.	D
10.	C		20.	A

21. C
22. C
23. D
24. D
25. C

EXAMINATION SECTION

TEST 1

DIRECTIONS: Each question or incomplete statement is followed by several suggested answers or completions. Select the one that BEST answers the question or completes the statement. *PRINT THE LETTER OF THE CORRECT ANSWER IN THE SPACE AT THE RIGHT.*

Questions 1-5.

DIRECTIONS: Questions 1 through 5 are to be answered on the basis of the following fact pattern.

Astrid's son, Carlos, attends the local high school. Carlos and another student, Manny, have been bullying another student both on and off school premises. The high school principal has notified the New York Police Department School Safety Unit of the issue. The principal has also been in touch with Astrid and Manny's mother, Mary. Mary believes Carlos is a bad influence to her son, Manny. After obtaining Astrid's phone number, Mary called Astrid and made threats towards her and Carlos. She indicated that if Carlos did not stay away from her son, Manny, she would have them both killed. The next day after school, Carlos is jumped by a group of teenagers and his leg is broken in the brawl. Astrid sues Manny, Mary, and the school district. Mary intends to countersue.

1. Who is the complainant?
   A. Manny   B. Mary   C. Astrid   D. Carlos

2. Which of the following is NOT a possible cause of action?
   A. Harassment
   B. Assault
   C. Negligence
   D. Breach of Contract

3. What key information is missing from the complaint?
   A. The name of the bullied student
   B. The location where Carlos was jumped
   C. The name of the high school principal
   D. The name of the police officer at the NYPD School Safety Unit who was originally notified on the issue

4. Is Mary obligated to countersue because she or her son, Manny, may have been involved in the assault against Carlos?
   A. Yes; she must answer the suit and countersue as required
   B. Yes; she must countersue to clear her son's name
   C. No; Mary is not obligated to countersue and can simply answer to the claims as alleged
   D. No; Mary is not obligated to countersue but she is obligated to countersue on Manny's behalf

5. Assume that Carlos and Manny are minors.
   What effect, if any, would this fact have on the lawsuit that is filed?
   A. The legal guardians of Carlos and Manny will need to file, and answer, the lawsuit on their behalf.
   B. Carlos and Manny do not need to appear in court.
   C. Minors cannot sue other people.
   D. The lawsuit is unaffected by their age.

6.
Mary Williams 1 Court Way Smithtown, NY 10170	Mary S. Williams 1 Court Way Smithtown, NY 10170	Mary S. Williams 1 Court Way Smith Town, NY 10170

   Which selection below accurately describes the addresses as listed above?
   A. All three addresses are the same.
   B. The first and the third address are the same.
   C. None of the addresses are the same.
   D. The second and third address are the same.

Questions 7-9.

DIRECTIONS: Questions 7 through 9 are to be answered on the basis of the following table.

Schedule – Judge Presser		
Petitioner	**Respondent**	**Status**
Williams	Smith	Dismissed with prejudice
Jones	Johnson	Continued
Adams	Doe	Dismissed with prejudice
Ash	Link	Adjourned
Lam	Garcia	Settled

7. How many cases were adjourned?
   A. 3   B. 1   C. 4   D. 5

8. In how many cases were money damages awarded by the judge?
   A. 0   B. 3   C. 4   D. 5

9. How many cases will be heard again?
   A. 2   B. 1   C. 3   D. 5

10. A warrant for the arrest of Benjamin Lang. Lang lives in Suffolk County, New York. What is recorded on the warrant?
    Lang's
    A. venue
    B. domicile
    C. jurisdiction
    D. subject matter jurisdiction

Questions 11-13.

DIRECTIONS: Questions 11 through 13 are to be answered on the basis of the following table.

455888912	455888812	455888912	455888812
Civil Court	Civil Court	Civil Court	Civil Court
Contract	Contract	Contract	Contract
Pam L. Williams	Pam Williams	Pam Williams	Pam L. Williams

11. Which selection below accurately describes the case captions as listed above?
    A. All of the captions are the same.
    B. Caption 1 and Caption 3 are the same.
    C. Caption 2 and Caption 4 are the same.
    D. None of the captions are the same.

11._____

12. Which digit above is dissimilar in two of the above captions?
    A. The seventh digit
    B. The fifth digit
    C. The sixth digit
    D. The eighth digit

12._____

13. The notation "contract" in each caption above describes the _____ of the case.
    A. Cause of action
    B. Remedy at issue
    C. Order of the court
    D. Disposition

13._____

14. Melinda was seen stealing money from a car on Atlantic Avenue in Brooklyn. Samuel witnessed the crime from his apartment and called the police. Officer Tang recorded the call in the police log. Samuel does not own a car and reported the crime anonymously. Later that same evening, Jeremy returned his car and found the passenger window had been broken and $500 was stolen from the glove compartment. Jeremy called the police to report the crime.
In the judge's docket, the petitioner of the case against Melinda is MOST likely
    A. Jeremy
    B. Samuel
    C. Officer Tang
    D. The petitioner is anonymous

14._____

15. Judge Oswald hears cases in the Surrogate Court.
Which of the following would NOT be in Judge Oswald's court calendar?
    A. Adoption
    B. Wills
    C. Estate and Probation
    D. Negligence

15._____

Questions 16-19.

DIRECTIONS: Questions 16 through 19 are to be answered on the basis of the following fact pattern.

Judge Laredo, Smith and Ora hear no-fault cases in the 10th Judicial District throughout the week. Judge Laredo hears cases the first Monday of each month. Judge Smith hears cases with amounts in dispute over $10,000 on Tuesday, Wednesday, and Friday. Judge Ora hears cases without amounts in dispute below $25,000 on Tuesdays only.

16. Geico and ABC Chiropractic are parties to a no-fault dispute with an amount in dispute of $8,500.
If Judge Laredo is unavailable, what day can the case be heard?
A. Wednesday   B. Friday   C. Monday   D. Tuesday

16.____

17. Blue Health Medical and Progressive Insurance are parties to a no-fault dispute which is scheduled to be heard February 18th. Blue Health demands Progressive reimburse the provider $5,000 for the primary surgeon fees and $12,000 in assistant surgeon fees.
Which judge will hear the matter and on which day?
A. Judge Smith on Friday   B. Judge Smith on Tuesday
C. Judge Smith on Wednesday   D. Judge Ora on Tuesday

17.____

18. A no-fault dispute is being heard on Monday, June 10th.
Which statement below must be TRUE?
A. The amount in dispute is above $10,000.
B. The amount in dispute is less than $25,000.
C. The amount in dispute is less than $10,000.
D. Judge Laredo is hearing the case.

18.____

19. What information must be obtained in order to properly schedule the court calendar?
A. The amount in dispute for each case
B. The parties in each case
C. Verification the dispute is "no-fault in nature"
D. All of the above

19.____

20. A victim impact statement is an oral or _____ statement that may be read in court.
A. recorded   B. transcribed   C. written   D. visualized

20.____

21. The clerk in the Surrogates Court will need to have access to what information in the preparation of adoption hearings?
A. Personal information of a child's current or prior legal guardian
B. Emancipation petition documentation
C. Deed or will
D. Probate documentation

21.____

Questions 22-25.

DIRECTIONS: Questions 22 through 25 are to be answered on the basis of the following table.

| Schedule – Judge Orlando ||||
Complainant/Plaintiff	Defendant	Case Type	Money Awarded
Williams	Smith	Civil	$5,000
Jones	Johnson	Criminal	No
Adams	Doe	Criminal	$10,000
Ash	Link	Civil	$15,000
Lam	Garcia	Civil	$25,000

22. What is the total amount of money damages from civil disputes? 22.____
    A. $45,000 B. $40,000 C. $5,000 D. 0

23. Which complainant/plaintiff was awarded less than $20,000? 23.____
    A. Williams, Adams, and Ash
    B. Jones, Adams, and Ash
    C. Lam, Williams, and Jones
    D. Jones, Adams, and Lam

24. How many criminal cases were heard by Judge Orlando? 24.____
    A. 4 B. 5 C. 2 D. 3

25. Which defendants are responsible for paying more than $10,000? 25.____
    A. Doe and Link
    B. Link and Garcia
    C. John and Doe
    D. Smith and Garcia

KEY (CORRECT ANSWERS)

1.	C		11.	D
2.	D		12.	A
3.	B		13.	A
4.	C		14.	A
5.	A		15.	D
6.	C		16.	D
7.	B		17.	D
8.	A		18.	D
9.	A		19.	D
10.	B		20.	C

21. A
22. A
23. A
24. C
25. B

TEST 2

DIRECTIONS: Each question or incomplete statement is followed by several suggested answers or completions. Select the one that BEST answers the question or completes the statement. *PRINT THE LETTER OF THE CORRECT ANSWER IN THE SPACE AT THE RIGHT.*

Questions 1-4.

DIRECTIONS: Questions 1 through 4 are to be answered on the basis of the following text.

After a lengthy trial with multiple ___1___, Jim was acquitted of armed robbery and conspiracy. On the other hand, his alleged partner, Bob, was ___2___ of armed robbery. The conspiracy charge was dropped against Bob since the 12-person ___3___ found he acted alone. Jim's attorney ___4___.

1. Fill in the blank for #1:
   A. witnesses B. evidence C. discretionary D. turbulent

2. Fill in the blank for #2:
   A. guilty B. convicted C. indicted D. surmised

3. Fill in the blank for #3:
   A. judge B. spectator C. jury D. bailiff

4. Fill in the blank for #4:
   A. appealed B. remanded C. reversed D. rescinded

Questions 5-10.

DIRECTIONS: Questions 5 through 10 are to be answered on the basis of the following table.

Court Schedule - Tuesday			
Judge	Total Cases	Cases Dismissed	Cases with Money Awarded
Presser	10	2	X
O'Dell	5	5	
Williams	6	6	
Sasha	8	7	X

5. How many cases were awarded money damages from Judge Presser's calendar?
   A. 2 B. 8 C. 6 D. 10

6. How many cases were awarded money damages from Judge Sasha's calendar?
   A. 8 B. 7 C. 1 D. 0

7. How many cases were dismissed on Tuesday? 7.____
   A. 11   B. 20   C. 7   D. 10

8. How many cases were awarded money damages on Tuesday? 8.____
   A. 9   B. 8   C. 1   D. 10

9. Which judge heard the MOST cases on Tuesday? 9.____
   A. Presser   B. O'Dell   C. Williams   D. Sasha

10. Which judge heard the LEAST cases on Tuesday? 10.____
    A. Presser   B. O'Dell   C. Willliams   D. Sasha

Questions 11-15.

DIRECTIONS: Questions 11 through 15 are to be answered on the basis of the following text.

Judge Smith hears adoption cases on Fridays. Judge Clark hears criminal cases every weekday except Tuesday in the New York City Criminal Court. Judge Clark hears felony criminal cases on Tuesday in Supreme Court. Judge Amy hears felony criminal cases on Thursday in Supreme Court.

11. Daniel is being charged with the murder of his cousin, Jerrell. 11.____
    Which judge can hear the case and on what day?
    A. Judge Smith on Friday   B. Judge Clark on Monday
    C. Judge Amy on Tuesday   D. Judge Clark on Tuesday

12. Jamal lives in Staten Island with his sister, Tisha, and Tisha's boyfriend, 12.____
    Hunter. Hunter and Jamal do not get along and one day last January, Hunter
    and Jamal were involved in a physical altercation. Hunter and Jamal both
    allege that the other assault and battered the other.
    Which judge can hear the case and on what day?
    A. Judge Clark on Tuesday   B. Judge Amy on Thursday
    C. Judge Smith on Friday   D. Judge Clark on Monday

13. Assuming the crime of assault and battery are not felonies, in which court 13.____
    will Jamal and Hunter's dispute be heard?
    A. Supreme Court   B. Surrogates Court
    C. New York City Criminal Court   D. Small Claims Court

14. Assume that Tisha and Hunter have a six-year-old daughter. 14.____
    If Hunter is incarcerated for his role in the physical altercation with Jamal,
    which court would have jurisdiction over Hunter's trial?
    A. Surrogates Court   B. New York City Criminal Court
    C. Bronx Housing Court   D. Richmond County Civil Court

15. What day of the week are the MOST cases heard between all three judges? 15.____
    A. Monday   B. Thursday   C. Tuesday   D. Friday

Questions 16-19.

DIRECTIONS: Questions 16 through 19 are to be answered on the basis of the following table.

Caption #1	Caption #2	Caption #3	Caption #4
Case 12-908	Case 12-909	Case 12-910	Case 12-911
Bronx Housing Court	Civil Court	Civil Court	Surrogates Court
Landlord/Tenant	Assault	Breach of Contract	Guardianship
ABC Property Mgmt v. Sam Smith	Jim Jones v. Sam Hunt	Terrell Williams v. Daniel Tang	In re: Jane Doe

16. Which caption above contains an INCORRECT cause of action?
    A. 1   B. 2   C. 3   D. 4

17. When were the cases in each of the captions above initiated?
    A. 2015
    B. 2016
    C. 2012
    D. Unable to determine based on the information provided

18. Which case caption above corresponds to a matter that will NOT have monetary damages awarded?
    A. 1   B. 2   C. 3   D. 4

19. Which case caption has a matter involving an institutional, rather than an individual, petitioner?
    A. 1   B. 2   C. 3   D. 4

20. A pro se litigant wants to initiate a lawsuit against his intrusive neighbor. Assuming the pro se litigant prevails, which form should be served against the neighbor after the judgment is entered?
    A. Notice of entry
    B. Notice of appeal
    C. Remand service
    D. Process discovery

21. A(n) _____ is a hearing for the purpose of determining the amount of damages sue on a claim. The clerk can enter the request on the judge's calendar after the opposing party has defaulted.
    A. imposition   B. inquest   C. tardy notice   D. reversal

22. After a judgment is entered, it becomes enforceable for a period of time. For real property, a transcript of _____ is filed with the County Clerk which makes the judgment enforceable for a period of ten years.
    A. enforcement
    B. judgment
    C. engagement
    D. affidavit

23. Sensitive information must be _____ before it becomes public record.
    A. retained   B. reposed   C. redacted   D. recanted

24. Service of process can be filed upon the individual or upon the _____. The affidavit of service will state the party that received the service.
    A. secretary of state
    B. guardian
    C. ad litem
    D. second most suitable person

24.____

25. A warrant can be issued to a sheriff or a marshal. The warrant clerk is responsible for reviewing the paperwork and ensuring that all is in order, including
    A. the names of the parties
    B. address of the premises
    C. the index number
    D. all of the above

25.____

KEY (CORRECT ANSWERS)

1.	A		11.	D
2.	B		12.	D
3.	C		13.	C
4.	A		14.	B
5.	B		15.	D
6.	C		16.	B
7.	B		17.	C
8.	A		18.	D
9.	A		19.	A
10.	B		20.	A

21.	B
22.	B
23.	C
24.	A
25.	D

TEST 3

DIRECTIONS: Each question or incomplete statement is followed by several suggested answers or completions. Select the one that BEST answers the question or completes the statement. *PRINT THE LETTER OF THE CORRECT ANSWER IN THE SPACE AT THE RIGHT.*

1. Supreme Court clerks need to be on notice when a(n) _____ is filed as a judge is not assigned until one that parties files this document and pays the filing fee. A case will never go to trial if this document is never filed.
   A. request for maintenance
   B. request for judicial intervention
   C. remediation
   D. arbitration

1.____

Questions 2-4.

DIRECTIONS: Questions 1 through 5 are to be answered on the basis of the following chart.

Row	Case Type	Court
1	Divorce	Supreme Court
2	Custody/Visitation	Family Court
3	Child Support	Family Court
4	Paternity	Family Court
5	When Someone Dies	Surrogates Court
6	Guardianship	Surrogate's Court
7	Name Change	Supreme Court
8	Housing	New York City Housing Court

2. Assume that you are advising a pro se litigant on the proper forms to file when representing him or herself. Where would John file a small estate affidavit?
   A. Family Court
   B. Supreme Court
   C. Surrogates Court
   D. New York Civil Court

2.____

3. Where would Tom's sister, Emmanuela, file a name change?
   A. Supreme Court
   B. Family Court
   C. Surrogates Court
   D. New York City Civil Court

3.____

4. Tara and her husband, Cassidy, share custody of their twin sons, Drake and Austin. Cassidy would like to petition the court for sole custody. Where would Cassidy file his petition?
   A. New York City Housing Court
   B. Supreme Court
   C. Family Court
   D. Surrogates Court

4.____

5. Richard is representing himself in a lawsuit against his landlord. Richard does not have the financial means to hire an attorney and would like to request a reduction in the court filing fees. Richard must file a request for a _____ which is made by filing a _____ and sworn _____ which explains his finances to the court.
   A. fee waiver; notice of motion; affirmation
   B. fee waiver, notice of motion, affidavit
   C. affidavit, notice of motion, fee waiver
   D. affidavit, fee waiver, notice of motion

Questions 6-10.

DIRECTIONS: Questions 6 through 10 are to be answered on the basis of the following text.

Daniel walks into this local supermarket after lunch and falls in one of the store aisles. Daniel lies on the floor – which is nearly empty – until one of the store managers finds him, helps him up, and offers to pay for his groceries. Daniel leaves the store bruised, but not seriously injured. Two days later, Daniel falls at another grocery store. This time, Daniel threatens to sue the grocery store. The second grocery store has heard about Daniel and is concerned that he is falsifying his injuries to gain sympathy and money. The second grocery store sues Daniel to get ahead of Daniel suing them.

6. Who is the plaintiff in the case?
   A. The first grocery store
   B. The second grocery store
   C. The grocery store manager
   D. Daniel

7. Which of the following is the MOST likely cause of action in a suit that Daniel initiates against the grocery store?
   A. Breach of contract
   B. Discrimination
   C. Negligence
   D. Assault

8. After the lawsuit has commenced, which party would respond or file an answer to the complaint?
   A. Daniel
   B. The first grocery store
   C. The second grocery store
   D. The grocery store manager

9. Which party is eligible to countersue?
   A. The first grocery store
   B. The second grocery store
   C. The grocery store manager
   D. Daniel

10. The lawsuit will likely be dismissed. Why?
    A. Daniel is clearly not exaggerating his injuries.
    B. Daniel has not sued either grocery store.
    C. The store manager did not take a report of Daniel's injuries.
    D. The first grocery store must sue Daniel first.

11. A settlement between parties is not a final and binding legal agreement until the _____ of settlement is signed by both parties.
    A. amendment   B. agreement   C. stipulation   D. simulation

12. Which of the following are appropriate reasons for filing an Order to Show Cause?
    A. Changing the terms of a court order
    B. Requesting the court to dismiss a case
    C. Bringing the case back to court for any reason
    D. All of the above

12.____

13. Which of the following is NOT an appropriate reason for filing an Order to Show Case?
    A. Asking for more time to do something previously agreed upon by court order
    B. Explaining why either party missed a court date
    C. Submitting financial information for a landlord/tenant dispute
    D. Fixing errors in a stipulation

13.____

Questions 14-17.

DIRECTIONS: Questions 14 through 17 are to be answered on the basis of the following text.

Judge Chin hears child neglect and abuse cases in Family Court on Mondays and Tuesdays. Judge Amy hears divorce cases on Mondays, Wednesdays, and Fridays. Judge Snell hears child support and visitation cases every day of the week except Thursday. Termination of parental rights, foster care placement, and other child support cases are scheduled on Thursdays only with any of the three judges.

14. Tim and Sarah would like to adjust their visitation schedule for their eight-year-old daughter, Samantha. They would like the courts to assist them with this issue as they have been unable to come to an agreement on their own.
    Which judge will hear the case and on what day?
    A. Judge Snell on Thursday   B. Judge Snell on Monday
    C. Judge Chin on Monday   D. Judge Chin on Friday

14.____

15. Amanda would like to file for emancipation from her parents.
    Which judge is MOST likely to hear her case?
    A. Judge Chin
    B. Judge Amy
    C. Judge Snell'
    D. Any of the judges can hear Amanda's case

15.____

16. Jimmy and Eva are legally separating. Which judge will hear their case and on what day?
    A. Judge Chin on Monday   B. Judge Snell on Monday
    C. Judge Amy on Monday   D. Judge Chin on Tuesday

16.____

4 (#3)

17. The State of New York intends to file a case against Eric for the abuses and neglect of his daughter, Clare. Eric, however, is not Clare's legal guardian. Clare's legal guardian is her grandmother, Allison. Even though it is not clear that Clare has been neglected, the courts have found that Clare should be placed into foster care until it can be determined who the ultimate caregiver should be.
Which judge will MOST likely hear this case?
    A. Judge Amy
    B. Judge Chin
    C. Judge Snell
    D. Any of the judges can hear this case

17._____

Questions 18-25.

DIRECTIONS: Questions 18 through 25 are to be answered on the basis of the following chart.

Item	Fee
Obtaining an index number	$210
RJI	$95
Note of Issue	$30
Motion or Cross-Motion	$45
Demand for Jury Trial	$65
Voluntary Discontinuance	$35
Notice of Appeal	$65

18. What is the final cost to obtain an index number, demand a jury trial, and file a notice of appeal?
    A. $210   B. $35   C. $65   D. $310

18._____

19. What is the final cost to obtain an RJI and note of issue?
    A. $125   B. $95   C. $30   D. $65

19._____

20. Which of the following is MOST likely to be filed with an RJI?
    A. Demand for jury trial
    B. Notice of appeal
    C. Voluntary discontinuance
    D. Obtaining an index number

20._____

21. Which of the following is the MOST likely outcome of filing a voluntary discontinuance?
The case
    A. is automatically appealed
    B. is dismissed
    C. is rescheduled
    D. will be remanded

21._____

22. What is the final cost of filing a notice of appeal?
    A. $35   B. $65   C. $95   D. $120

22._____

23. What is the final cost of all items prior to filing a motion or cross-motion?
    A. $210   B. $95   C. $45   D. $335

23._____

69

24. Jamal would like to petition the court to compel discovery from his adversary and former friend, Bob. He would also like to speed up the date of trial by filing a demand for jury trial and RJI.
What is the final cost to do so?
A. $160   B. $95   C. $65   D. $205

24.____

25. What is the LEAST costly court document filing fee?
A. Notice of motion
B. Demand for jury trial
C. Note of issue
D. RJI

25.____

KEY (CORRECT ANSWERS)

1.	B		11.	C
2.	C		12.	D
3.	A		13.	C
4.	C		14.	B
5.	B		15.	D
6.	B		16.	C
7.	C		17.	D
8.	A		18.	D
9.	D		19.	A
10.	B		20.	D

21. B
22. B
23. D
24. D
25. C

TEST 4

DIRECTIONS: Each question or incomplete statement is followed by several suggested answers or completions. Select the one that BEST answers the question or completes the statement. *PRINT THE LETTER OF THE CORRECT ANSWER IN THE SPACE AT THE RIGHT.*

1. A lawsuit for money damages amounting to more than $25,000 can be heard in which court?
    A. Surrogates Court
    B. Supreme Court
    C. New York City Civil Court
    D. New York City Criminal Court

2. Which of the following will NOT be on a Notice of Entry?
    A. Name of plaintiff
    B. Name of defendant
    C. Index number
    D. Social Security number

3. Court clerks are prohibited from which of the following?
    A. Predicting the judgment of the court
    B. Explaining available options for a case or problem
    C. Providing past rulings
    D. Providing citations or copies of the law

4. Court clerks are permitted to do all of the following EXCEPT
    A. provide forms with instructions
    B. instruct an individual on how to make a complaint
    C. analyze the law based on the specifics of a case
    D. describe court records and their availability

5. Mary would like to sue her neighbor, Jacob, for money damages. Mary claims Jacob ran his car into Mary's garage door while it was down and caused $5,000 in damages. For claims below $1,000, the filing fee is $15, while the filing fee is $5 more for claims above $1,000.
   How much is Mary's filing fee?
    A. $15   B. $10   C. $20   D. $25

Questions 6-10.

DIRECTIONS: Questions 6 through 10 are to be answered on the basis of the following table.

| Schedule – Judge O'Neill |||
Wednesday	Thursday	Friday
Continued	Dismissed with prejudice	Dismissed with prejudice
Continued	Adjourned	Continued
Settled	Dismissed with prejudice	Dismissed without prejudice
Settled	Continued	Settled
Settled	Continued	Settled

6. How many cases were adjourned this week?
    A. 5   B. 6   C. 1   D. 2

7. How many cases settled this week?
   A. 5   B. 4   C. 3   D. 8

8. How many cases were dismissed this week?
   A. 6   B. 4   C. 5   D. 7

9. How many cases will likely be heard again or, in other words, how many cases can be re-filed or are otherwise continued?
   A. 6   B. 5   C. 7   D. 8

10. Which day was Judge O'Neill the LEAST busy?
    A. Thursday
    B. Friday
    C. Wednesday
    D. Each day was equally busy

Questions 11-15.

DIRECTIONS: Questions 11 through 15 are to be answered on the basis of the following text.

At Alex's arraignment, he pled ___1___ to the charge of driving under the influence and vehicular manslaughter. At trial, the prosecutor presented evidence from several ___2___ that testified Alex had a drinking problem. While Alex's defense attorneys ___3___ to that testimony and argued it was hearsay, the judge overruled those objections and allowed the testimony to be entered in the record as originally spoken. At the conclusion of the trial, Alex was found ___4___ and sentenced to community service.

11. Fill in the blank for #1:
    A. nolo   B. contendere   C. not guilty   D. guilty

12. Fill in the blank for #2:
    A. witnesses   B. evidence   C. testimony   D. bearer

13. Fill in the blank for #3:
    A. disagreed   B. objected   C. qualified   D. disclaimed

14. Fill in the blank for #4:
    A. arraigned   B. protested   C. remanded   D. guilty

15. An acquittal can also be recorded in court documentation as a finding of
    A. reversal   B. recusal   C. not guilty   D. remand

16. Evidence must be found _____ before it can be marked and evaluated by the fact finder, either a judge or jury, in civil and criminal cases.
    A. relevant   B. redacted   C. qualified   D. admissible

17. The party who seeks an appeal from a decision of a court is deemed a(n) _____ and is recorded in court documentation as such.
    A. petitioner   B. respondent   C. appellant   D. re-respondent

18. How would a condominium be recorded in a bankruptcy proceeding? 18.____
    A. Real property B. Personal property
    C. Intangible asset D. chattel

19. Which of the following is LEAST likely to be recorded as a written statement describing one's legal and factual arguments? 19.____
    A. Attorney's brief B. Motion
    C. Summons D. Complaint

20. A lawsuit where one or more members of a large group of individuals sues on behalf of the other individuals in the large group is recorded as a _____ lawsuit. 20.____
    A. introductory B. class action C. municipality D. winning

21. Jamal has filed for bankruptcy. After the trustee has reviewed Jamal's assets, the trustee proposes a plan to the court where Jamal promises property that he already owns to satisfy the major of his debt. 21.____
    The property Jamal owns that will satisfy the debt is recorded as
    A. demerits B. collateral C. debris D. probate

22. Judge Presser has rendered Emilio's sentence for the charges of armed robbery and kidnapping. Emilio will serve 10 years for armed robbery and 12 years for kidnapping. 22.____
    If Emilio's total time in prison is 12 years, his sentence is recorded as
    A. consecutive B. demonstrative
    C. concurrent D. rebated

23. Assume the same facts as the previous question, but assume Emilio serves 22 years in prison. 23.____
    In this instance, his sentence is recorded as
    A. consecutive B. demonstrative
    C. concurrent D. rebated

24. A conviction can also be recorded in court records as a judgment of _____ against a defendant. 24.____
    A. guilt B. remorse C. retaliation D. acquittal

25. In bankruptcy, Jamal sells his house to his mother for $5 in an effort to hide it from creditors who will require that he sell it to satisfy his debts. 25.____
    This sale is recorded as a
    A. fraudulent transfer B. falsified sale
    C. remarkable trade D. clawback trade

KEY (CORRECT ANSWERS)

1.	B		11.	C
2.	D		12.	A
3.	A		13.	B
4.	C		14.	D
5.	C		15.	C
6.	C		16.	D
7.	A		17.	C
8.	B		18.	A
9.	A		19.	C
10.	C		20.	B

21.	B
22.	C
23.	A
24.	A
25.	A

OFFICE RECORD KEEPING
EXAMINATION SECTION
TEST 1

DIRECTIONS: Each question or incomplete statement is followed by several suggested answers or completions. Select the one that BEST answers the question or completes the statement. *PRINT THE LETTER OF THE CORRECT ANSWER IN THE SPACE AT THE RIGHT.*

Questions 1-5.

DIRECTIONS: Questions 1 through 5 are to be answered on the basis of the following chart to check for address and zip code errors.

    A. No errors
    B. Address only
    C. Zip code only
    D. Both

	Correct List Address	Zip Code	List to be Checked Address	Zip Code	
1.	44-A Western Avenue Bethesda, MD	65564	44-A Western Avenue Bethesda, MD	65654	1.____
2.	567 Opera Lane Jackson, MO	28218	567 Opera Lane Jacksen, MO	28218	2.____
3.	200 W. Jannine Dr. Missoula, MT	30707	200 W. Jannine Dr. Missoula, MT	30307	3.____
4.	28 Champaline Dr. Reno, NV	34101	28 Champaine Way Reno, NV	43101	4.____
5.	65156 Rodojo Parsimony, KY	44590-7326	65156 Rodojo Parsimony, KY	44590-7326	5.____

6. When alphabetized correctly, which of the following would be second?   6.____
   A. flame   B. herring   C. decadence   D. emoticon

7. Which one of the following letters is as far after E as K is before R in the alphabet?   7.____
   A. J   B. K   C. H   D. M

8. How many pairs of the following sets of numbers are exactly alike?   8.____
    134232   123456   432512   561343
    564643   432123   132439   438318

   A. 0   B. 2   C. 3   D. 4

9. When alphabetized correctly, which of the following would be FOURTH?   9.____
   A. microcosm   B. natural   C. lithe   D. nature

10. When alphabetized correctly, which of the following would be THIRD?   10.____
    A. exoskeleton   B. euthanize   C. Europe   D. eurythmic

11. Which one of the following letters is as far before T as S is after I in the alphabet?   11.____
    A. j   B. K   C. M   D. N

12. How many pairs of the following sets of letters are exactly ALIKE?   12.____
    GIHEKE   GIHEKE
    KIWNEB   KWINEB
    PQMZJI   PMQZJI
    OPZIBS   OBZIBS
    PONEHE   POENHE

    A. 0   B. 1   C. 2   D. 4

13. When alphabetized correctly, which of the following would be FIRST?   13.____
    A. Catalina   B. catcher   C. caustic   D. curious

14. Which of the following letters is as far after D as U is after B in the alphabet?   14.____
    A. R   B. V   C. W   D. Z

Questions 15-19.

DIRECTIONS: Use the following information and chart to complete Questions 15 through 19.

Every theft reported to an adjuster needs to be assigned a six-letter code containing the following:

First Letter: Type of theft
Second Letter: Witnesses
Third Letter: Value of stolen item
Fourth Letter: Location
Fifth Letter: Time of theft
Sixth Letter: Elapsed between theft and report

<u>Type of Theft:</u>
A. Breaking and Entering
B. Retail Theft
C. Armed robbery
D. Grand Theft Auto

<u>Witnesses</u>
A. None
B. 1 witness
C. Multiple witnesses
D. Security camera

3 (#1)

Location
A. Single Family Home
B. Apartment Building
C. Store
D. Office
E. Vehicle
F. Public Space (Parking Garage, Park, etc.)

Time of Theft
A. 7 AM – 1 PM
B. 1 PM – 6 PM
C. 6 PM – 11 PM
D. 11 PM – 3 AM
E. 3 AM – 7 AM

Time Elapsed Between Theft and Report
A. 0-1 hour
B. 1-4 hours
C. 4-12 hours
D. 12-24 hours
E. 24 Hours

Value of Stolen Items
A. $0-$100
B. $101-$250
C. $251-$500
D. $500-$1000
E. $1001-$5000
F. $5000 or more

15. At 9:30 PM, $175 worth of clothing was stolen from a store. The crime was reported right away by a single store associate. Which of the following would be the CORRECT code?
   A. BCCABB   B. BBBCCA   C. ACCBAB   D. CBCABB

16. A Crossover vehicle worth $4,500 was stolen from a park at approximately 6:45 AM this morning. It was reported stolen at 11:00 AM later that morning by the owner. There were no witnesses. What is the CORRECT code?
   A. DEECAF   B. CFECAE   C. DEFECA   D. DAEFEC

17. Although it was just reported, a breaking and entering occurred 5 days ago at 1:30 AM, according to security cameras that recorded the theft at the accounting firm. Although locks and doors were damaged, nothing was stolen. Which of the following would be the CORRECT code?
   A. ADDEEA   B. ADDDAE   C. ADADDE   D. ADEADE

18. Jill Wagner was held at knifepoint this morning at 11:30 AM when she was walking out of her apartment complex. The thief demanded money, and she gave him $54. She was the only witness and reported the crime immediately. Which of the following would be the CORRECT code?
   A. CBABAA   B. BBABAA   C. CBBABB   D. ABBBCA

19. An artifact worth $5,500 was stolen from the home of Chad Judea this early evening while he was out to dinner from 5:30 PM to 6 PM. When he arrived home at 6 PM, he immediately called the police. There were no witnesses. Which of the following would be the CORRECT code?
   A. AABBAF   B. AABFAF   C. AABABF   D. AAFABA

20. Diatribe means MOST NEARLY
   A. argument   B. cooperation   C. delicate   D. arrogance

77

21. Vitriolic means MOST NEARLY 21.____
    A. flammable   B. fearful   C. spiteful   D. asinine

22. Aplomb means MOST NEARLY 22.____
    A. self-righteous   B. respectable   C. dispirited   D. self-confidence

23. Pervicacious means MOST NEARLY 23.____
    A. rotten   B. immoral   C. stubborn   D. immortal

24. Detrimental means MOST NEARLY 24.____
    A. valuable   B. selfish   C. hopeless   D. harmful

25. Heinous means MOST NEARLY 25.____
    A. sweating   B. glorious   C. atrocious   D. moderate

KEY (CORRECT ANSWERS)

1.	C		11.	A
2.	B		12.	B
3.	C		13.	A
4.	D		14.	C
5.	A		15.	B
6.	D		16.	D
7.	B		17.	C
8.	A		18.	A
9.	D		19.	D
10.	B		20.	A

21. C
22. D
23. C
24. D
25. C

TEST 2

DIRECTIONS: Each question or incomplete statement is followed by several suggested answers or completions. Select the one that BEST answers the question or completes the statement. *PRINT THE LETTER OF THE CORRECT ANSWER IN THE SPACE AT THE RIGHT.*

Questions 1-7.

DIRECTIONS: In answering Questions 1 through 7, you will be presented with analogies (known as word relationships). Select the answer choice that BEST completes the analogy.

1. Coordinated is related to movement as speech is related to
   A. predictive   B. rapid   C. prophetic   D. articulate

2. Pottery is related to shard as wood is related to
   A. acorn   B. chair   C. smoke   D. kiln

3. Poverty is related to money as famine is related to
   A. nourishment   B. infirmity   C. illness   D. care

4. Farmland is related to arable as waterway is related to
   A. impenetrable   B. maneuverable
   C. fertile   D. deep

5. 19 is related to 17 as 37 is related to
   A. 39   B. 36   C. 34   D. 31

6. Cup is related to lip as bird is related to
   A. beak   B. grass   C. forest   D. bush

7. ZRYQ is related to KCJB as PWOV is related to
   A. GBHA   B. ISJT   C. ELDK   D. EOFP

Questions 8-12.

DIRECTIONS: In answering Questions 8 through 12, each of the questions has a group. Find out which one of the given alternatives will be another member of that group.

8. Springfield, Sacramento, Tallahassee
   A. Buffalo   B. Bangor   C. Pittsburgh   D. Providence

9. Lock, Shut, Fasten
   A. Window   B. Iron   C. Door   D. Block

10. Pathology, Radiology, Ophthalmology
    A. Zoology   B. Hematology   C. Geology   D. Biology

79

11. Karate, Jujitsu, Boxing   11._____
    A. Polo   B. Pole-vault   C. Judo   D. Swimming

12. Newspaper, Hoarding, Television   12._____
    A. Press   B. Rumor   C. Media   D. Broadcast

Questions 13-18.

DIRECTIONS: Questions 13 through 18 are to be answered on the basis of the following pie chart.

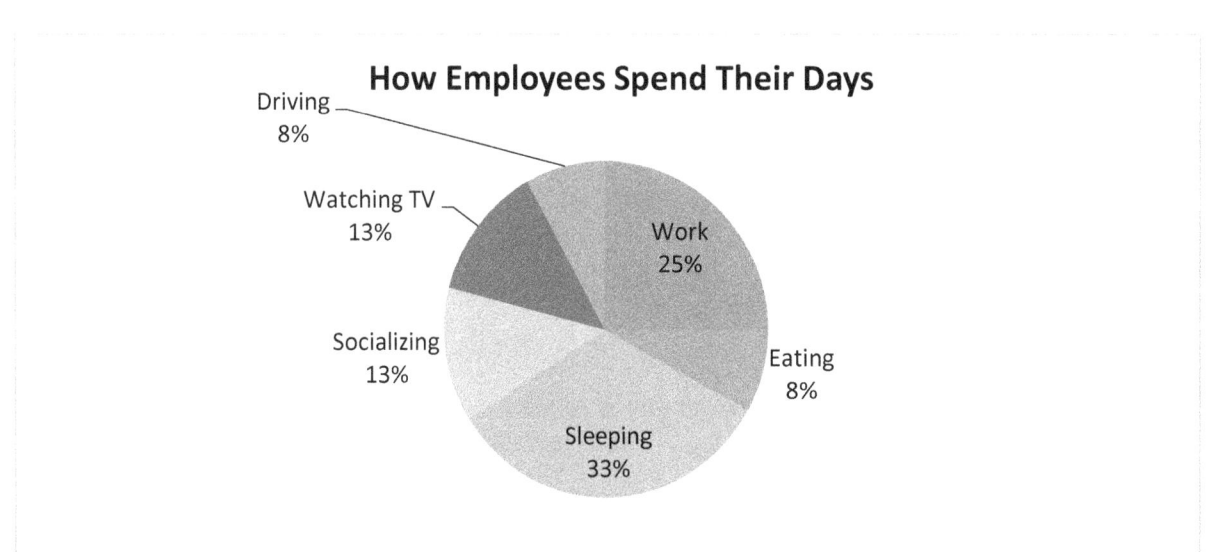

How Employees Spend Their Days

- Driving 8%
- Watching TV 13%
- Work 25%
- Socializing 13%
- Eating 8%
- Sleeping 33%

13. Approximately how many hours a day are spent eating?   13._____
    A. 2 hours   B. 5 hours   C. 1 hour   D. 30 minutes

14. According to the graph, for each 48 hour period, about how many hours are   14._____
    spent socializing and watching TV?
    A. 9 hours   B. 6 hours   C. 12 hours   D. 3 hours

15. If an employee ate two-thirds of their meals at a restaurant, what percentage   15._____
    of the total day is spent eating at home?
    A. 2.5%   B. 5.3%   C. 8%   D. 1.4%

16. About how many hours a day are spent working and sleeping?   16._____
    A. 7   B. 10   C. 12   D. 14

17. Which of the following equations could be used to figure out how much time   17._____
    an employee spends watching TV during a week? T equals the total amount of
    time watching TV during the week.
    A. T = 13% x 24 x 7   B. T = 24 x 13 x 7
    C. T = 24/13% x 7   D. T = 1.3 x 7 x 24

18. How many hours a week does the average employee spend socializing?   18._____
    A. 20   B. 22   C. 23   D. 24

Questions 19-25.

DIRECTIONS: Questions 19 through 25 are to be answered on the basis of the following charts.

DIAL DIRECT	WEEKDAY FULL RATE		EVENING 40% DISCOUNT		WEEKEND 60% DISCOUNT	
SAMPLE RATES FROM SEATTLE TO	FIRST MINUTE	EACH ADDITIONAL MINUTE	FIRST MINUTE	EACH ADDITIONAL MINUTE	FIRST MINUTE	EACH ADDITIONAL MINUTE
Savannah, GA	.52	.23	.31	.14	.21	.08
Providence, RI	.52	.223	.31	.14	.21	.08
Golden, CO	.52	.23	.31	.14	.21	.08
Indianapolis, IN	.48	.19	.29	.11	.19	.07
San Diego, CA	.54	.24	.32	.14	.22	.09
Tallahassee, FL	.54	.24	.32	.14	.22	.09
Milwaukee, WI	.57	.27	.34	.16	.23	.09
Minneapolis, MN	.49	.22	.29	.13	.20	.08
Baton Rouge, LA	.52	.23	.31	.14	.21	.08
Buffalo, NY	.52	.23	.31	.14	.21	.08
Annapolis, MD	.54	.24	.32	.14	.22	.09
Washington, DC	.52	.23	.31	.14	.21	.08

OPERATOR ASSISTED		
STATION-TO-STATION		PERSON-TO-PERSON
1 – 10 MILES	$.75	$3.00 FEE FOR ALL MILEAGES
11 - 22 MILES	$1.10	*NOTE: Add to this base charge – the minute rates from the above chart
23-3000 MILES	$1.55	

19. What is the price of a 6-minute dial direct call to Annapolis, MD when you call on a weekend?
    A. $0.59   B. $0.54   C. $0.67   D. $0.49

20. What is the difference in cost between a 10 minute dial direct to Buffalo, NY and a 10 minute person-to-person call to Buffalo, NY?
    A. $1.55   B. $3.00   C. $0.55   D. $4.55

21. What is the price of a 15-minute operator-assisted Station-to-Station call to Indianapolis, IN on a Monday at noon?
    A. $3.74   B. $7.80   C. $3.45   D. $4.69

22. What is the difference in price between an 11-minute dial direct call to Milwaukee, WI at 11:00 AM on a Wednesday and the same call made at 9 PM that night?
    A. $2.27   B. $3.00   C. $1.55   D. $1.336

23. Which of the following is NOT a type of charge for a dial direct call?   23._____
    A. Holiday   B. Evening   C. Weekend   D. Weekday

24. If a 3.5% tax applied to the total cost of any call, what would be the TOTAL   24._____
    cost of a 13-minute weekday, dial direct call to Golden, CO?
    A. $3.28   B. $3.39   C. $4.94   D. $6.39

25. What is the amount of discount from a dial direct, weekday call to   25._____
    Tallahassee, FL cost as compared to a dial direct, weekend call to
    Tallahassee?
    A. 45%   B. 30%   C. 60%   D. 20%

KEY (CORRECT ANSWERS)

1.	D	11.	C
2.	B	12.	D
3.	A	13.	A
4.	C	14.	C
5.	D	15.	A
6.	A	16.	D
7.	C	17.	A
8.	D	18.	B
9.	D	19.	C
10.	B	20.	B

21. D
22. D
23. A
24. B
25. C

TEST 3

DIRECTIONS: Each question or incomplete statement is followed by several suggested answers or completions. Select the one that BEST answers the question or completes the statement. *PRINT THE LETTER OF THE CORRECT ANSWER IN THE SPACE AT THE RIGHT.*

Questions 1-7.

DIRECTIONS: Questions 1 through 7 are to be answered on the basis of the following graph.

Corporate Fundraiser – Candy Sales by the Case

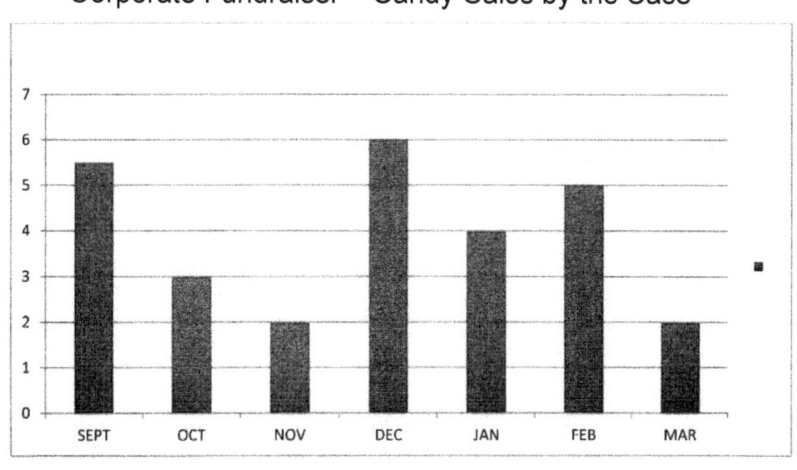

1. The vertical scale ranging from 0 to 7 represents the number of   1.____
   A. students selling candy
   B. candy sold in each case
   C. days each month that candy was sold
   D. cases of candy sold

2. Which two months had approximately the same amount of candy sold?   2.____
   A. November and March   B. September and February
   C. November and October   D. October and March

3. Which month showed a 100% increase in sales over the month of November?   3.____
   A. March   B. January   C. April   D. December

4. From month-to-month, which month saw an approximate 33% drop in sales from the previous month?   4.____
   A. March   B. September   C. January   D. October

5. The amount of candy sold in December is twice the amount of candy sold in which other month?   5.____
   A. October   B. March   C. January   D. September

83

6. What was the total amount of candy sold during the months shown on the graph? 6._____
   A. 44 cases   B. 35.5 cases   C. 23.5 cases   D. 27.5 cases

7. If the fundraiser extended the additional five months of the year and added an additional 65% in sales, approximately how many cases would be sold in total for an entire year? 7._____
   A. 40.5 cases   B. 37 cases   C. 45 cases   D. 27.5 cases

Questions 8-11.

DIRECTIONS: Questions 8 through 11 are to be answered on the basis of the following chart.

S = 10 students
s = 5 students

Mr. Hucklebee	S S S S s
Ms. Shopenhauer	S S S
Mr. White	S S S s
Mrs. Mulrooney	S S S

8. The size of Mr. White's class is _____ students. 8._____
   A. 30   B. 35   C. 40   D. 4

9. The total of all students in all four classes is _____ students. 9._____
   A. 150   B. 140   C. 125   D. 14

10. The average class size based on the above chart is _____ students. 10._____
    A. 140   B. 45   C. 35   D. 30

11. In order to ensure each teacher has the same amount of students in each class, how many students would need to transfer out of Mr. Hucklebee's class? 11._____
    A. 10
    B. 5
    C. 0
    d. 15 would need to transfer into his class

12. When alphabetized correctly, which of the following would be THIRD? 12._____
    A. box   B. departed   C. electrical   D. elemental

13. When alphabetized correctly, which of the following would be SECOND? 13._____
    A. polarize   B. omnipotent   C. polygraph   D. omniscient

14. When alphabetized correctly, which of the following would be THIRD? 14._____
    A. Macklemore, Jonathan   B. Macklemore, J.
    C. DiCastro, Darian   D. Castro, Darren Henry

15. The group fought through the fog, *shambling* through the night, doing their best to stay upright. 15.____
    The word *shambling* means
    A. frozen in place
    B. running
    C. walking awkwardly
    D. shivering uncontrollably

16. Many doctors agree that Gen-aspirin is the best for fighting headaches. It comes in different flavors and is easy to swallow. 16.____
    Is this a valid or invalid argument?
    A. Invalid
    B. Valid

Questions 17-21.

DIRECTIONS: Questions 17 through 21 are to be answered on the basis of the following paragraph.

Hospital workers and volunteers often ask Mr. Ansley to educate children who are hospitalized with primary ciliary dyskinesia (PCD). As he goes through the precautionary cleaning process (scrubbing, donning sterilized clothes, etc.) in order to see his students, Mr. Ansley wonders why their parents add the stress and pressure of schooling and trying to play catch-up because of the amount of time spent in the hospital and not in the classroom, which is an unfortunate side effect of patients with PCD. These children go through so many painful treatments on a given day that it seems punishing to subject them to schooling as normal children do, especially with life expectancy being as short as it is.

17. What is meant by *precautionary* in the second sentence? 17.____
    A. Careful   B. Protective   C. Sterilizing   D. Medical

18. What is the MAIN idea of this passage? 18.____
    A. The preparation to visit a patient with primary ciliary dyskinesia is extensive.
    B. Children with PCD are unable to live normal lives.
    C. Children with PCD die young.
    D. Certain allowances should be made for children with PCD.

19. What is the author's purpose? 19.____
    A. To advise
    B. To educate
    C. To establish credibility
    D. To amuse

20. What is the author's tone? 20.____
    A. Cruel
    B. Sympathetic
    C. Disbelieving
    D. Cheerful

21. How is Mr. Ansley so familiar with the procedures used when visiting a child with PCD? 21.____
    A. He has read about it
    B. He works in the hospital.
    C. His child has PCD.
    D. He tutors them on a regular basis.

Questions 22-25.

DIRECTIONS: One of the underlined words in Questions 22 through 25 should be changed. Select the one that should be changed and print the letter of the word that would change the underlined word.

22. After we <u>washed</u> the fruit that had <u>growing</u> in the garden, we knew there <u>was</u> a store that would buy them.
   A. washing   B. grown   C. is   D. No change

22.____

23. When the temperature <u>drops</u> under 32 degrees (F), the water on the lake <u>freezes</u>, which <u>allowed</u> children to skate across it.
   A. dropped   B. froze   C. allows   D. No change

23.____

24. My friend's bulldog, while <u>chasing</u> cars in the street, always <u>manages</u> to <u>knock</u> over our garbage bins.
   A. chased   B. manage   C. knocks   D. No change

24.____

25. Some of the ice on the driveway <u>has melted</u>.
   A. having melted   B. have melted
   C. has melt   D. No change

25.____

KEY (CORRECT ANSWERS)

1.	D		11.	A
2.	A		12.	C
3.	B		13.	D
4.	C		14.	B
5.	A		15.	C
6.	D		16.	A
7.	C		17.	C
8.	B		18.	D
9.	B		19.	A
10.	C		20.	B

21. D
22. B
23. C
24. D
25. D

TEST 4

DIRECTIONS: Each question or incomplete statement is followed by several suggested answers or completions. Select the one that BEST answers the question or completes the statement. *PRINT THE LETTER OF THE CORRECT ANSWER IN THE SPACE AT THE RIGHT.*

Questions 1-2.

DIRECTIONS: One of the underlined words in Questions 1 and 2 should be changed. Select the one that should be changed and print the letter of the word that would change the underlined word.

1. <u>You</u> can get to Martha's Vineyard by driving from Boston to Woods Hole. Once there, you can travel over on a boat, but <u>you</u> may find traveling by airplane to be more exciting.
   A. they   B. visitors   C. it   D. No change

   1.____

2. When John wants to go to the store looking for <u>milk and eggs</u>, <u>you</u> must remember to bring <u>his</u> wallet.
   A. them   B. he   C. its   D. No change

   2.____

3. An item that sells for $400 is put on sale at $145. What is the percentage of decrease?
   A. 25%   B. 28%   C. 64%   D. 36%

   3.____

4. Two Junior College Mathematics courses have a total of 510 students. The 9:00 AM class has 60 more than the 12:30 PM class. How many students are in the 12:30 class?
   A. 225   B. 285   C. 255   D. 205

   4.____

5. If a car gets 26 miles per gallon and it has driven 75,210 miles, approximately what is the number of gallons of gas that it has used?
   A. 3,000   B. 2,585   C. 165   D. 1,800

   5.____

6. Which one of the following sentences about proper telephone usage is NOT always correct? When answering a telephone, you should
   A. know who you are speaking to
   B. give the caller your undivided attention
   C. identify yourself to the caller
   D. obtain the information your caller wishes before you do other work

   6.____

7. You are part of the "Safety at Work" committee, which is dedicated to ensuring safety of employees. During your regular shift, you notice an employee in violation of one of your committee's rules. Which of the following actions should you take FIRST?
   A. Speak with the employee about the safety rules and mandate them to stop breaking the rules.
   B. Speak to the employee about safety rules and point out the rule they violated.
   C. Bring up the issue during the next committee meeting.
   D. Report the violation to the employee's superiors.

7.____

8. Part of your duties is overseeing employee confidential information. A friend and coworker of yours asks to obtain information concerning another employee. Which is the BEST action to take?
   A. Ask the coworker if you can share the information.
   B. Ask your supervisor if you can give the information to your friend.
   C. Refuse to give the information to your friend.
   D. Give the information to your friend.

8.____

9. Which of the following words means the OPPOSITE of protract?
   A. Extend   B. Hesitant   C. Curtail   D. Plethora

9.____

10. Which of the following words means the OPPOSITE of conserve?
    A. Relinquish   B. Waste   C. Proficient   D. Rigid

10.____

11. Which of the following words means the SAME as dissipate?
    A. Scatter   B. Emancipate
    C. Engage   D. Accumulate

11.____

12. Your office just purchased 14 fax machines. Each fax machine costs $79.99. How much did the 14 fax machines cost?
    A. $1,119.86   B. $1,108.77   C. $1,201.44   D. $1,788.22

12.____

Questions 13-19.

DIRECTIONS: Questions 13 through 19 are to be answered on the basis of the following chart.

Office City	Sales Rank	Production Materials Produced	Rank for Production	Damaged Materials	Employees	Percent of Profit	Sales Points	Weeks Without Injuries
Springfield	13.6	271	12	1	34	35	36	7
Philadelphia	17	274	4	3	25	41	20	4
Gary	16	260	10	5	34	34	21	3
Boulder	5	10	6	9	38	15	20	8
Miami	81	3	81	77	133	4	2	0
Houston	2	370	2	0	95	66	100	16
Battle Creek	82	290	82	81	91	13	9	2

13. Between Philadelphia and Battle Creek, how many damaged materials were there? 13._____
    A. 84 B. 78 C. 45 D. 86

14. How many offices have had 5 or more weeks without injuries? 14._____
    A. 3 B. 4 C. 2 D. 0

15. What was the TOTAL number of damaged materials for the offices in Boulder, Miami, Houston, and Springfield offices? 15._____
    A. 91 B. 87 C. 80 D. 77

16. What were the TOTAL sales points of Houston, Battle Creek, and Gary? 16._____
    A. 115 B. 145 C. 160 D. 130

17. Which of the offices had the LOWEST number of weeks without an injury? 17._____
    A. Battle Creek B. Miami C. Gary D. Philadelphia

18. If worker efficiency is a percentage based on the number of workers at an office and the amount of materials produced, which office has the GREATEST worker efficiency? 18._____
    A. Philadelphia B. Springfield C. Boulder D. Gary

19. If the company was looking to close a facility, which of the following factors would NOT be a reason to close the Miami office? 19._____
    A. Weeks without injury B. Sales rank
    C. Production materials produced D. Employees

Questions 20-25.

DIRECTIONS: In answering Questions 20 through 25, select the sentence in which the underlined word is used correctly.

20. A. Jon needs to increase his capitol by 30% to invest in my business. 20._____
    B. The organization is reevaluating it's decision to purchase the building.
    C. The office supply store sells computer paper and stationery.
    D. The quarterback and running back left there helmets on the bus.

21. A. The police sergeant sited me for disorderly conduct and driving without a license. 21._____
    B. The votes have already been counted.
    C. The professor's theory contradicts the principals of Einstein and Newton.
    D. Who's glass of water is on the table?

22. A. The board of trustees decided to accept the CEO's resignation. 22._____
    B. Lose hats will help keep your head from hurting.
    C. She complemented me on my exquisite dinner tastes.
    D. Jamaal offered him some sound advise.

23.
   A. In class today, Maya lead us in the reciting of the pledge.
   B. Doctors worry about the affects of drinking red wine right before bed.
   C. The workers used sledge hammers to break up the pavement.
   D. The teacher gave her students wise council.

   23._____

24.
   A. This building was formerly the site of one of the city's oldest department stores.
   B. In his position, Albert must be very discrete in handling confidential information.
   C. He was to tired to continue the race.
   D. Each of his mortgage payments as about evenly divided between principle and interest.

   24._____

25.
   A. The police spent several hours at the cite of the accident.
   B. A majority of the public support capitol punishment.
   C. The magician used mirrors to create a convincing illusion.
   D. The heiress flouted her wealth by wearing expensive jewelry.

   25._____

KEY (CORRECT ANSWERS)

1.	D		11.	A
2.	B		12.	A
3.	C		13.	A
4.	A		14.	A
5.	A		15.	B
6.	D		16.	D
7.	B		17.	B
8.	C		18.	A
9.	C		19.	D
10.	B		20.	C

21. B
22. A
23. C
24. A
25. C

CLERICAL ABILITIES
EXAMINATION SECTION
TEST 1

DIRECTIONS: Each question or incomplete statement is followed by several suggested answers or completions. Select the one that BEST answers the question or completes the statement. *PRINT THE LETTER OF THE CORRECT ANSWER IN THE SPACE AT THE RIGHT.*

Questions 1-4.

DIRECTIONS: Questions 1 through 4 are to be answered on the basis of the information given below.

    The most commonly used filing system and the one that is easiest to learn is alphabetical filing. This involves putting records in an A to Z order, according to the letters of the alphabet. The name of a person is filed by using the following order: first, the surname or last name; second, the first name; third, the middle name or middle initial. For example, *Henry C. Young* is filed under *Y* and thereafter under *Young, Henry C.* The name of a company is filed in the same way. For example, *Long Cabinet Co.* is filed under *L* while *John T. Long Cabinet Co.* is filed under *L* and thereafter under *Long, John T. Cabinet Co.*

1. The one of the following which lists the names of persons in the CORRECT alphabetical order is:
   A. Mary Carrie, Helen Carrol, James Carson, John Carter
   B. James Carson, Mary Carrie, John Carter, Helen Carrol
   C. Helen Carrol, James Carson, John Carter, Mary Carrie
   D. John Carter, Helen Carrol, Mary Carrie, James Carson

   1.____

2. The one of the following which lists the names of persons in the CORRECT alphabetical order is:
   A. Jones, John C.; Jones, John A.; Jones, John P.; Jones, John K.
   B. Jones, John P.; Jones, John K.; Jones, John C.; Jones, John A.
   C. Jones, John A.; Jones, John C.; Jones, John K.; Jones, John P.
   D. Jones, John K.; Jones, John C.; Jones, John A.; Jones, John P.

   2.____

3. The one of the following which lists the names of the companies in the CORRECT alphabetical order is:
   A. Blane Co., Blake Co., Block Co., Blear Co.
   B. Blake Co., Blane Co., Blear Co., Block Co.
   C. Block Co., Blear Co., Blane Co., Blake Co.
   D. Blear Co., Blake Co., Blane Co., Block Co.

   3.____

4. You are to return to the file an index card on *Barry C. Wayne Materials and Supplies Co.*
Of the following, the CORRECT alphabetical group that you should return the index card to is
   A. A to G   B. H to M   C. N to S   D. T to Z

4.____

Questions 5-10.

DIRECTIONS: In each of Questions 5 through 10, the names of four people are given. For each question, choose as your answer the one of the four names given which should be filed FIRST according to the usual system of alphabetical filing of names, as described in the following paragraph.

In filing names, you must start with the last name. Names are filed in order of the first letter of the last name, then the second letter, etc. Therefore, BAILY would be filed before BROWN, which would be filed before COLT. A name with fewer letters of the same type comes first, i.e., Smith before Smithe. If the last names are the same, the names are filed alphabetically by the first name. If the first name is an initial, a name with an initial would come before a first name that starts with the same letter as the initial. Therefore, I. BROWN would come before IRA BROWN. Finally, if both last name and first name are the same, the name would be filed alphabetically by the middle name, once again an initial coming before a middle name which starts with the same letter as the initial. If there is no middle name at all, the name would come before those with middle initials or names.

SAMPLE QUESTION: A. Lester Daniels
                   B. William Dancer
                   C. Nathan Danzig
                   D. Dan Lester

The last names beginning with D are filed before the last name beginning with L. Since DANIELS, DANCER, and DANZIG all begin with the same three letters, you must look at the fourth letter of the last name to determine which name should be filed first. C comes before I or Z in the alphabet, so DANCER is filed before DANIELS or DANZIG. Therefore, the answer to the above sample question is B.

5. A. Scott Biala
    B. Mary Byala
    C. Martin Baylor
    D. Francis Bauer

5.____

6. A. Howard J. Black
    B. Howard Black
    C. J. Howard Black
    D. John H. Black

6.____

7. A. Theodora Garth Kingston
    B. Theadore Barth Kingston
    C. Thomas Kingston
    D. Thomas T. Kingston

7.____

8. A. Paulette Mary Huerta
    B. Paul M. Huerta
    C. Paulette L. Huerta
    D. Peter A. Huerta

9. A. Martha Hunt Morgan
    B. Martin Hunt Morgan
    C. Mary H. Morgan
    D. Martine H. Morgan

10. A. James T. Meerschaum
    B. James M. Mershum
    C. James F. Mearshaum
    D. James N. Meshum

Questions 11-14.

DIRECTIONS: Questions 11 through 14 are to be answered SOLELY on the basis of the following information.

You are required to file various documents in file drawers which are labeled according to the following pattern:

DOCUMENTS

MEMOS		LETTERS	
File	Subject	File	Subject
84PM1	(A-L)	84PC1	(A-L)
84PM2	(M-Z)	84PC2	(M-Z)

REPORTS		INQUIRIES	
File	Subject	File	Subject
84PR1	(A-L)	84PQ1	(A-L)
84PR2	(M-Z)	84PQ2	(M-Z)

11. A letter dealing with a burglary should be filed in the drawer labeled
    A. 84PM1   B. 84PC1   C. 84PR1   D. 84PQ2

12. A report on Statistics should be found in the drawer labeled
    A. 84PM1   B. 84PC2   C. 84PR2   D. 84PQS

13. An inquiry is received about parade permit procedures. It should be filed in the drawer labeled
    A. 84PM2   B. 84PC1   C. 84PR1   D. 84PQ2

14. A police officer has a question about a robbery report you filed. You should pull this file from the drawer labeled
    A. 84PM1   B. 84PM2   C. 84PR1   D. 84PR2

Questions 15-22.

DIRECTIONS: Each of Questions 15 through 22 consists of four or six numbered names. For each question, choose the option (A, B, C, or D) which indicates the order in which the names should be filed in accordance with the following filing instructions:
- File alphabetically according to last name, then first name, then middle initial.
- File according to each successive letter within a name.
- When comparing two names in which the letters in the longer name are identical to the corresponding letters in the shorter name, the shorter name is filed first.
- When the last names are the same, initials are always filed before names beginning with the same letter.

15. I.   Ralph Robinson
     II. Alfred Ross
     III. Luis Robles
     IV. James Roberts

   The CORRECT filing sequence for the above names should be
     A. IV, II, I, III   B. I, IV, III, II   C. III, IV, I, II   D. IV, I, III, II

16. I.   Irwin Goodwin
     II. Inez Gonzalez
     III. Irene Goodman
     IV. Ira S. Goodwin
     V.   Ruth I. Goldstein
     VI. M.B. Goodman

   The CORRECT filing sequence for the above names should be
     A. V, II, I, IV, III, VI   B. V, II, VI, III, IV, I
     C. V, II, III, VI, IV, I   D. V, II, III, VI, I, IV

17. I.   George Allan
     II. Gregory Allen
     III. Gary Allen
     IV. George Allen

   The CORRECT filing sequence for the above names should be
     A. IV, III, I, II   B. I, IV, II, III   C. III, IV, I, II   D. I, III, IV, II

18. I. Simon Kauffman
    II. Leo Kaufman
    III. Robert Kaufmann
    IV. Paul Kauffmann

    The CORRECT filing sequence for the above names should be
    A. I, IV, II, III   B. II, IV, III, I   C. III, II, IV, I   D. I, II, III, IV

19. I. Roberta Williams
    II. Robin Wilson
    III. Roberta Wilson
    IV. Robin Williams

    The CORRECT filing sequence for the above names should be
    A. III, II, IV, I   B. I, IV, III, II   C. I, II, III, IV   D. III, I, II, IV

20. I. Lawrence Shultz
    II. Albert Schultz
    III. Theodore Schwartz
    IV. Thomas Schwarz
    V. Alvin Schultz
    VI. Leonard Shultz

    The CORRECT filing sequence for the above names should be
    A. II, V, III, IV, I, VI
    B. IV, III, V, I, II, VI
    C. II, V, I, VI, III, IV
    D. I, VI, II, V, III, IV

21. I. McArdle
    II. Mayer
    III. Maletz
    IV. McNiff
    V. Meyer
    VI. MacMahon

    The CORRECT filing sequence for the above names should be
    A. I, IV, VI, III, II, V
    B. II, I, IV, VI, III, V
    C. VI, III, II, I, IV, V
    D. VI, III, II, V, I, IV

22. I. Jack E. Johnson
    II. R.H. Jackson
    III. Bertha Jackson
    IV. J.T. Johnson
    V. Ann Johns
    VI. John Jacobs

    The CORRECT filing sequence for the above names should be
    A. II, III, VI, V, IV, I
    B. III, II, VI, V, IV, I
    C. VI, II, III, I, V, IV
    D. III, II, VI, IV, V, I

Questions 23-30.

DIRECTIONS: The code table below shows 10 letters with matching numbers. For each question, there are three sets of letters. Each set of letters is followed by a set of numbers which may or may not match their correct letter according to the code table. For each question, check all three sets of letters and numbers and mark your answer:
  A. if no pairs are correctly matched
  B. if only one pair is correctly matched
  C. if only two pairs are correctly matched
  D. if all three pairs are correctly matched

CODE TABLE

T	M	V	D	S	P	R	G	B	H
1	2	3	4	5	6	7	8	9	0

SAMPLE QUESTION: TMVDSP – 123456
                    RGBHTM – 789011
                    DSPRGB – 256789

In the sample question above, the first set of numbers correctly match its set of letters. But the second and third pairs contain mistakes. In the second pair, M is correctly matched with number 1. According to the code table, letter M should be correctly matched with number 2. In the third pair, the letter D is incorrectly matched with number 2. According to the code table, letter D should be correctly matched with number 4. Since only one of the pairs is correctly matched, the answer to this sample question is B.

23. RSBMRM – 759262   23._____
     GDSRVH – 845730
     VDBRTM - 349713

24. TGVSDR – 183247   24._____
     SMHRDP – 520647
     TRMHSR - 172057

25. DSPRGM – 456782   25._____
     MVDBHT – 234902
     HPMDBT - 062491

26. BVPTRD – 936184   26._____
     GDPHMB – 807029
     GMRHMV - 827032

27. MGVRSH – 283750   27._____
     TRDMBS – 174295
     SPRMGV – 567283

28. SGBSDM – 489542
    MGHPTM – 290612
    MPBMHT - 269301

    28.____

29. TDPBHM – 146902
    VPBMRS – 369275
    GDMBHM - 842902

    29.____

30. MVPTBV – 236194
    PDRTMB – 47128
    BGTMSM - 981232

    30.____

KEY (CORRECT ANSWERS)

1.	A	11.	B	21.	C
2.	C	12.	C	22.	B
3.	B	13.	D	23.	B
4.	D	14.	D	24.	B
5.	D	15.	D	25.	C
6.	B	16.	C	26.	A
7.	B	17.	D	27.	D
8.	B	18.	A	28.	A
9.	A	19.	B	29.	D
10.	C	20.	A	30.	A

TEST 2

DIRECTIONS: Each question or incomplete statement is followed by several suggested answers or completions. Select the one that BEST answers the question or completes the statement. *PRINT THE LETTER OF THE CORRECT ANSWER IN THE SPACE AT THE RIGHT.*

Questions 1-10.

DIRECTIONS: Questions 1 through 10 each consists of two columns, each containing four lines of names, numbers and/or addresses. For each question, compare the lines in Column I with the lines in Column II to see if they match exactly, and mark your answer A, B, C, or D, according to the following instructions:
- A. all four lines match exactly
- B. only three lines match exactly
- C. only two lines match exactly
- D. only one line matches exactly

	COLUMN I	COLUMN II	
1.	I. Earl Hodgson II. 1409870 III. Shore Ave. IV. Macon Rd.	Earl Hodgson 1408970 Schore Ave. Macon Rd.	1.____
2.	I. 9671485 II. 470 Astor Court III. Halprin, Phillip IV. Frank D. Poliseo	9671485 470 Astor Court Halperin, Phillip Frank D. Poliseo	2.____
3.	I. Tandem Associates II. 144-17 Northern Blvd. III. Alberta Forchi IV. Kings Park, NY 10751	Tandom Associates 144-17 Northern Blvd. Albert Forchi Kings Point, NY 10751	3.____
4.	I. Bertha C. McCormack II. Clayton, MO III. 976-4242 IV. New City, NY 10951	Bertha C. McCormack Clayton, MO 976-4242 New City, NY 10951	4.____
5.	I. George C. Morill II. Columbia, SC 29201 III. Louis Ingham IV. 3406 Forest Ave.	George C. Morrill Columbia, SD 29201 Louis Ingham 3406 Forest Ave.	5.____
6.	I. 506 S. Elliott Pl. II. Herbert Hall III. 4712 Rockaway Pkwy IV. 169 E. 7 St.	506 S. Elliott Pl. Hurbert Hall 4712 Rockaway Pkwy 169 E. 7 St.	6.____

2 (#2)

7.	I.	345 Park Ave.	345 Park Pl.	7.____
	II.	Colman Oven Corp.	Coleman Oven Corp.	
	III.	Robert Conte	Robert Conti	
	IV.	6179846	6179846	
8.	I.	Grigori Schierber	Grigori Schierber	8.____
	II.	Des Moines, Iowa	Des Moines, Iowa	
	III.	Gouverneur Hospital	Gouverneur Hospital	
	IV.	91-35 Cresskill Pl.	91-35 Cresskill Pl.	
9.	I.	Jeffery Janssen	Jeffrey Janssen	9.____
	II.	8041071	8041071	
	III.	40 Rockefeller Plaza	40 Rockafeller Plaza	
	IV.	407 6 St.	406 7 St.	
10.	I.	5971996	5871996	10.____
	II.	3113 Knickerbocker Ave.	31123 Knickerbocker Ave.	
	III.	8434 Boston Post Rd.	8424 Boston Post Rd.	
	IV.	Penn Station	Penn Station	

Questions 11-14.

DIRECTIONS: Questions 11 through 14 are to be answered by looking at the four groups of names and addresses listed below (I, II, III, and IV), and then finding out the number of groups that have their corresponding numbered lies exactly the same.

GROUP I
Line 1. Richmond General Hospital
Line 2. Geriatric Clinic
Line 3. 3975 Paerdegat St.
Line 4. Loudonville, New York 11538

GROUP II
Line 1. Richman General Hospital
Line 2. Geriatric Clinic
Line 3. 3975 Peardegat St.
Line 4. Londonville, New York 11538

GROUP III
Line 1. Richmond General Hospital
Line 2. Geriatric Clinic
Line 3. 3795 Paerdegat St.
Line 4. Loudonville, New York 11358

GROUP IV
Line 1. Richmend General Hospital
Line 2. Geriatric Clinic
Line 3. 3975 Paerdegat St.
Line 4. Loudonville, New York 11538

1. In how many groups is line one exactly the same? 11.____
    A. Two   B. Three   C. Four   D. None

12. In how many groups is line two exactly the same? 12.____
    A. Two   B. Three   C. Four   D. None

13. In how many groups is line three exactly the same? 13.____
    A. Two   B. Three   C. Four   D. None

14. In how many groups is line four exactly the same? 14.____
    A. Two   B. Three   C. Four   D. None

Questions 15-18.

DIRECTIONS: Each of Questions 15 through 18 has two lists of names and addresses. Each list contains three sets of names and addresses. Check each of the three sets in the list on the right to see if they are the same as the corresponding set in the list on the left. Mark your answers:
  A. if none of the sets in the right list are the same as those in the left list
  B. if only one of the sets in the right list is the same as those in the left list
  C. if only two of the sets in the right list are the same as those in the left list
  D. if all three sets in the right list are the same as those in the left list

15. Mary T. Berlinger   Mary T. Berlinger   15.____
    2351 Hampton St.   2351 Hampton St.
    Monsey, N.Y. 20117   Monsey, N.Y. 20117

    Eduardo Benes   Eduardo Benes
    483 Kingston Avenue   473 Kingston Avenue
    Central Islip, N.Y. 11734   Central Islip, N.Y. 11734

    Alan Carrington Fuchs   Alan Carrington Fuchs
    17 Gnarled Hollow Road   17 Gnarled Hollow Road
    Los Angeles, CA 91635   Los Angeles, CA 91685

16. David John Jacobson   David John Jacobson   16.____
    178 34 St. Apt. 4C   178 53 St. Apt. 4C
    New York, N.Y. 00927   New York, N.Y. 00927

    Ann-Marie Calonella   Ann-Marie Calonella
    7243 South Ridge Blvd.   7243 South Ridge Blvd.
    Bakersfield, CA 96714   Bakersfield, CA 96714

    Pauline M. Thompson   Pauline M. Thomson
    872 Linden Ave.   872 Linden Ave.
    Houston, Texas 70321   Houston, Texas 70321

17. Chester LeRoy Masterton   Chester LeRoy Masterson   17.____
    152 Lacy Rd.   152 Lacy Rd.
    Kankakee, Ill. 54532   Kankakee, Ill. 54532

    William Maloney   William Maloney
    S. LaCrosse Pla.   S. LaCross Pla.
    Wausau, Wisconsin 52136   Wausau, Wisconsin 52146

    Cynthia V. Barnes   Cynthia V. Barnes
    16 Pines Rd.   16 Pines Rd.
    Greenpoint, Miss. 20376   Greenpoint,, Miss. 20376

4 (#2)

18. Marcel Jean Frontenac   Marcel Jean Frontenac   18.____
    8 Burton On The Water   6 Burton On The Water
    Calender, Me. 01471   Calender, Me. 01471

    J. Scott Marsden   J. Scott Marsden
    174 S. Tipton St.   174 Tipton St.
    Cleveland, Ohio   Cleveland, Ohio

    Lawrence T. Haney   Lawrence T. Haney
    171 McDonough St.   171 McDonough St.
    Decatur, Ga. 31304   Decatur, Ga. 31304

Questions 19-26.

DIRECTIONS: Each of Questions 19 through 26 has two lists of numbers. Each list contains three sets of numbers. Check each of the three sets in the list on the right to see if they are the same as the corresponding set in the list on the left. Mark your answers:
- A. if none of the sets in the right list are the same as those in the left list
- B. if only one of the sets in the right list is the same as those in the left list
- C. if only two of the sets in the right list are the same as those in the left list
- D. if all three sets in the right list are the same as those in the left lists

19. 7354183476   7354983476   19.____
     4474747744   4474747774
     5791430231   57914302311

20. 7143592185   7143892185   20.____
     8344517699   8344518699
     9178531263   9178531263

21. 2572114731   257214731   21.____
     8806835476   8806835476
     8255831246   8255831246

22. 331476853821   331476858621   22.____
     6976658532996   6976655832996
     3766042113715   3766042113745

23. 8806663315   88066633115   23.____
     74477138449   74477138449
     211756663666   211756663666

24. 990006966996   99000696996   24.____
     53022219743   53022219843
     4171171117717   4171171177717

25. 24400222433004   24400222433004   25.____
     5300030055000355   5300030055500355
     20000075532002022   20000075532002022

26. 6111666406600011116   61116664066001116   26.____
     7111300117001100733   7111300117001100733
     26666446664476518   26666446664476518

Questions 27-30.

DIRECTIONS: Questions 27 through 30 are to be answered by picking the answer which is in the correct numerical order, from the lowest number to the highest number, in each question.

27. A. 44533, 44518, 44516, 44547   27.____
     B. 44516, 44518, 44533, 44547
     C. 44547, 44533, 44518, 44516
     D. 44518, 44516, 44547, 44533

28. A. 95587, 95593, 95601, 95620   28.____
     B. 95601, 95620, 95587, 95593
     C. 95593, 95587, 95601. 95620
     D. 95620, 95601, 95593, 95587

29. A. 232212, 232208, 232232, 232223   29.____
     B. 232208, 232223, 232212, 232232
     C. 232208, 232212, 232223, 232232
     D. 232223, 232232, 232208, 232208

30. A. 113419, 113521, 113462, 113462   30.____
     B. 113588, 113462, 113521, 113419
     C. 113521, 113588, 113419, 113462
     D. 113419, 113462, 113521, 113588

KEY (CORRECT ANSWERS)

1.	C	11.	A	21.	C
2.	B	12.	C	22.	A
3.	D	13.	A	23.	D
4.	A	14.	A	24.	A
5.	C	15.	C	25.	C
6.	B	16.	B	26.	C
7.	D	17.	B	27.	B
8.	A	18.	B	28.	A
9.	D	19.	B	29.	C
10.	C	20.	B	30.	D

NAME AND NUMBER CHECKING
EXAMINATION SECTION
TEST 1

DIRECTIONS: Questions 1 through 17 consist of sets of names and addresses. In each question, the name and address in Column II should be an exact copy of the name and address in Column I.
If there is:
a mistake only in the name, mark your answer A;
a mistake only in the address, mark your answer B;
a mistake in both name and address, mark your answer C;
No mistake in either name or address, mark your answer D.

Sample Question

Column I
Christina Magnusson
288 Greene Street
New York, N.Y. 10003

Column II
Christina Magnusson
288 Greene Street
New York, N.Y. 10013

Since there is a mistake only in the address (the zip code should be 10003 instead of 10013), the answer to the sample question is B.

COLUMN I | COLUMN II

1. Ms. Joan Kelly
313 Franklin Avenue
Brooklyn, N.Y. 11202

   Ms. Joan Kielly
   318 Franklin Ave.
   Brooklyn, N.Y. 11202

   1.____

2. Mrs. Eileen Engel
47-24 86 Road
Queens, N.Y. 11122

   Mrs. Ellen Engel
   47-24 86 Road
   Queens, New York 11122

   2.____

3. Marcia Michaels
213 E. 81 St.
New York, N.Y. 10012

   Marcia Michaels
   213 E. 81 St.
   New York, N.Y. 10012

   3.____

4. Rev. Edward J. Smyth
1401 Brandeis Street
San Francisco, Calif. 96201

   Rev. Edward J. Smyth
   1401 Brandies Street
   San Francisco, Calif. 96201

   4.____

5. Alicia Rodriguez
24-68 82 St.
Elmhurst, N.Y. 11122

   Alicia Rodriguez
   2468 81 St.
   Elmhurst, N.Y. 11122

   5.____

2 (#1)

COLUMN I	COLUMN II	
6. Ernest Eisemann 21 Columbia St. New York, N.Y. 10007	Ernest Eisermann 21 Columbia St. New York, N.Y. 10007	6._____
7. Mr. & Mrs. George Petersson 87-11 91st Avenue Woodhaven, N.Y. 11421	Mr. & Mrs. George Peterson 87-11 91st Avenue Woodhaven, N.Y. 11421	7._____
8. Mr. Ivan Klebnikov 1848 Newkirk Avenue Brooklyn, N.Y. 11226	Mr. Ivan Klebikov 1848 Newkirk Avenue Brooklyn, N.Y. 11622	8._____
9. Mr. Samuel Rothfleisch 71 Pine Street New York, N.Y. 10005	Samuel Rothfleisch 71 Pine Street New York, N.Y. 100005	9._____
10. Mrs. Isabel Tonnessen 198 East 185th Street Bronx, N.Y. 10458	Mrs. Isabel Tonnessen 189 East 185th Street Bronx, N.Y. 10348	10._____
11. Esteban Perez 173 Eighth Street Staten Island, N.Y. 10306	Estaban Perez 173 Eighth Street Staten Island, N.Y. 10306	11._____
12. Esta Wong 141 West 68 St. New York, N.Y. 10023	Esta Wang 141 West 68 St. New York, N.Y. 10023	12._____
13. Dr. Alberto Grosso 3475 12th Avenue Brooklyn, N.Y. 11218	Dr. Alberto Grosso 3475 12th Avenue Brooklyn, N.Y. 11218	13._____
14. Mrs. Ruth Bortias 482 Theresa Ct. Far Rockaway, N.Y. 11691	Ms. Ruth Bortlas 482 Theresa Ct. Far Rockaway, N.Y. 11169	14._____
15. Mr. & Mrs. Howard Fox 2301 Sedgwick Ave. Bronx, N.Y. 10468	Mr. & Mrs. Howard Fox 231 Sedgwick Ave. Bronx, N.Y. 10468	15._____
16. Miss Marjorie Black 223 East 23 Street New York, N.Y. 10010	Miss Margorie Black 223 East 23 Street New York, N.Y. 10010	16._____

3 (#1)

COLUMN I	COLUMN II	
17. Michelle Herman 806 Valley Rd. Old Tappan, N.J. 07675	Michelle Hermann 806 Valley Dr. Old Tappan, N.J. 07675	17.____

KEY (CORRECT ANSWERS)

1.	C	7.	A	13.	D
2.	A	8.	C	14.	C
3.	D	9.	D	15.	B
4.	B	10.	B	16.	A
5.	B	11.	A	17.	C
6.	A	12.	D		

TEST 2

DIRECTIONS: Questions 1 through 15 are to be answered SOLELY on the instructions given below. *PRINT THE LETTER OF THE CORRECT ANSWER IN THE SPACE AT THE RIGHT.*

INSTRUCTIONS

In each of the following questions, the 3-line name and address in Column I is the master-list entry, and the 3-line entry in Column II is the information to be checked against the master list. If there is one line that does not match, mark your answer A; if there are two lines that do not match, mark your answer B; if all three lines do not match, mark your answer C; if the lines all match exactly, mark your answer D.

Sample Question

Column I
Mark L. Field
11-09 Price Park Blvd.
Bronx, N.Y. 11402

Column II
Mark L. Field
11-99 Prince Park Way
Bronx, N.Y. 11401

The first lines in each column match exactly. The second lines do not match since 11-09 does not match 11-99; and Blvd. does not match Way. The third lines do not match either since 11402 does not match 11401. Therefore, there are two lines that do not match, and the CORRECT answer is B.

	COLUMN I	COLUMN II	
1.	Jerome A. Jackson 1243 14th Avenue New York, N.Y. 10023	Jerome A. Johnson 1234 14th Avenue New York, N.Y. 10023	1.____
2.	Sophie Strachtheim 33-28 Connecticut Ave. Far Rockaway, N.Y. 11697	Sophie Strachtheim 33-28 Connecticut Ave. Far Rockaway, N.Y. 11697	2.____
3.	Elisabeth N.T. Gorrell 256 Exchange St. New York, N.Y. 10013	Elizabeth N.T. Gorrell 256 Exchange St. New York, N.Y. 10013	3.____
4.	Maria J. Gonzalez 7516 E. Sheepshead Rd. Brooklyn, N.Y. 11240	Maria J. Gonzalez 7516 N. Shepshead Rd. Brooklyn, N.Y. 11240	4.____
5.	Leslie B. Brautenweiler 21 57A Seiler Terr. Flushing, N.Y. 11367	Leslie B. Brautenwieler 21-75A Seiler Terr. Flushing, N.J. 11367	5.____

2 (#2)

	COLUMN I	COLUMN II	
6.	Rigoberto J. Peredes 157 Twin Towers, #18F Tottenville, S. I., N.Y,	Rigoberto J. Peredes 157 Twin Towers, #18F Tottenville, S.I., N.Y.	6.____
7.	Pietro F. Albino P.O. Box 7548 Floral Park, N.Y. 11005	Pietro F. Albina P.O. Box 7458 Floral Park, N.Y. 11005	7.____
8.	Joanne Zimmerman Bldg. SW, Room 314 532-4601	Joanne Zimmermann Bldg. SW, Room 314 532-4601	8.____
9.	Carlyle Whetstone Payroll Div. –A, Room 212A 262-5000, ext. 471	Carlyle Whetstone Payroll Div. –A, Room 212A 262-5000, ext. 417	9.____
10.	Kenneth Chiang Legal Council, Room 9745 (201) 416-9100, ext. 17	Kenneth Chiang Legal Counsel, Room 9745 (201) 416-9100, Ext. 17	10.____
11.	Ethel Koenig Personnel Services Division, Room 433; 635-7572	Ethel Hoenig Personal Services Division, Room 433; 635-7527	11.____
12.	Joyce Ehrhardt Office of the Administrator, Room W56; 387-8706	Joyce Ehrhart Office of the Administrator, Room W56; 387-7806	12.____
13.	Ruth Lang EAM Bldg., Room C101 625-2000, ext. 765	Ruth Lang EAM Bldg., Room C110 625-2000, ext. 765	13.____
14.	Anne Marie Ionozzi Investigations, Room 827 576-4000, ext. 832	Anna Marie Ionozzi Investigation, Room 827 566-4000, ext. 832	14.____
15.	Willard Jameson Fm C Bldg., Room 687 454-3010	Willard Jamieson Fm C Bldg., Room 687 454-3010	15.____

KEY (CORRECT ANSWERS)

1.	B	6.	D		C
2.	D	7.	B	12.	B
3.	A	8.	D	13.	A
4.	A	9.	B	14.	C
5.	C	10.	A	15.	A

TEST 3

DIRECTIONS: Questions 1 through 10 are to be answered on the basis of the following instructions. *PRINT THE LETTER OF THE CORRECT ANSWER IN THE SPACE AT THE RIGHT.*

INSTRUCTIONS

For each such set of names, addresses, and numbers listed in Columns I and II, select your answer from the following options:
The names in Columns I and II are different,
The addresses in Columns I and II are different,
The numbers in Columns I and II are different,
The names, addresses, and numbers in Columns I and II are identical.

	COLUMN I	COLUMN II	
1.	Francis Jones 62 Stately Avenue 96-12446	Francis Jones 62 Stately Avenue 96-21446	1.____
2.	Julio Montez 19 Ponderosa Road 56-73161	Julio Montez 19 Ponderosa Road 56-71361	2.____
3.	Mary Mitchell 2314 Melbourne Drive 68-92172	Mary Mitchell 2314 Melbourne Drive 68-92172	3.____
4.	Harry Patterson 25 Dunne Street 14-33430	Harry Patterson 25 Dunne Street 14-34330	4.____
5.	Patrick Murphy 171 West Hosmer Street 93-81214	Patrick Murphy 171 West Hosmer Street 93-18214	5.____
6.	August Schultz 816 St. Clair Avenue 53-40149	August Schultz 816 St. Claire Avenue 53-40149	6.____
7.	George Taft 72 Runnymede Street 47-04033	George Taft 72 Runnymede Street 47-04023	7.____
8.	Angus Henderson 1418 Madison Street 81-76375	Angus Henderson 1318 Madison Street 81-76375	8.____

COLUMN I	COLUMN II	
9. Carolyn Mazur 12 Riverview Road 38-99615	Carolyn Mazur 12 Rivervane Road 38-99615	9.____
10. Adele Russell 1725 Lansing Lane 72-91962	Adela Russell 1725 Lansing Lane 72-91962	10.____

KEY (CORRECT ANSWERS)

1.	C	6.	B
2.	C	7.	C
3.	D	8.	D
4.	C	9.	B
5.	C	10.	A

TEST 4

DIRECTIONS: Questions 1 through 20 test how good you are at catching mistakes in typing or printing. In each question, the name and address in Column II should be an exact copy of the name and address in Column I. Mark your answer
A. If there is no mistake in either name or address;
B. If there is a mistake in both name and address;
C. If there is a mistake only in the name;
D. If there is a mistake only in the address.
PRINT THE LETTER OF THE CORRECT ANSWER IN THE SPACE AT THE RIGHT.

COLUMN I

COLUMN II

1. Milos Yanocek
33-60 14 Street
Long Island City, N.Y. 11011

   Milos Yanocek
33-60 14 Street
Long Island City, N.Y. 11001

   1._____

2. Alphonse Sabattelo
24 Minnetta Lane
New York, N.Y. 10006

   Alphonse Sabbattelo
24 Minetta Lane
New York, N.Y. 10006

   2._____

3. Helen Steam
5 Metropolitan Oval
Bronx, N.Y. 10462

   Helene Stearn
5 Metropolitan Oval
Bronx, N.Y. 10462

   3._____

4. Jacob Weisman
231 Francis Lewis Boulevard
Forest Hills, N.Y. 11325

   Jacob Weisman
231 Francis Lewis Boulevard
Forest Hills, N.Y. 11325

   4._____

5. Riccardo Fuente
134 West 83 Street
New York, N.Y. 10024

   Riccardo Fuentes
134 West 88 Street
New York, N.Y. 10024

   5._____

6. Dennis Lauber
52 Avenue D
Brooklyn, N.Y. 11216

   Dennis Lauder
52 Avenue D
Brooklyn, N.Y. 11216

   6._____

7. Paul Cutter
195 Galloway Avenue
Staten Island, N.Y. 10356

   Paul Cutter
175 Galloway Avenue
Staten Island, N.Y. 10365

   7._____

8. Sean Donnelly
45-58 41 Avenue
Woodside, N.Y. 11168

   Sean Donnelly
45-58 41 Avenue
Woodside, N.Y. 11168

   8._____

9. Clyde Willot
1483 Rockaway Avenue
Brooklyn, N.Y. 11238

   Clyde Willat
1483 Rockaway Avenue
Brooklyn, N.Y. 11238

   9._____

2 (#4)

COLUMN I	COLUMN II	
10. Michael Stanakis 419 Sheriden Avenue Staten Island, N.Y. 10363	Michael Stanakis 419 Sheraden Avenue Staten Island, N.Y. 10363	10.____
11. Joseph DiSilva 63-84 Saunders Road Rego Park, N.Y. 11431	Joseph Disilva 64-83 Saunders Road Rego Park, N.Y. 11431	11.____
12. Linda Polansky 2224 Fendon Avenue Bronx, N.Y. 20464	Linda Polansky 2255 Fenton Avenue Bronx, N.Y. 10464	12.____
13. Alfred Klein 260 Hillside Terrace Staten Island, N.Y. 15545	Alfred Klein 260 Hillside Terrace Staten Island, N.Y. 15545	13.____
14. William McDonnell 504 E. 55 Street New York, N.Y. 10103	William McConnell 504 E. 55 Street New York, N.Y. 10108	14.____
15. Angela Cipolla 41-11 Parson Avenue Flushing, N.Y. 11446	Angela Cipola 41-11 Parsons Avenue Flushing, N.Y. 11446	15.____
16. Julie Sheridan 1212 Ocean Avenue Brooklyn, N.Y. 11237	Julia Sheridan 1212 Ocean Avenue Brooklyn, N.Y. 11237	16.____
17. Arturo Rodriguez 2156 Cruger Avenue Bronx, N.Y. 10446	Arturo Rodrigues 2156 Cruger Avenue Bronx, N.Y. 10446	17.____
18. Helen McCabe 2044 East 19 Street Brooklyn, N.Y. 11204	Helen McCabe 2040 East 19 Street Brooklyn, N.Y. 11204	18.____
19. Charles Martin 526 West 160 Street New York, N.Y. 10022	Charles Martin 526 West 160 Street New York, N.Y. 10022	19.____
20. Morris Rabinowitz 31 Avenue M Brooklyn, N.Y. 11216	Morris Rabinowitz 31 Avenue N Brooklyn, N.Y. 11216	20.____

KEY (CORRECT ANSWERS)

1.	D	11.	B
2.	B	12.	D
3.	C	13.	A
4.	A	14.	B
5.	B	15.	B
6.	C	16.	C
7.	D	17.	C
8.	A	18.	D
9.	B	19.	A
10.	D	20.	D

TEST 5

DIRECTIONS: In copying the addresses below from Column A to the same line in Column B, an Agent-in-Training made some errors. For Questions 1 through 5, if you find that the agent made an error in
only one line, mark your answer A;
only two lines, mark your answer B;
only three lines, mark your answer C;
all four lines, mark your answer D.

EXAMPLE

COLUMN A	COLUMN B
24 Third Avenue	24 Third Avenue
5 Lincoln Road	5 Lincoln Street
50 Central Park West	6 Central Park West
37-21 Queens Boulevard	21-37 Queens Boulevard

Since errors were made on only three lines, namely the second, third, and fourth, the CORRECT answer is C.
PRINT THE LETTER OF THE CORRECT ANSWER IN THE SPACE AT THE RIGHT.

	COLUMN A	COLUMN B	
1.	57-22 Springfield Boulevard 94 Gun Hill Road 8 New Dorp Lane 36 Bedford Avenue	75-22 Springfield Boulevard 94 Gun Hill Avenue 8 New Drop Lane 36 Bedford Avenue	1.____
2.	538 Castle Hill Avenue 54-15 Beach Channel Drive 21 Ralph Avenue 162 Madison Avenue	538 Castle Hill Avenue 54-15 Beach Channel Drive 21 Ralph Avenue 162 Morrison Avenue	2.____
3.	49 Thomas Street 27-21 Northern Blvd. 86 125th Street 872 Atlantic Ave.	49 Thomas Street 21-27 Northern Blvd. 86 125th Street 872 Baltic Ave,	3.____
4.	261-17 Horace Harding Expwy. 191 Fordham Road 6 Victory Blvd. 552 Oceanic Ave.	261-17 Horace Harding Pkwy. 191 Fordham Road 6 Victoria Blvd. 552 Ocean Ave.	4.____
5.	90-05 38th Avenue 19 Central Park West 9281 Avenue X 22 West Farms Square	90-05 36th Avenue 19 Central Park East 9281 Avenue X 22 West Farms Square	5.____

KEY (CORRECT ANSWERS)

1. C
2. A
3. B
4. C
5. B

TEST 6

DIRECTIONS: For Questions 1 through 10, choose the letter in Column II next to the number which EXACTLY matches the number in Column I. *PRINT THE LETTER OF THE CORRECT ANSWER IN THE SPACE AT THE RIGHT.*

COLUMN I   COLUMN II

1. 14235
   A. 13254
   B. 12435
   C. 13245
   D. 14235

   1.____

2. 70698
   A. 90768
   B. 60978
   C. 70698]
   D. 70968

   2.____

3. 11698
   A. 11689
   B. 11986
   C. 11968
   D. 11698

   3.____

4. 50497
   A. 50947
   B. 50497
   C. 50749
   D. 54097

   4.____

5. 69635
   A. 60653
   B. 69630
   C. 69365
   D. 69635

   5.____

6. 1201022011
   A. 1201022011
   B. 1201020211
   C. 1202012011
   D. 1021202011

   6.____

7. 3893981389
   A. 3893891389
   B. 3983981389
   C. 3983891389
   D. 3893981389

   7.____

8. 4765476589
   A. 4765476598
   B. 4765476588
   C. 4765476589
   D. 4765746589

   8.____

9. 8679678938
    A. 8679687938
    B. 8679678938
    C. 8697678938
    D. 8678678938

10. 6834836932
    A. 6834386932
    B. 6834836923
    C. 6843836932
    D. 6834836932

Questions 11-15.

DIRECTIONS: For Questions 11 through 15, determine how many of the symbols in Column Z are exactly the same as the symbol in Column Y.
If none is exactly the same, answer A;
If only one symbol is exactly the same, answer B;
If two symbols are exactly the same, answer C;
If three symbols are exactly the same, answer D.

COLUMN Y	COLUMN Z
11. A123B1266	A123B1366 A123B1266 A133B1366 A123B1266
12. CC28D3377	CD22D3377 CC38D3377 CC28C3377 CC28D2277
13. M21AB201X	M12AB201X M21AB201X M21AB201Y M21BA201X
14. PA383Y744	AP383Y744 PA338Y744 PA388Y744 PA383Y774
15. PB2Y8893	PB2Y8893 PB2Y8893 PB3Y8898 PB2Y8893

KEY (CORRECT ANSWERS)

1.	D	6.	A	11.	C
2.	C	7.	D	12.	A
3.	D	8.	C	13.	B
4.	B	9.	B	14.	A
5.	D	10.	D	15.	D

CODING

COMMENTARY

An ingenious question-type called coding, involving elements of alphabetizing, filing, name and number comparison, and evaluative judgment and application, has currently won wide acceptance in testing circles for measuring clerical aptitude and general ability, particularly on the senior (middle) grades (levels).

While the directions for this question usually vary in detail, the candidate is generally asked to consider groups of names, codes, and numbers, and, then, according to a given plan, to arrange codes in alphabetic order; to arrange these in numerical sequence; to re-arrange columns of names and numbers in correct order; to espy errors in coding; to choose the correct coding arrangement in consonance with the given directions and examples, etc.

This question-type appears to have few paramaters in respect to form, substance, or degree of difficulty.

Accordingly, acquaintance with, and practice in, the coding question is recommended for the serious candidate.

EXAMINATION SECTION
TEST 1

DIRECTIONS:

CODE TABLE

Name of Applicant	H	A	N	G	S	B	R	U	K	E
Test Code	c	o	m	p	l	e	x	i	t	y
File Number	0	1	2	3	4	5	6	7	8	9

Assume that each of the above *capital letters* is the first letter of the Name of an Applicant, that the *small letter* directly beneath each capital letter is the Test Code for the Applicant, and that the *number* directly beneath each code letter is the File Number for the Applicant.
In each of the following questions, the test code letters and the file numbers in Columns 2 and 3 should correspond to the capital letters in Column 1. For each question, look at each column carefully and mark your answer as follows:

If there is an error only in Column 2, mark your answer A.
If there is an error only in Column 3, mark your answer B.
If there is an error in both Columns 2 and 3, mark your answer C.
If both Columns 2 and 3 are correct, mark your answer D.

The following sample question is given to help you understand the procedure.

SAMPLE QUESTION

Column 1	Column 2	Column 3
AKEHN	otyci	18902

In Column 2, the final test code letter "i" should be "m." Column 3 is correctly coded to Column 1. Since there is an error only in Column 2, the answer is A

	Column 1	Column 2	Column 3	
1.	NEKKU	mytti	29987	1.___
2.	KRAEB	txlye	86095	2.___
3.	ENAUK	ymoit	92178	3.___
4.	REANA	xeomo	69121	4.___
5.	EKHSE	ytcxy	97049	5.___

KEY (CORRECT ANSWERS)

1. B
2. C
3. D
4. A
5. C

TEST 2

DIRECTIONS: The employee identification codes in Column I begin and end with a capital letter and have an eight-digit number in between. In Questions 1 through 8, employee identification codes in Column I are to be arranged according to the following rules:

First: Arrange in alphabetical order according to the first letter.

Second: When two or more employee identification codes have the same first letter, arrange in alphabetical order according to the last letter.

Third: When two or more employee codes have the same first and last letters, arrange in numerical order beginning with the lowest number.

The employee identification codes in Column I are numbered 1 through 5 in the order in which they are listed. In Column II the numbers 1 through 5 are arranged in four different ways to show different arrangements of the corresponding employee identification numbers. Choose the answer in Column II in which the employee identification numbers are arranged according to the above rules.

SAMPLE QUESTION

Column I
1. E75044127B
2. B96399104A
3. B93939086A
4. B47064465H
5. B99040922A

Column II
A. 4, 1, 3, 2, 5
B. 4, 1, 2, 3, 5
C. 4, 3, 2, 5, 1
D. 3, 2, 5, 4, 1

In the sample question, the four employee identification codes starting with B should be put before the employee identification code starting with E. The employee identification codes starting with B and ending with A should be put before the employee identification codes starting with B and ending with H. The three employee identification codes starting with B and ending with A should be listed in numerical order, beginning with the lowest number. The correct way to arrange the employee identification codes, therefore, is 3, 2, 5, 4, 1 shown below.

3. B93939086A
2. B96399104A
5. B99040922A
4. B47064465H
1. E75044127B

Therefore, the answer to the sample question is D. Now answer the following questions according to the above rules.

Column I

1. 1. G42786441J
    2. H45665413J
    3. G43117690J
    4. G435466981
    5. G416799421

Column II

A. 2, 5, 4, 3, 1
B. 5, 4, 1, 3, 2
C. 4, 5, 1, 3, 2
D. 1, 3, 5, 4, 2

2 (#2)

2. 1. S44556178T
    2. T43457169T
    3. S53321176T
    4. T53317998S
    5. S67673942S

    A. 1, 3, 5, 2, 4
    B. 4, 3, 5, 2, 1
    C. 5, 3, 1, 2, 4
    D. 5, 1, 3, 4, 2

    2.____

3. 1. R63394217D
    2. R63931247D
    3. R53931247D
    4. R66874239D
    4. R46799366D

    A. 5, 4, 2, 3, 1
    B. 1, 5, 3, 2, 4
    C. 5, 3, 1, 2, 4
    D. 5, 1, 2, 3, 4

    3.____

4. 1. A35671968B
    2. A35421794C
    3. A35466987B
    4. C10435779A
    5. C00634779B

    A. 3, 2, 1, 4, 5
    B. 2, 3, 1, 5, 4
    C. 1, 3, 2, 4, 5
    D. 3, 1, 2, 4, 5

    4.____

5. 1. I99746426Q
    2. I10445311Q
    3. J63749877P
    4. J03421739Q
    5. J00765311Q

    A. 2, 1, 3, 5, 4
    B. 5, 4, 2, 1, 3
    C. 4, 5, 3, 2, 1
    D. 2, 1, 4, 5, 3

    5.____

6. 1. M33964217N
    2. N33942770N
    3. N06155881M
    4. M00433669M
    5. M79034577N

    A. 4, 1, 5, 2, 3
    B. 5, 1, 4, 3, 2
    C. 4, 1, 5, 3, 2
    D. 1, 4, 5, 2, 3

    6.____

7. 1. D77643905C
    2. D44106788C
    3. D13976022F
    4. D97655430E
    5. D00439776F

    A. 1, 2, 5, 3, 4
    B. 5, 3, 2, 1, 4
    C. 2, 1, 5, 3, 4
    D. 2, 1, 4, 5, 3

    7.____

8. 1. W22746920A
    2. W22743720A
    3. W32987655A
    4. W43298765A
    5. W30987433A

    A. 2, 1, 3, 4, 5
    B. 2, 1, 5, 3, 4
    C. 1, 2, 3, 4, 5
    D. 1, 2, 5, 3, 4

    8.____

KEY (CORRECT ANSWERS)

1. B 5. A
2. D 6. C
3. C 7. D
4. D 8. B

TEST 3

DIRECTIONS: Each of the following equestions consists of three sets of names and name codes. In each question, the two names and name codes on the same line are supposed to be exactly the same.

Look carefully at each set of names and codes and mark your answer:
- A. if there are mistakes in all three sets
- B. if there are mistakes in two of the sets
- C. if there is a mistake in only one set
- D. if there are no mistakes in any of the sets

The following sample question is given to help you understand the procedure.

Macabe, John N. - V	53162	Macade, John N. - V	53162
Howard, Joan S. - J	24791	Howard, Joan S. - J	24791
Ware, Susan B. - A	45068	Ware, Susan B. - A	45968

In the above sample question, the names and name codes of the first set are not exactly the same because of the spelling of the last name (Macabe - Macade). The names and name codes of the second set are exactly the same. The names and name codes of the third set are not exactly the same because the two name codes are different (A 45068 - A 45968), Since there are mistakes in only 2 of the sets, the answer to the sample question is B.

1. Powell, Michael C. - 78537 F   Powell, Michael C. - 78537 F   1.____
    Martinez, Pablo, J. - 24435 P   Martinez, Pablo J. - 24435 P
    MacBane, Eliot M. - 98674 E   MacBane, Eliot M. - 98674 E

2. Fitz-Kramer Machines Inc. - 259090   Fitz-Kramer Machines Inc. - 259090   2.____
    Marvel Cleaning Service - 482657   Marvel Cleaning Service - 482657
    Donate, Carl G. - 637418   Danato, Carl G. - 687418

3. Martin Davison Trading Corp. - 43108 T   Martin Davidson Trading Corp. - 43108 T   3.____
    Cotwald Lighting Fixtures - 76065 L   Cotwald Lighting Fixtures - 70056 L
    R. Crawford Plumbers - 23157 C   R. Crawford Plumbers - 23157 G

4. Fraiman Engineering Corp. - M4773   Friaman Engineering Corp. -M4773   4.____
    Neuman, Walter B. - N7745   Neumen, Walter B. - N7745
    Pierce, Eric M. - W6304   Pierce, Eric M. - W6304

5. Constable, Eugene - B 64837   Comstable, Eugene - B 64837   5.____
    Derrick, Paul - H 27119   Derrik, Paul - H 27119
    Heller, Karen - S 49606   Heller, Karen - S 46906

6. Hernando Delivery Service Co. - D 7456   Hernando Delivery Service Co. - D 7456   6.____
    Barettz Electrical Supplies - N 5392   Barettz Electrical Supplies - N 5392
    Tanner, Abraham - M 4798   Tanner, Abraham - M 4798

7. Kalin Associates - R 38641   Kaline Associates - R 38641   7.____
    Sealey, Robert E. - P 63533   Sealey, Robert E. - P 63553
    Scalsi Office Furniture   Scalsi Office Furniture

2 (#3)

8. Janowsky, Philip M.- 742213　　　　　Janowsky, Philip M.- 742213　　　　　8.____
    Hansen, Thomas H. - 934816　　　　　Hanson, Thomas H. - 934816
    L. Lester and Son Inc. - 294568　　　L. Lester and Son Inc. - 294568

KEY (CORRECT ANSWERS)

1. D
2. C
3. A
4. B
5. A

6. D
7. B
8. C

TEST 4

DIRECTIONS: The following questions are to be answered on the basis of the following Code Table. In this table, for each number, a corresponding code letter is given. Each of the questions contains three pairs of numbers and code letters. In each pair, the code letters should correspond with the numbers in accordance with the Code Table.

CODE TABLE

Number	1	2	3	4	5	6	7	8	9	0
Corresponding Code Letter	Y	N	Z	X	W	T	U	P	S	R

In some of the pairs below, an error exists in the coding. Examine the pairs in each question carefully. If an error exists in:
    Only one of the pairs in the question, mark your answer A.
    Any two pairs in the question, mark your answer B.
    All three pairs in the question, mark your answer C.
    None of the pairs in the question, mark your answer D.

SAMPLE QUESTION
37258 - ZUNWP
948764 - SXPTTX
73196 - UZYSP

In the above sample, the first pair is correct since each number, as listed, has the correct corresponding code letter. In the second pair, an error exists because the number 7 should have the code letter U instead of the letter T. In the third pair, an error exists because the number 6 should have the code letter T instead of the letter P. Since there are errors in two of the three pairs, the correct answer is B.

1. 493785 - XSZUPW
   86398207 - PTUSPNRU
   5943162 - WSXZYTN

2. 5413968412 - WXYZSTPXYR
   8763451297 - PUTZXWYZSU
   4781965302 - XUPYSUWZRN

3. 79137584 - USYRUWPX
   638247 - TZPNXS
   49679312 - XSTUSZYN

4. 37854296 - ZUPWXNST
   09183298 - RSYXZNSP
   91762358 - SYUTNXWP

5. 3918762485 - ZSYPUTNXPW
   1578291436 - YWUPNSYXZT
   2791385674 - NUSYZPWTUX

6. 197546821   -   YSUWSTPNY   6.____
   873024867   -   PUZRNWPTU
   583179246   -   WPZYURNXT

7. 510782463   -   WYRUSNXTZ   7.____
   478192356   -   XUPYSNZWT
   961728532   -   STYUNPWXN

KEY (CORRECT ANSWERS)

1. A
2. C
3. B
4. B
5. D

6. C
7. B

TEST 5

DIRECTIONS: Assume that each of the capital letters is the first letter of the name of a city using EAM equipment. The number directly beneath each capital letter is the code number for the city. The small letter beneath each code number is the code letter for the number of EAM divisions in the city and the + or - symbol directly beneath each code letter is the code symbol which signifies whether or not the city uses third generation computers with the EAM equipment.

The questions that follow show City Letters in Column I, Code Numbers in Column II, Code Letters in Column III, and Code Symbols in Column IV. If correct. each City Letter in Column I should correspond by position with each of the three codes shown in the other three columns, in accordance with the coding key shown. *BUT* there are some errors. For each question,

If there is a total of ONE error in Columns 2, 3, and 4, mark your answer A.
If there is a total of TWO errors in Columns 2, 3, and 4, mark your answer B.
If there is a total of THREE errors in Columns 2, 3, and 4, mark your answer C.
If Columns 2, 3, and 4 are correct, mark your answer D.

SAMPLE QUESTION

I	II	III	IV
City Letter	Code Numbers	Code Letters	Code Symbols
Y J M O S	5 3 7 9 8	e b g i h	- - + + -

The errors are as follows: In Column 2, the Code Number should be "2" instead of "3" for City Letter "J," and in Column 4 the Code Symbol should be "+" instead of "-" for City Letter "Y." Since there is a total of two errors in Columns 2, 3, and 4, the answer to this sample question is B.

Now answer questions 1 through 9 according to these rules.

CODING KEY

City Letter	P	J	R	T	Y	K	M	S	O
Code Number	1	2	3	4	5	6	7	8	9
Code Letter	a	b	c	d	e	f	g	h	i
Code Symbol	+	-	+	-	+	-	+	-	+

	I City Letters	II Code Numbers	III Code Letters	IV Code Symbols	
1.	K O R M P	6 9 3 7 1	f i e g a	- - + + +	1.____
2.	O T P S Y	9 4 1 8 6	b d a h e	+ - - - +	2.____
3.	R S J T M	3 8 1 4 7	c h b e g	- - - - +	3.____
4.	P M S K J	1 7 8 6 2	a g h f b	+ + - - -	4.____
5.	M Y T J R	7 5 4 2 3	g e d f c	+ + - - +	5.____
6.	T P K Y O	4 1 6 7 9	d a f e i	- + - + -	6.____
7.	S K O R T	8 6 9 3 5	h f i c d	- - + + -	7.____
8.	J R Y P K	2 3 5 1 9	b d e a f	- + + + -	8.____
9.	R O M P Y	4 9 7 1 5	c i g a d	+ + - + +	9.____

KEY (CORRECT ANSWERS)

1. B
2. C
3. C
4. D
5. A

6. B
7. A
8. B
9. C

TEST 6

Assume that each of the capital letters is the first letter of the name of an offense, that the small letter directly beneath each capital letter is the code letter for the offense, and that the number directly beneath each code letter is the file number for the offense.

DIRECTIONS: In each of the following questions, the code letters and file numbers should correspond to the capital letters.

If there is an error only in Column 2, mark your answer A.
If there is an error only in Column 3, mark your answer B.
If there is an error in both Column 2 and Column 3, mark your answer C.
If both Columns 2 and 3 are correct, mark your answer D.

SAMPLE QUESTION

Column 1	Column 2	Column 3
BNARGHSVVU	emoxtylcci	6357905118

The code letters in Column 2 are correct but the first "5" in Column 3 should be "2." Therefore, the answer is B. Now answer the following questions according to the above rules.

CODE TABLE

Name of Offense	V A N D S B R U G H
Code Letter	c o m p l e x i t y
File Number	1 2 3 4 5 6 7 8 9 0

	Column 1	Column 2	Column 3	
1.	HGDSBNBSVR	ytplxmelcx	0945736517	1.____
2.	SDGUUNHVAH	lptiimycoy	5498830120	2.____
3.	BRSNAAVUDU	exlmooctpi	6753221848	3.____
4.	VSRUDNADUS	cleipmopil	1568432485	4.____
5.	NDSHVRBUAG	mplycxeiot	3450175829	5.____
6.	GHUSNVBRDA	tyilmcexpo	9085316742	6.____
7.	DBSHVURANG	pesycixomt	4650187239	7.____
8.	RHNNASBDGU	xymnolepti	7033256398	8.____

KEY (CORRECT ANSWERS)

1. C
2. D
3. A
4. C
5. B
6. D
7. A
8. C

TEST 7

DIRECTIONS: Each of the following questions contains three sets of code letters and code numbers. In each set, the code numbers should correspond with the code letters as given in the Table, but there is a coding error in some of the sets. Examine the sets in each question carefully.

Mark your answer A if there is a coding error in only *ONE* of the sets in the question.
Mark your answer B if there is a coding error in any *TWO* of the sets in the question.
Mark your answer C if there is a coding error in all *THREE* sets in the question.
Mark your answer D if there is a coding error in *NONE* of the sets in the question.

SAMPLE QUESTION

fgzduwaf - 35720843
uabsdgfw - 04262538
hhfaudgs - 99340257

In the above sample question, the first set is right because each code number matches the code letter as in the Code Table. In the second set, the corresponding number for the code letter b is wrong because it should be 1 instead of 2. In the third set, the corresponding number for the last code letter s is wrong because it should be 6 instead of 7. Since there is an error in two of the sets, the answer to the above sample question is B.

In the Code Table below, each code letter has a corresponding code number directly beneath it.

CODE TABLE

Code Letter	b	d	f	a	g	s	z	w	h	u
Code Number	1	2	3	4	5	6	7	8	9	0

1. fsbughwz - 36104987   zwubgasz - 78025467
   ghgufddb - 59583221

2. hafgdaas - 94351446   ddsfabsd - 22734162
   wgdbssgf - 85216553

3. abfbssbd - 41316712   ghzfaubs - 59734017
   sdbzfwza - 62173874

4. whfbdzag - 89412745   daaszuub - 24467001
   uzhfwssd - 07936623

5. zbadgbuh - 71425109   dzadbbsz - 27421167
   gazhwaff - 54798433

6. fbfuadsh - 31304265   gzfuwzsb - 57300671
   bashhgag - 14699535

KEY (CORRECT ANSWERS)

1. B
2. C
3. B
4. B
5. D
6. C

TEST 8

DIRECTIONS: The following questions are to be answered on the basis of the following Code Table. In this table every letter has a corresponding code number to be punched. Each question contains three pairs of letters and code numbers. In each pair, the code numbers should correspond with the letters in accordance with the Code Table.

CODE TABLE

Letter	P	L	A	N	D	C	O	B	U	R
Corresponding Code Number	1	2	3	4	5	6	7	8	9	0

In some of the pairs below, an error exists in the coding. Examine the pairs in each question. Mark your answer

A if there is a mistake in only *one* of the pairs
B if there is a mistake in only *two* of the pairs
C if there is a mistake in *all three* of the pairs
D if there is a mistake in *none* of the pairs

SAMPLE QUESTION

LCBPUPAB - 26819138
ACOABOL - 3683872
NDURONUC - 46901496

In the above sample, the first pair is correct since each letter as listed has the correct corresponding code number. In the second pair, an error exists because the letter O should have the code number 7, instead of 8. In the third pair, an error exists because the letter D should have the code number 5, instead of 6. Since there are errors in two of the three pairs, your answer should be B.

1. ADCANPLC - 35635126   DORURBBO - 57090877   1.____
   PNACBUCP - 14368061

2. LCOBLRAP - 26782931   UPANUPCD - 91349156   2.____
   RLDACLRO - 02536207

3. LCOROPAR - 26707130   BALANRUP - 83234091   3.____
   DOPOAULL - 57173922

4. ONCRUBAP - 74609831   DCLANORD - 56243705   4.____
   AORPDUR - 3771590

5. PANRBUCD - 13408965   UAOCDPLR - 93765120   5.____
   OPDDOBRA - 71556803

6. BAROLDCP - 83072561   PNOCOBLA - 14767823   6.____
   BURPDOLA - 89015723

7. ANNCPABO - 34461387   DBALDRCP - 58325061   7.____
   ACRPOUL - 3601792

135

2 (#8)

8. BLAPOUR - 8321790   NOACNPL - 4736412   8.____
   RODACORD - 07536805

9. ADUBURCL - 3598062   NOCOBAPR - 47578310   9.____
   PRONDALU - 10754329

10. UBADCLOR - 98356270   NBUPPARA - 48911033   10.____
    LONDUPRC - 27459106

KEY (CORRECT ANSWERS)

1. C
2. B
3. D
4. B
5. A

6. D
7. B
8. B
9. C
10. A

TEST 9

DIRECTIONS: Answer questions 1 through 10 ONLY on the basis of the following information.

Column I consists of serial numbers of dollar bills. Column II shows different ways of arranging the corresponding serial numbers.

The serial numbers of dollar bills in Column I begin and end with a capital letter and have an eight-digit number in between. The serial numbers in Column I are to be arranged according to the following rules:

FIRST: In alphabetical order according to the first letter.

SECOND: When two or more serial numbers have the same first letter, in alphabetical order according to the last letter.

THIRD: When two or more serial numbers have the same first and last letters, in numerical order, beginning with the lowest number.

The serial numbers in Column I are numbered (1) through (5) in the order in which they are listed. In Column II the numbers (1) through (5) are arranged in four different ways to show different arrangements of the corresponding serial numbers. Choose the answer in Column II in which the serial numbers are arranged according to the above rules.

SAMPLE QUESTION

	COLUMN I		COLUMN II
(1)	E75044127B	(A)	4, 1, 3, 2, 5
(2)	B96399104A	(B)	4, 1, 2, 3, 5
(3)	B93939086A	(C)	4, 3, 2, 5, 1
(4)	B47064465H	(D)	3, 2, 5, 4, 1
(5)	B99040922A		

In the sample question, the four serial numbers starting with B should be put before the serial number starting with E. The serial numbers starting with B and ending with A should be put before the serial number starting with B and ending with H. The three serial numbers starting with B and ending with A should be listed in numerical order, beginning with the lowest number. The correct way to arrange the serial numbers, therefore, is:

(3) B93939086A
(2) B96399104A
(5) B99040922A
(4) B47064465H
(1) E75044127B

Since the order of arrangement is 3, 2, 5, 4, 1, the answer to the sample question is (D).

	COLUMN I		COLUMN II
1. (1)	P44343314Y	A.	2, 3, 1, 4, 5
(2)	P44141341S	B.	1, 5, 3, 2, 4
(3)	P44141431L	C.	4, 2, 3, 5, 1
(4)	P41143413W	D.	5, 3, 2, 4, 1
(5)	P44313433H		
2. (1)	D89077275M	A.	3, 2, 5, 4, 1
(2)	D98073724N	B.	1, 4, 3, 2, 5
(3)	D90877274N	C.	4, 1, 5, 2, 3
(4)	D98877275M	D.	1, 3, 2, 5, 4
(5)	D98873725N		

3.	(1)	H32548137E	A.	2,	4,	5,	1,	3
	(2)	H35243178A	B.	1,	5,	2,	3,	4
	(3)	H35284378F	C.	1,	5,	2,	4,	3
	(4)	H35288337A	D.	2,	1,	5,	3,	4
	(5)	H32883173B						
4.	(1)	K24165039H	A.	4,	2,	5,	3,	1
	(2)	F24106599A	B.	2,	3,	4,	1,	5
	(3)	L21406639G	C.	4,	2,	5,	1,	3
	(4)	C24156093A	D.	1,	3,	4,	5,	2
	(5)	K24165593D						
5.	(1)	H79110642E	A.	2,	1,	3,	5,	4
	(2)	H79101928E	B.	2,	1,	4,	5,	3
	(3)	A79111567F	C.	3,	5,	2,	1,	4
	(4)	H79111796E	D.	4,	3,	5,	1,	2
	(5)	A79111618F						
6.	(1)	P16388385W	A.	3,	4,	5,	2,	1
	(2)	R16388335V	B.	2,	3,	4,	5,	1
	(3)	P16383835W	C.	2,	4,	3,	1,	5
	(4)	R18386865V	D.	3,	1,	5,	2,	4
	(5)	P18686865W						
7.	(1)	B42271749G	A.	4,	1,	5,	2,	3
	(2)	B42271779G	B.	4,	1,	2,	5,	3
	(3)	E43217779G	C.	1,	2,	4,	5,	3
	(4)	B42874119C	D.	5,	3,	1,	2,	4
	(5)	E42817749G						
8.	(1)	M57906455S	A.	4,	1,	5,	3,	2
	(2)	N87077758S	B.	3,	4,	1,	5,	2
	(3)	N87707757B	C.	4,	1,	5,	2,	3
	(4)	M57877759B	D.	1,	5,	3,	2,	4
	(5)	M57906555S						
9.	(1)	C69336894Y	A.	2,	5,	3,	1,	4
	(2)	C69336684V	B.	3,	2,	5,	1,	4
	(3)	C69366887W	C.	3,	1,	4,	5,	2
	(4)	C69366994Y	D.	2,	5,	1,	3,	4
	(5)	C69336865V						
10.	(1)	A56247181D	A.	1,	5,	3,	2,	4
	(2)	A56272128P	B.	3,	1,	5,	2,	4
	(3)	H56247128D	C.	3,	2,	1,	5,	4
	(4)	H56272288P	D.	1,	5,	2,	3,	4
	(5)	A56247188D						

KEY (CORRECT ANSWERS)

1. D 6. D
2. B 7. B
3. A 8. A
4. C 9. A
5. C 10. D

TEST 10

DIRECTIONS: Answer the following questions on the basis of the instructions, the code, and the sample questions given below. Assume that an officer at a certain location is equipped with a two-way radio to keep him in constant touch with his security headquarters. Radio messages and replies are given in code form, as follows:

CODE TABLE

Radio Code for Situation	J	P	M	F	B
Radio Code for Action to be Taken	o	r	a	z	q
Radio Response for Action Being Taken	1	2	3	4	5

Assume that each of the above capital letters is the radio code for a particular type of situation, that the small letter below each capital letter is the radio code for the action an officer is directed to take, and that the number directly below each small letter is the radio response an officer should make to indicate what action was actually taken.

In each of the following questions, the code letter for the action directed (Column 2) and the code number for the action taken (Column 3) should correspond to the capital letters in Column 1.

INSTRUCTIONS: If only Column 2 is different from Column 1, mark your answer I.
If only Column 3 is different from Column 1, mark your answer II.
If both Column 2 and Column 3 are different from Column I, mark your answer III.
If both Columns 2 and 3 are the same as Column 1, mark your answer IV.

SAMPLE QUESTION

Column 1	Column 2	Column 3
JPFMB	orzaq	12453

The CORRECT answer is: A. I B. II C. III D. IV

The code letters in Column 2 are correct, but the numbers "53" in Column 3 should be "35." Therefore, the answer is B. Now answe the following questions according to the above rules.

	Column 1	Column 2	Column 3	
1.	PBFJM	rqzoa	25413	1.____
2.	MPFBJ	zrqao	32541	2.____
3.	JBFPM	oqzra	15432	3.____
4.	BJPMF	qaroz	51234	4.____
5.	PJFMB	rozaq	21435	5.____
6.	FJBMP	zoqra	41532	6.____

KEY (CORRECT ANSWERS)

1. D
2. C
3. B
4. A
5. D
6. A

FILING
EXAMINATION SECTION
TEST 1

Questions 1-9.

DIRECTIONS: An important part of the duties of an office worker in a public agency is to file office records. Questions 1 through 9 are designed to determine whether you can file records correctly. Each of these questions consists of four names. For each question, select the one of the four names that should be FOURTH if the four names were arranged in alphabetical order. *PRINT THE LETTER OF THE CORRECT ANSWER IN THE SPACE AT THE RIGHT.*

1. A. 6th National Bank   B. Sexton Lock Co.   1.____
   C. The 69th Street League D. Thomas Saxon Corp.

2. A. 4th Avenue Printing Co. B. The Four Corners Corp. 2.____
   C. Dr. Milton Fournet   D. The Martin Fountaine Co.

3. A. Mr. Chas. Le Mond   B. Model Express, Inc.   3.____
   C. Lenox Enterprises   D. Mobile Supply Co.

4. A. Frank Waller Johnson   B. Frank Walter Johnson   4.____
   C. Wilson Johnson   D. Frank W. Johnson

5. A. Miss Anne M. Carlsen   B. Mrs. Albert S. Carlson 5.____
   C. Mr. Alan Ross Carlsen   D. Dr. Anthony Ash Carlson

6. A. Delaware Paper Co.   B. William Del Ville   6.____
   C. Ralph A. Delmar   D. Wm. K. Del Ville

7. A. The Lloyd Disney Co.   B. Mrs. Raymond Norris   7.____
   C. Oklahoma Envelope, Inc. D. Miss Esther O'Neill

8. A. The Olympic Eraser Co. B. Mrs. Raymond Norris   8.____
   C. Oklahoma Envelope, Inc. D. Miss Esther O'Neill

9. A. Patricia MacNamara   B. Eleanor McNally   9.____
   C. Robt. MacPherson, Jr.   D. Helen McNair

Questions 10-21.

DIRECTIONS: Questions 10 through 21 are to be answered on the basis of the usual rules for alphabetical filing. For each question, indicate in the space at the right the letter preceding the name which should be THIRD in alphabetical order.

10. A. Russell Cohen B. Henry Cohn 10.____
    C. Wesley Chambers D. Arthur Connors

11. A. Wanda Jenkins B. Pauline Jennings 11.____
    C. Leslie Jantzenberg D. Rudy Jensen

12. A. Arnold Wilson B. Carlton Willson 12.____
    C. Duncan Williamson D. Ezra Wilston

13. A. Joseph M. Buchman B. Gustave Bozzerman 13.____
    C. Constantino Brunelli D. Armando Buccino

14. A. Barbara Waverly B. Corinne Warterdam 14.____
    C. Dennis Waterman D. Harold Wartman

15. A. Jose Mejia B. Bernard Mendelsohn 15.____
    C. Antonio Mejias D. Richard Mazzitelli

16. A. Hesselberg, Norman J. B. Hesselman, Nathan B. 16.____
    C. Hazel, Robert S. D. Heintz, August J.

17. A. Oshins, Jerome B. Ohsie, Marjorie 17.____
    C. O'Shaugn, F.J. D. O'Shea, Frances

18. A. Petrie, Joshua A. B. Pendleton, Oscar 18.____
    C. Pertwee, Joshua D. Perkins, Warren G.

19. A. Morganstern, Alfred B. Morganstern, Albert 19.____
    C. Monroe, Mildred D. Modesti, Ernest

20. A. More, Stewart B. Moorhead, Jay 20.____
    C. Moore, Benjamin D. Moffat, Edith

21. A. Ramirez, Paul B. Revere, Pauline 21.____
    C. Ramos, Felix D. Ramazotti, Angelo

KEY (CORRECT ANSWERS)

1.	C		11.	B
2.	A		12.	A
3.	B		13.	D
4.	B		14.	C
5.	D		15.	C
6.	A		16.	A
7.	C		17.	D
8.	D		18.	C
9.	B		19.	B
10.	B		20.	B

21. C

TEST 2

DIRECTIONS: Each question or incomplete statement is followed by several suggested answers or completions. Select the one that BEST answers the question or completes the statement. *PRINT THE LETTER OF THE CORRECT ANSWER IN THE SPACE AT THE RIGHT.*

Questions 1-4.

DIRECTIONS: Questions 1 through 4 are to be answered on the basis of the following alphabetical rules.

RULES FOR ALPHABETICAL FILING

Names of Individuals

The names of individuals are filed in strict alphabetical order, *first* according to the last name, *then* according to first name or initial, and *finally* according to middle name or initial. For example: George Allen precedes Edward Bell and Leonard Reston precedes Lucille Reston.

When last names are the same, for example, A. Green and Agnes Green, the one with the initial comes before the one with the name written out when the first initials are identical.

Prefixes such as De, O', Mac, Mc and Van are filed as written and are treated as part of the names to which they are connected. For example, Gladys McTeaque is filed before Frances Meadows.

1. If the following four names were put into an alphabetical list, what would the FIRST name on the list be?
   A. Wm. C. Paul
   B. W. Paul
   C. Alice Paul
   D. Alyce Paule

2. If the following four names were put into an alphabetical list, what would the THIRD name on the list be?
   A. I. MacCarthy
   B. Irene MacKarthy
   C. Ida McCaren
   D. I.A. McCarthy

3. If the following four names were put into an alphabetical list, what would the SECOND name on the list be?
   A. John Gilhooley
   B. Ramon Gonzalez
   C. Gerald Gilholy
   D. Samuel Gilvecchio

4. If the following four names were put into an alphabetical list, what would the FOURTH name on the list be?
   A. Michael Edwinn
   B. James Edwards
   C. Mary Edwin
   D. Carlo Edwards

2 (#2)

Questions 5-9.

DIRECTIONS: Questions 5 through 9 consist of a group of names which are to be arranged in alphabetical order for filing.

5. Of the following, the name which should be filed FIRST is 5._____
   A. Joseph J. Meadeen
   B. Gerard L. Meader
   C. John F. Madcar
   D. Philip F. Malder

6. Of the following, the name which should be filed LAST is 6._____
   A. Stephen Fischer
   B. Benjamin Fitchmann
   C. Thomas Fishman
   D. Augustus S. Fisher

7. The name which should be filed SECOND is 7._____
   A. Yeatman, Frances
   B. Yeaton, C.S.
   C. Yeatman, R.M.
   D. Yeats, John

8. The name which should be filed THIRD is 8._____
   A. Hauser, Ann
   B. Hauptmann, Jane
   C. Hauster, Mary
   D. Rauprich, Julia

9. The name which should be filed SECOND is 9._____
   A. Flora McDougall
   B. Fred E. MacDowell
   C. Juanita Mendez
   D. James A. Madden

Questions 10-14.

DIRECTIONS: Questions 10 through 14 are to be answered based on an alphabetical arrangement of the following list of names.

Walker, Carol J.	Wacht, Michael	Wade, Ethel
Wall, Fredrick	Wall, Francis	Wall, Frank
Wachs, Paul	Walker, Carol L.	Wagner, Arthur
Walters, Daniel	Wade, Ellen	Wald, William
Wagner, Allen	Walters, David	Walker, Carmen

10. The 4th name on the alphabetized list would be 10._____
    A. Wade, Ellen
    B. Wade, Ethel
    C. Wagner, Allen
    D. Wagner, Arthur

11. The 7th name on the alphabetized list would be 11._____
    A. Walker, Carmen
    B. Walker, Carol J.
    C. Walker, Carol L.
    D. Wald, William

12. The name that would come immediately AFTER Wagner, Arthur on the alphabetized list would be 12._____
    A. Wade, Ethel
    B. Wagner, Allen
    C. Wald, William
    D. Walker, Carol L.

145

13. The name that would come immediately BEFORE Wall, Frank would be 13.____
    A. Wall, Francis
    B. Wall, Fredrick
    C. Walters, David
    D. Walters, Daniel

14. The 12th name on the alphabetized list would be 14.____
    A. Walker, Carol L.
    B. Wald, William
    C. Wall, Francis
    D. Wall, Frank

KEY (CORRECT ANSWERS)

1.	C	6.	B	11.	D
2.	C	7.	C	12.	C
3.	A	8.	A	13.	A
4.	A	9.	D	14.	D
5.	C	10.	B		

TEST 3

DIRECTIONS: Each question or incomplete statement is followed by several suggested answers or completions. Select the one that BEST answers the question or completes the statement. *PRINT THE LETTER OF THE CORRECT ANSWER IN THE SPACE AT THE RIGHT.*

Questions 1-8.

DIRECTIONS: Questions 1 through 8 are based on the Rules of Alphabetical Filing given below. Read these rules carefully before answering the questions.

Names of People
1. The names of people are filed in strict alphabetical order, first according to the last name, then according to first name or initial, and finally according to middle name or initial. For example: George Allen comes before Edward Bell, and Leonard P. Reston comes before Lucille B. Reston.

2. When last names are the same, for example, A. Green and Agnes Green, the one with the initial comes before the one with the name written out when the first initials are identical.

3. When first and last names are alike and the middle name is given, for example, John David Doe and John Devoe Doe, the names should be filed in alphabetical order of the middle names.

4. When first and last names are the same, a name without a middle initial comes before one with a middle name or initial. For example, John Doe comes before John A. Doe and John Alan Doe.

5. When first and last names are the same, a name with a middle initial comes before one with a middle name beginning with the same initial. For example, Jack R. Hertz comes before Jack Richard Hertz.

6. Prefixes such as De, O', Mac, Mc, and Van are filed as written and are treated as part of the names to which they are connected. For example, Robert O'Dea is filed before David Olsen.

7. Abbreviated names are treated as if they were spelled out. For example: Chas. is filed as Charles and Thos. is filed as Thomas.

8. Titles and designations such as Dr., Mr., and Prof. are disregarded in filing.

Names of Organizations
1. The names of business organizations are filed according to the order in which each word in the name appears. When an organization name bears the name of a person, it is filed according to the rules for filing names of people as given above. For example: William Smith Service Co. comes before Television Distributors, Inc.

2. Where bureau, board, office or department appears as the first part of the title of a governmental agency, that agency should be filed under the word in the title expressing the chief function of the agency. For example, Bureau of Budget would be filed as if written Budget, (Bureau of the). The Department of Personnel would be filed as if written Personnel, (Department of).

3. When the following words are part of an organization, they are disregarded: the, of, and.

4. When there are numbers in a name, they are treated as if they were spelled out. For example: 10th Street Bootery is filed as Tenth Street Bootery.

Each question from 1 through 8 contains four names numbered from 1 through 4 but not necessarily numbered in correct filing order. Answer each question by choosing the letter corresponding to the CORRECT filing order of the four names in accordance with the above rules.

SAMPLE QUESTION:
   I. Robert J. Smith
   II. R. Jeffrey Smith
   III. Dr. A. Smythe
   IV. Allen R. Smithers

   A. I, II, III, IV   B. III, I, II, IV   C. II, I, IV, III   D. III, II, I, IV

Since the correct filing order, in accordance with the above rules is II I, IV, III, the correct answer is C.

1.   I. J. Chester VanClief   II. John C. Van Clief
   III. J. VanCleve   IV. Mary L. Vance

   The CORRECT answer is:
   A. IV, III, I, II   B. IV, III, II, I   C. III, I, II, IV   D. III, IV, I, II

2.   I. Community Development Agency   II. Department of Social Services
   III. Board of Estimate   IV. Bureau of Gas and Electricity

   The CORRECT answer is:
   A. III, IV, I, II   B. 1, II, IV, III   C. II, I, III, IV   D. I, III, IV, II

3.   I. Dr. Chas. K. Dahlman   II. F. & A. Delivery Service
   III. Department of Water Supply   IV. Demano Men's Custom Tailors

   The CORRECT answer is:
   A. I, II, III, IV   B. I, IV, II, III   C. IV, I, II, III   D. IV, I, III, II

4. I. 48th Street Theater   II. Fourteenth Street Day Care Center   4.____
   III. Professor A. Cartwright   IV. Albert F. McCarthy

   The CORRECT answer is:
   A. IV, II, I, III   B. IV, III, I, II   C. III, II, I, IV   D. III, I, II, IV

5. I. Frances D'Arcy   II. Mario L. DelAmato   5.____
   III. William R. Diamond   IV. Robert J. DuBarry

   The CORRECT answer is:
   A. I, II, IV, III   B. II, I, III, IV   C. I, II, III, IV   D. II, I, III, IV

6. I. Evelyn H. D'Amelio   II. Jane R. Bailey   6.____
   III. Robert Bailey   IV. Frank Baily

   The CORRECT answer is:
   A. I, II, III, IV   B. I, III, II, IV   C. II, III, IV, I   D. III, II, IV, I

7. I. Department of Markets   7.____
   II. Bureau of Handicapped Children
   III. Housing Authority Administration Building
   IV. Board of Pharmacy

   The CORRECT answer is:
   A. II, I, III, IV   B. I, II, IV, III   C. I, II, III, IV   D. III, II, I, IV

8. I. William A. Shea Stadium   II. Rapid Speed Taxi Co. 8.____
   III. Harry Stampler's Rotisserie III. Wilhelm Albert Shea

   The CORRECT answer is:
   A. II, III, IV, I   B. IV, I, III, II   C. II, IV, I, III   D. III, IV, I, II

Questions 9-18.

DIRECTIONS: Questions 9 through 18 each show in Column I names written on four ledger cards (lettered w, x, y, z) which have to be filed. You are to choose the option (lettered A, B, C, or D) in Column II which BEST represents the proper order for filing the cards.

SAMPLE

	COLUMN I		COLUMN II
w.	John Stevens	A.	w, y, z, x
x.	John D. Stevenson	B.	y, w, z, x
y.	Joan Stevens	C.	x, y, w, z
z.	J. Stevenson	D.	x, w, y, z

3 (#3)

The correct way to file the cards is:
y. Joan Stevens
w. John Stevens
z. J. Stevenson
x. John D. Stevenson

The correct order is shown by the letters y, w, z, x in that sequence. Since, in Column II, B appears in front of the letters y, w, z, x in that sequence, B is the correct answer to the sample question.

Now answer the following questions, using the same procedure.

9. COLUMN I
    w. Juan Montoya
    x. Manuel Montenegro
    y. Victor Matos
    z. Victoria Maltos

    COLUMN II
    A. y, z, x, w
    B. z, y, x, w
    C. z, y, w, x
    D. y, x, z, w

9.____

10. COLUMN I
    w. Frank Carlson
    x. Robert Carlson
    y. George Carlson
    z. Frank Carlton

    COLUMN II
    A. z, x, w, y
    B. z, y, x, w
    C. w, y, z, x
    D. w, z, y, x

10.____

11. COLUMN I
    w. Carmine Rivera
    x. Jose Rivera
    y. Frank River
    z. Joan Rivers

    COLUMN II
    A. y, w, x, z
    B. y, x, w, z
    C. w, x, y, z
    D. w, x, z, y

11.____

12. COLUMN I
    w. Jerome Mathews
    x. Scott A. Matthew
    y. Charles B. Matthew
    z. Scott C. Mathewsw

    COLUMN II
    A. w, y, z, x
    B. z, y, x, w
    C. z, w, x, y
    D. w, z, y, x

12.____

13. COLUMN I
    w. John McMahan
    x. John P. MacMahan
    y. Joseph DeMayo
    z. Joseph D. Mayo

    COLUMN II
    A. w, x, y, z
    B. y, x, z, w
    C. x, w, y, z
    D. y, x, w, z

13.____

14. COLUMN I
    w. Raymond Martinez
    x. Ramon Martinez
    y. Prof. Ray Martinez
    z. Dr. Raymond Martin

    COLUMN II
    A. z, x, y, w
    B. z, y, x, w
    C. z, w, y, x
    D. y, x, w, z

14.____

4 (#3)

15. COLUMN I
    w. Mr. Robert Vincent Mackintosh
    x. Robert Reginald Macintosh
    y. Roger V. McIntosh
    z. Robert R. Mackintosh

    COLUMN II
    A. y, x, z, w
    B. x, w, z, y
    C. x, w, y, z
    D. x, z, w, y

15.____

16. COLUMN I
    w. Dr. D. V. Facsone
    x. Prof. David Fascone
    y. Donald Facsone
    z. Mrs. D. Fascone

    COLUMN II
    A. y, w, z, x
    B. w, y, x, z
    C. w, y, z, x
    D. z, w, x, y

16.____

17. COLUMN I
    w. Johnathan Q. Addams
    x. John Quincy Adams
    y. J. Quincy Addams
    z. Jerimiah Adams

    COLUMN II
    A. z, x, w, y
    B. z, x, y, w
    C. y, w, x, z
    D. x, w, z, y

17.____

18. COLUMN I
    w. Nehimiah Persoff
    x. Newton Pershing
    y. Newman Perring
    z. Nelson Persons

    COLUMN II
    A. w, z, x, y
    B. x, z, y, w
    C. y, x, w, z
    D. z, y, w, x

18.____

KEY (CORRECT ANSWERS)

1.	A	6.	D	11.	A	16.	C
2.	D	7.	D	12.	D	17.	B
3.	B	8.	C	13.	B	18.	C
4.	D	9.	B	14.	A		
5.	C	10.	C	15.	D		

TEST 4

Questions 1-13.

DIRECTIONS: Each question from 1 through 13 contains four names. For each question, choose the name that should be FIRST if he four names are to be arranged in alphabetical order in accordance with the Rule for Alphabetical Filing of Names of People given below. Read this rule carefully. Then, for each question, mark your answer space with the letter that is next to the name that should be first in alphabetical order.

<u>RULE FOR ALPHABETICAL FILING OF NAMES OF PEOPLE</u>

The names of people are filed in strict alphabetical order, first according to the last name, then according to the first name. For example; George Allen comes before Edward Bell, and Alice Reston comes before Lucille Reston.

<u>SAMPLE QUESTION</u>
A. Roger Smith (2)
B. Joan Smythe (4)
C. Alan Smith (1)
D. James Smithe (3)

The number in parentheses show the proper alphabetical order in which these names should be filed. Since the name that should be filed FIRST is Alan Smith, the correct answer to the sample question is C.

1. A. William Claremont B. Antonio Clements 1.____
   C. Anthony Clemente D. William Claymont

2. A. Wayne Fumando B. Sarah Femando 2.____
   C. Susan Fumando D. Wilson Femando

3. A. Wilbur Hanson B. Wm. Hansen 3.____
   C. Robert Hansen D. Thomas Hanson

4. A. George St. John B. Thomas Santos 4.____
   C. Frances Starks D. Mary S. Stranum

5. A. Franklin Carrol B. Timothy Carrol 5.____
   C. Timothy S. Carol D. Frank F. Carroll

6. A. Christie-Barry Storage B. John Christie-Barry 6.____
   C. The Christie-Barry Company D. Anne Christie-Barrie

7. A. Inter State Travel Co. A. Interstate Car Rental 7.____
   C. Inter State Trucking D. Interstate Lending Inst.

2 (#4)

8. A. The Los Angeles Tile Co. 8.____
   B. Anita F. Los
   C. The Lost & Found Detective Agency
   D. Jason Los-Brio

9. A. Prince Charles   B. Prince Charles Coiffures   9.____
   C. Chas. F. Prince   D. Thomas A. Charles

10. A. U.S. Dept. of Agriculture   B. United States Aircraft Co.   10.____
    C. U.S. Air Transport, Inc.   D. The United Union

11. A. Meyer's Art Shop   B. Frank B. Meyer   11.____
    C. Meyers' Paint Store   D. Meyer and Goldberg

12. A. David Des Laurier   B. Des Moines Flower Shop   12.____
    C. Henry Desanto   D. Mary L. Desta

13. A. Jeffrey Van Der Meer   B. Jeffrey M. Vander   13.____
    C. Jeffrey Van   D. Wallace Meer

KEY (CORRECT ANSWERS)

1.	A	6.	D	11.	A
2.	B	7.	B	12.	C
3.	C	8.	B	13.	D
4.	A	9.	D		
5.	C	10.	C		

TEST 5

Questions 1-10.

DIRECTIONS: Questions 1 through 10 are to be answered on the basis of the usual rules of filing. Column I lists, next to the numbers 1 to 10, the names of 10 clinic patients. Column II lists, next to the letters A to D, the headings of file drawers into which you are to place the records of these patients. For each question, indicate in the space at the right the letter preceding the heading of the file drawer in which the record should be filed.

	COLUMN I		COLUMN II	
1.	Charles Coughlin	A.	Cab-Cep	1.____
2.	Mary Carstairs	B.	Ceq-Cho	2.____
3.	Joseph Collin	C.	Chr-Coj	3.____
4.	Thomas Chelsey	D.	Cok-Czy	4.____
5.	Cedric Chalmers			5.____
6.	Mae Clarke			6.____
7.	Dora Copperhead			7.____
8.	Arnold Cohn			8.____
9.	Charlotte Crumboldt			9.____
10.	Frances Celine			10.____

Questions 11-18.

DIRECTIONS: Questions 11 to 18 are to be answered on the basis of the usual rules of filing. Column I lists, next to the numbers 11 to 18, the names of 8 clinic patients. Column II lists, next to the letters A to O, the headings of file drawers into which you are to place the records of these patients. For each question, indicate in the space at the right the letter preceding the heading of the file drawer in which the record should be filed.

COLUMN I	COLUMN II	
11. Thomas Adams	A. Aab-Abi	11.____
	B. Abj-Ach	
12. Joseph Albert	C. Aci-Aco	12.____
	D. Acp-Ada	
13. Frank Anaster	E. Adb-Afr	13.____
	F. Afs-Ago	
14. Charles Abt	G. Agp-Ahz	14.____
	H. Aia-Ako	
15. John Alfred	I. Akp-Ald	15.____
	J. Ale-Amo	
16. Louis Aron	K. Amp-Aor	16.____
	L. Aos-Apr	
17. Francis Amos	M. Aps-Asi	17.____
	N. Asj-Ati	
18. William Adler	O. Atj-Awz	18.____

Questions 19-28.

DIRECTIONS: Questions 19 through 28 are to be answered on the basis of the usual rules of filing. Column I lists, next to the numbers 19 through 28, the names of 10 clinic patients. Column II lists, next to the letters A to D the headings of file drawers into which you are to place the medical records of these patients. For each question, indicate in the space at the right the letter preceding the heading of the file drawer in which the record should be filed.

COLUMN I	COLUMN II	
19. Frank Shea	A. Sab-Sej	19.____
20. Rose Seaborn	B. Sek-Sio	20.____
21. Samuel Smollin	C. Sip-Soo	21.____
22. Thomas Shur	D. Sop-Syz	22.____
23. Ben Schaefer		23.____
24. Shirley Strauss		24.____
25. Harry Spiro		25.____
26. Dora Skelly		26.____
27. Sylvia Smith		27.____
28. Arnold Selz		28.____

KEY (CORRECT ANSWERS)

1.	D	11.	D	21.	C
2.	A	12.	I	22.	B
3.	D	13.	K	23.	A
4.	B	14.	B	24.	D
5.	B	15.	J	25.	D
6.	C	16.	M	26.	C
7.	D	17.	J	27.	C
8.	C	18.	E	28.	B
9.	D	19.	B		
10.	A	20.	A		

PREPARING WRITTEN MATERIAL

PARAGRAPH REARRANGEMENT
COMMENTARY

The sentences that follow are in scrambled order. You are to rearrange them in proper order and indicate the letter choice containing the correct answer at the space at the right.

Each group of sentences in this section is actually a paragraph presented in scrambled order. Each sentence in the group has a place in that paragraph; no sentence is to be left out. You are to read each group of sentences and decide upon the best order in which to put the sentences so as to form a well-organized paragraph.

The questions in this section measure the ability to solve a problem when all the facts relevant to its solution are not given.

More specifically, certain positions of responsibility and authority require the employee to discover connection between events sometimes, apparently, unrelated. In order to do this, the employee will find it necessary to correctly infer that unspecified events have probably occurred or are likely to occur. This ability becomes especially important when action must be taken on incomplete information.

Accordingly, these questions require competitors to choose among several suggested alternatives, each of which presents a different sequential arrangement of the events. Competitors must choose the MOST logical of the suggested sequences.

In order to do so, they may be required to draw on general knowledge to infer missing concepts or events that are essential to sequencing the given events. Competitors should be careful to infer only what is essential to the sequence. The plausibility of the wrong alternatives will always require the inclusion of unlikely events or of additional chains of events which are NOT essential to sequencing the given events.

It's very important to remember that you are looking for the best of the four possible choices, and that the best choice of all may not even be one of the answers you're given to choose from.

There is no one right way to solve these problems. Many people have found it helpful to first write out the order of the sentences, as they would have arranged them, on their scrap paper before looking at the possible answers. If their optimum answer is there, this can save them some time. If it isn't, this method can still give insight into solving the problem. Others find it most helpful to just go through each of the possible choices, contrasting each as they go along. You should use whatever method feels comfortable and works for you.

While most of these types of questions are not that difficult, we've added a higher percentage of the difficult type, just to give you more practice. Usually there are only one or two questions on this section that contain such subtle distinctions that you're unable to answer confidently. And you then may find yourself stuck deciding between two possible choices, neither of which you're sure about.

EXAMINATION SECTION

TEST 1

DIRECTIONS: The sentences listed below are part of a meaningful paragraph, but they are not given in their proper order. You are to decide what would be the BEST order to put sentences to form a well-organized paragraph. Each sentence has a place in the paragraph; there are no extra sentences. *PRINT THE LETTER OF THE CORRECT ANSWER IN THE SPACE AT THE RIGHT.*

1. I. He came on a winter's eve.
    II. Akira came directly, breaking all tradition.
    III. He pounded on the door while a cold rain beat on the shuttered veranda, so at first Chie thought him only the wind.
    IV. Was that it?
    V. Had he followed form—had he asked his mother to speak to his father to approach a go-between—would Chie have been more receptive?
    The CORRECT answer is:
    A. II, IV, V, I, III   B. I, III, II, IV, V   C. V, IV, II, III, I   D. III, V, I, II, IV

2. I. We have an understanding.
    II. Either method comes down to the same thing: a matter of parental approval.
    III. If you give your consent, I become Naomi's husband.
    IV. Please don't judge my candidacy by the unseemliness of this proposal.
    V. I ask directly because the use of a go-between takes much time.
    The CORRECT answer is:
    A. III, IV, II, V, I   B. I, V, II, III, IV   C. I, IV, V, II, III   D. V, III, I, IV, II

3. I. Many relish the opportunity to buy presents because gift-giving offers a powerful means to build stronger bonds with one's closest peers.
    II. Aside from purchasing holiday gifts, most people regularly buy presents for other occasions throughout the year, including weddings, birthdays, anniversaries, graduations, and baby showers.
    III. Last year, Americans spent over $30 billion at retail stores in the month of December alone.
    IV. This frequent experience of gift-giving can engender ambivalent feelings in gift-givers.
    V. Every day, millions of shoppers hit the stores in full force—both online and on foot—searching frantically for the perfect gift.
    The CORRECT answer is:
    A. II, III, V, I, IV   B. IV, V, I, III, II   C. III, II, V, I, IV   D. V, III, II, IV, I

159

4. I. Why do gift-givers assume that gift price is closely linked to gift-recipients' feelings of appreciation?
    II. Perhaps givers believe that bigger (i.e., more expensive) gifts convey stronger signals of thoughtfulness and consideration.
    III. In this sense, gift-givers may be motivated to spend more money on a gift in order to send a "stronger signal" to their intended recipient.
    IV. According to Camerer (1988) and others, gift-giving represents a symbolic ritual, whereby gift-givers attempt to signal their positive attitudes toward the intended recipient and their willingness to invest resources in a future relationship.
    V. As for gift-recipients, they may not construe smaller and larger gifts as representing smaller and larger signals of thoughtfulness and consideration.
    The CORRECT answer is:
    A. V, III, II, IV, I   B. I, II, IV, III, V   C. IV, I, III, V, II   D. II, V, I, IV, III

5. I. But when the spider is not hungry, the stimulation of its hairs merely causes it to shake the touched limb.
    II. Touching this body hair produces one of two distinct reactions.
    III. The entire body of a tarantula, especially its legs, is thickly clothed with hair.
    IV. Some of it is short and wooly, some long and stiff.
    V. When the spider is hungry, it responds with an immediate and swift attack.
    The CORRECT answer is:
    A. IV, II, I, III, V   B. V, I, III, IV, II   C. III, IV, II, V, I   D. I, II, IV, III, V

6. I. That tough question may be just one question away from an easy one.
    II. They tend to be arranged sequentially: questions on the first paragraph come before questions on the second paragraph.
    III. In summation, it is important not to forget that there is no penalty for guessing.
    IV. Try *all* questions on the passage.
    V. Remember, the critical reading questions after each passage are not arranged in order of difficulty.
    The CORRECT answer is:
    A. I, III, IV, II, V   B. II, I, V, III, IV   C. III, IV, I, V, II   D. V, II, IV, I, III

7. I. This time of year clients come to me with one goal in mind: losing weight.
    II. I usually tell them that their goal should be focused on fat loss instead of weight loss.
    III. Converting and burning fat while maintaining or building muscle is an art, which also happens to be my job.
    IV. What I love about this line of work is that *everyone* benefits from healthy eating and supplemental nutrition.
    V. This is because most of us have more stored fat than we prefer, but we do not want to lose muscle in addition to the fat.
    The CORRECT answer is:
    A. V, III, I, II, IV   B. I, IV, V, III, IV   C. II, I, III, IV, V   D. II, V, IV, I, II

8.
   I. In Tierra del Fuego, "invasive" describes the beaver perfectly.
   II. What started as a small influx of 50 beavers has since grown to a number over 200,000.
   III. Unlike in North America where the beaver has several natural predators that help to maintain manageable population numbers, Tierra del Fuego has no such luxury.
   IV. An invasive species is a non-indigenous animal, fungus, or plant species introduced to an area that has the potential to inflict harm upon the native ecosystem.
   V. It was first introduced in 1946 by the Argentine government in an effort to catalyze a fur trading industry in the region.
   The CORRECT answer is:
   A. IV, I, V, II, III   B. I, IV, II, III, V   C. II, V, III, I, IV   D. V, II, IV, III, I

8.____

9.
   I. The words ensure that we are all part of something much larger than the here and now.
   II. Literature might be thought of as the creative measure of history.
   III. It seems impossible to disconnect most literary works from their historical context.
   IV. Great writers, poets, and playwrights mold their sense of life and the events of their time into works of art.
   V. However, the themes that make their work universal and enduring perhaps do transcend time.
   The CORRECT answer is:
   A. I, III, II, V, IV   B. IV, I, V, II, III   C. II, IV, III, V, I   D. III, V, I, IV, II

9.____

10.
   I. If you don't already have an exercise routine, try to build up to a good 20- to 45-minute aerobic workout.
   II. When your brain is well oxygenated, it works more efficiently, so you do your work better and faster.
   III. Your routine will help you enormously when you sit down to work on homework or even on the day of a test.
   IV. Twenty minutes of cardiovascular exercise is a great warm-up before you start your homework.
   V. Exercise does not just help your muscles; it also helps your brain.
   The CORRECT answer is:
   A. I, IV, II, IV, III   B. IV, V, II, I, III   C. V, III, IV, II, I   D. III, IV, I, V, II

10.____

11.
   I. Experts often suggest that crime resembles an epidemic, but what kind?
   II. If it travels along major transportation routes, the cause is microbial.
   III. Economics professor Karl Smith has a good rule of thumb for categorizing epidemics: if it is along the lines of communication, he says the cause is information.
   IV. However, if it spreads everywhere all at once, the cause is a molecule.
   V. If it spreads out like a fan, the cause is an insect.
   The CORRECT answer is:
   A. I, III, II, V, IV   B. II, I, V, IV, III   C. V, III, I, II, IV   D. IV, V, I, III, II

11.____

12. I. A recent study had also suggested a link between childhood lead exposure and juvenile delinquency later on.
     II. These ideas all caused Nevin to look into other sources of lead-based items as well, such as gasoline.
     III. In 1994, Rick Nevin was a consultant working for the U.S Department of Housing and Urban Development on the costs and benefits of removing lead paint from old houses.
     IV. Maybe reducing lead exposure could have an effect on violent crime too?
     V. A growing body of research had linked lead exposure in small children with a whole raft of complications later in life, including lower IQ and behavioral problems.
     The CORRECT answer is:
     A. I, III, V, II, IV   B. IV, I, II, V, III   C. I, III, V, IV, II   D. III, V, I, IV, II

13. I. Like Lord Byron a century earlier, he had learn to play himself, his own best hero, with superb conviction.
     II. Or maybe he was Tarzan Hemingway, crouching in the African bush with elephant gun at the ready.
     III. He was Hemingway of the rugged outdoor grin and the hairy chest posing beside the lion he had just shot.
     IV. But even without the legend, the chest-beating, wisecracking pose that was later to seem so absurd, his impact upon us was tremendous.
     V. By the time we were old enough to read Hemingway, he had become legendary.
     The CORRECT answer is:
     A. I, V, II, IV, III   B. II, I, III, IV, V   C. IV, II, V, III, I   D. V, I, III, II, IV

14. I. Why do the electrons that inhabit atoms jump around so strangely, from one bizarrely shaped orbital to another?
     II. And most importantly, why do protons, the bits that give atoms their heft and personality, stick together at all?
     III. Why are some atoms, like sodium, so hyperactive while others, like helium, are so aloof?
     IV. As any good contractor will tell you, a sound structure requires stable materials.
     V. But atoms, the building blocks of everything we know and love—brownies and butterflies and beyond—do not appear to be models of stability.
     The CORRECT answer is:
     A. IV, V, III, I, II   B. V, III, I, II, IV   C. I, IV, II, V, III   D. III, I, IV, II, V

15. I. Current atomic theory suggests that the strong nuclear force is most likely conveyed by massless particles called "gluons".
     II. According to quantum chromodynamics (QCD), protons and neutrons are composed of smaller particles called quarks, which are held together by the gluons.
     III. As a quantum theory, it conceives of space and time as tiny chunks that occasionally misbehave, rather than smooth predictable quantities.

IV. If you are hoping that QCD ties up atomic behavior with a tidy little bow, you will be disappointed.
V. This quark-binding force has "residue" that extends beyond protons and neutrons themselves to provide enough force to bind the protons and neutrons together.
The CORRECT answer is:
   A. III, IV, II, V, I   B. II, I, IV, III, V   C. I, II, V, IV, III   D. V, III, I, IV, II

16.
I. I have seen him whip a woman, causing the blood to run half an hour at a time.
II. Mr. Severe, the overseer, used to stand by the door of the quarter, armed with a large hickory stick, ready to whip anyone who was not ready to start at the sound of the horn.
III. This was in the midst of her crying children, pleading for their mother's release.
IV. He seemed to take pleasure in manifesting his fiendish barbarity.
V. Mr. Severe was rightly named: he was a cruel man.
The CORRECT answer is:
   A. I, IV, III, II, I   B. II, V, I, III, IV   C. II, V, III, I, IV   D. IV, III, I, V, II

16.____

17.
I. His death was recorded by the slaves as the result of a merciful providence.
II. His career was cut short.
III. He died very soon after I went to Colonel Lloyd's; and he died as he lived, uttering bitter curses and horrid oaths.
IV. Mr. Severe's place was filled by a Mr. Hopkins.
V. From the rising till the going down of the sun, he was cursing, raving, cutting, and slashing among the slaves in the field.
The CORRECT answer is:
   A. V, II, III, I, IV   B. IV, I, III, II, V   C. III, I, IV, V, II   D. I, II, V, III, IV

17.____

18.
I. The primary reef-building organisms are invertebrate animals known as corals.
II. They are located in warm, shallow, tropical marine waters with enough light to stimulate the growth of reef organisms.
III. Coral reefs are highly diverse ecosystems, supporting greater numbers of fish species than any other marine ecosystem.
IV. They belong to the class Anthozoa and are subdivided into stony corals, which have six tentacles.
V. These corals are small colonial, marine invertebrates.
The CORRECT answer is:
   A. I, IV, V, II, III   B. V, I, III, IV, II   C. III, II, I, V, IV   D. IV, V, II, III, I

18.____

19.
I. Jane Goodall, an English ethologist, is famous for her studies of the chimpanzees of the Gombe Stream Reserve in Tanzania.
II. As a result of her studies, Goodall concluded that chimpanzees are an advanced species closely related to humans.
III. Ultimately, Goodall's observations led her to write *The Chimpanzee Family Book*, which conveys a new, more humane view of wildlife.

19.____

IV. She is credited with the first recorded observation of chimps eating meat and using and making tools.
V. Her observations have forced scientists to redefine the characteristics once considered as solely human traits.
The CORRECT answer is:
A. V, II, IV, III, I   B. I, IV, II, V, III   C. I, II, V, IV, III   D. III, V, II, I, IV

20.
I. Since then, research has demonstrated that the deposition of atmospheric chemicals is causing widespread acidification of lakes, streams, and soil.
II. "Acid rain" is a popularly used phrase that refers to the deposition of acidifying substances from the atmosphere.
III. This phenomenon became a prominent issue around 1970.
IV. Of the many chemicals that are deposited from the atmosphere, the most important in terms of causing acidity in soil and surface waters are dilute solutions of sulfuric and nitric acids.
V. These chemicals are deposited as acidic rain or snow and include sulfur dioxide, oxides of nitrogen, and tiny particulates such as ammonium sulfate.
The CORRECT answer is:
A. III, IV, I, II, V   B. IV, III, I, IV, V   C. V, I, IV, III, II   D. II, III, I, IV, V

21.
I. Programmers wrote algorithmic software that precisely specified both the problem and how to solve it.
II. AI programmers, in contrast, have sought to program computers with flexible rules for seeking solutions to problems.
III. In the 1940 and 1950s, the first large, electronic, digital computers were designed to perform numerical calculations set up by a human programmer.
IV. The computers did so by completing a series of clearly defined steps, or algorithms.
V. An AI program may be designed to modify the rules it is given or to develop entirely new rules.
The CORRECT answer is:
A. I, III, II, V, IV   B. IV, I, III, V, II   C. III, IV, I, II, V   D. III, I, II, IV, V

22.
I. Wildfire is a periodic ecological disturbance, associated with the rapid combustion of much of the biomass of an ecosystem.
II. Wildfires themselves are both routine and ecologically necessary.
III. It is where they encounter human habitation, of course, that dangers quickly escalate,
IV. Once ignited by lightning or by humans, the biomass oxidizes as an uncontrolled blaze.
V. This unfettered burning continues until the fire either runs out of fuel or is quenched.
The CORRECT answer is:
A. V, IV, I, II, III   B. I, II, V, III, IV   C. III, II, I, IV, V   D. IV, V, III, I, II

23.
  I. His arguments supported the positions advanced by the Democratic Party's southern wing and sharply challenged the constitutionality of the Republican Party's emerging political platform.
  II. Beginning in the mid-1840s as a simple freedom suit, the case ended with the Court's intervention in the central political issues of the 1850s and the intensification of the sectional crisis that ultimately led to civil war.
  III. During the Civil War, the decision quickly fell into disrepute, and its major rulings were overruled by ratification of the 13th and 14th Amendments.
  IV. *Dred Scott v. Sandford* ranks as one of the worst decisions in the Supreme Court's history.
  V. Chief Justice Roger Taney, speaking for a deeply divided Court, brought about this turn of events by ruling that no black American—whether free or enslaved—could be a U.S. citizen and that Congress possessed no legitimate authority to prohibit slavery's expansion into the federal territories.

  The CORRECT answer is:
  A. II, IV, I, III, V   B. V, I, III, IV, II   C. I, V, II, V, III   D. IV, II, V, I, III

24.
  I. Considered the last battle between the U.S. Army and American Indians, the Wounded Knee Massacre took place on the morning of 29 December 1890 beside Wounded Knee Creek on South Dakota's Pine Ridge Reservation.
  II. This was the culmination of the Ghost Dance religion that had started with a Paiute prophet from Nevada named Wovoka (1856-1932), who was also known as Jack Wilson.
  III. During the previous year, U.S. government officials had reduced Sioux lands and cut back rations so severely that the Sioux people were starving.
  IV. These conditions encouraged the desperate embrace of the Ghost Dance.
  V. This pan-tribal ritual had historical antecedents that go much further back than its actual founder.

  The CORRECT answer is:
  A. I, II, III, IV, V   B. V, IV, II, III, I   C. IV, III, I, V, II   D. III, I, V, II, IV

25.
  I. Their actions, which became known as the Boston Tea Party, set in motion events that led directly to the American Revolution.
  II. Urged on by a crowd of cheering townspeople, the disguised Bostonians destroyed 342 chests of tea estimated to be worth between $10,000 an $18,000.
  III. The Americans, who numbered around 70, shared a common aim: to destroy the ships' cargo of British East India Company tea.
  IV. Many years later, George Hewes, a 31-year-old shoemaker and participant, recalled "We then were ordered by our commander to open the hatches and take out all the chests of tea and throw them overboard. And we immediately proceeded to execute his orders, first cutting and splitting the chests with our tomahawks, so as thoroughly to expose them to the effects of the water.

V. At nine o'clock on the night of December 16, 1773, a band of Bostonians disguised as Native Americans boarded the British merchant ship Dartmouth and two companion vessels anchored at Griffin's Wharf in Boston harbor.

The CORRECT answer is:

A. V, III, IV, II, I   B. IV, II, III, I, V   C. III, IV, V, II, I   D. V, II, IV, III, I

KEY (CORRECT ANSWERS)

1.	A		11.	A
2.	C		12.	D
3.	D		13.	D
4.	B		14.	A
5.	C		15.	C
6.	D		16.	B
7.	B		17.	A
8.	A		18.	C
9.	C		19.	B
10.	B		20.	D

21. C
22. B
23. D
24. A
25. A

TEST 2

DIRECTIONS: The sentences listed below are part of a meaningful paragraph, but they are not given in their proper order. You are to decide what would be the BEST order to put sentences to form a well-organized paragraph. Each sentence has a place in the paragraph; there are no extra sentences. *PRINT THE LETTER OF THE CORRECT ANSWER IN THE SPACE AT THE RIGHT.*

1. I. Recently, some U.S. cities have added a new category: compost, organic matter such as food scraps and yard debris.
    II. For example, paper may go in one container, glass and aluminum in another, regular garbage in a third.
    III. Like paper or glass recycling, composting demands a certain amount of effort from the public in order to be successful.
    IV. Over the past generation, people in many parts of the United States have become accustomed to dividing their household waste products into different categories for recycling.
    V. But the inconveniences of composting are far outweighed by its benefits.
    The CORRECT answer is:
    A. V, II, III, IV, I   B. I, III, IV, V, II   C. IV, II, I, III, V   D. III, I, V, II, IV

1.____

2. I. It also enhances soil texture, encouraging healthy roots and minimizing the need for chemical fertilizers.
    II. Most people think of banana peels, eggshells, and dead leaves as "waste," but compost is actually a valuable resource with multiple practical uses.
    III. When utilized as a garden fertilizer, compost provides nutrients to soil and improves plant growth while deterring or killing pests and preventing some plant diseases.
    IV. In large quantities, compost can be converted into a natural gas that can be used as fuel for transportation or heating and cooling systems.
    V. Better than soil at holding moisture, compost minimizes water waste and storm runoff, increases savings on watering costs, and helps reduce erosion on embankments near bodies of water.
    The CORRECT answer is:
    A. II, III, I, V, IV   B. I, IV, V, III, II   C. V, II, IV, I, III   D. III, V, II, IV, I

2.____

3. I. The street is a sea of red, the traditional Chinese color of luck and happiness.
    II. Buildings are draped with festive, red banners and garlands.
    III. Crowds gather then to celebrate Lunar New Year.
    IV. Lamp posts are strung with crimson paper lanterns, which bob in the crisp winter breeze.
    V. At the beginning of February, thousands of people line H Street, the heart of Chinatown in Washington, D.C.
    The CORRECT answer is:
    A. I, V, II, III, IV   B. IV, II, V, I, III   C. III, I, II, IV, V   D. V, III, I, II, IV

3.____

167

4. I. Experts agree that the lion dance originated in the Han dynasty; however, there is little agreement about the dance's original purpose.
   II. Another theory is that an emperor, upon waking from a dream about a lion, hired an artist to choreograph the dance.
   III. Dancers must be synchronized with the music accompanying the dance, as well as with each other, in order to fully realize the celebration.
   IV. Whatever the origins are, the current function of the dance is celebration.
   V. Some evidence suggests that the earliest version of the dance was an attempt to ward off an evil spirt.
   The CORRECT answer is:
   A. V, II, IV, III, I   B. I, V, II, IV, III   C. II, I, III, V, IV   D. IV, III, V, I, II

   4.____

5. I. Half the population of New York, Toronto, and London do not own cars; instead they use public transport.
   II. Every day, subway systems carry 155 million passengers, thirty-four times the number carried by all the world's airplanes.
   III. Though there are 600 million cars on the planet, and counting, there are also seven billion people, which means most of us get around taking other modes of transportation.
   IV. All of that is to say that even a century and a half after the invention of the internal combustion engine, private car ownership is still an anomaly.
   V. In other words, traveling to work, school, or the market means being a straphanger: someone who relies on public transport.
   The CORRECT answer is:
   A. I, II, IV, V, III   B. III, V, I, II, IV   C. III, I, II, IV, V   D. II, IV, V, III, I

   5.____

6. I. "They jumped up like popcorn," he said, describing how they would flap their half-formed wings and take short hops into the air.
   II. Dan settled on the Chukar Partridge as a model species, but he might not have made his discovery without the help of a local rancher that supplied him with the birds.
   III. At field sites around the world, Dan Kiel saw a pattern in how young ground birds ran along behind their parents.
   IV. So when a group of graduate students challenged him to come up with new data on the age-old ground-up-tree-down debate, he designed a project to see what clues might lie in how baby game birds learned to fly.
   V. When the rancher stopped by to see how things were progressing, he yelled at Dan to give the birds something to climb on.
   The CORRECT answer is:
   A. IV, II, V, I, III   B. III, II, I, V, IV   C. III, I, IV, II, V   D. I, II, IV, V, III

   6.____

7. I. Honey bees are hosts to the pathogenic large ectoparasitic mite, *Varroa destructor*.
   II. These mites feed on bee hemolymph (blood) and can kill bees directly or by increasing their susceptibility to secondary infections.
   III. Little is known about the natural defenses that keep the mite infections under control.

   7.____

IV. Pyrethrums are a group of flowering plants that produce potent insecticides with anti-mite activity.
V. In fact, the human mite infestation known as scabies is treated with a topical pyrethrum cream.
The CORRECT answer is:
   A. I, II, III, IV, V   B. V, IV, II, I, III   C. III, IV, V, I, II   D. II, IV, I, III, V

8. I. He hardly ever allowed me to pay for the books he placed in my hands, but when he wasn't looking I'd leave the coins I'd managed to collect on the counter.
    II. My favorite place in the whole city was the Sempere & Sons bookshop on Calle Santa Ana.
    III. It smelled of old paper and dust and it was my sanctuary, my refuge.
    IV. The bookseller would let me sit on a chair in a corner and read any book I liked to my heart's content.
    V. It was only small change—if I'd had to buy a book with that pittance, I would probably have been able to afford only a booklet of cigarette papers.
    The CORRECT answer is:
       A. I, III, V, II, IV   B. II, IV, I, III, V   C. V, I, III, IV, II   D. II, III, IV, I, V

9. I. At school, I had learned to read and write long before the other children.
    II. My father, however, did not see things the way I did; he did not like to see books in the house.
    III. Where my school friends saw notches of ink on incomprehensible pages, I saw light, streets, and people.
    IV. Back then my only friends were made of paper and ink.
    V. Words and the mystery of their hidden science fascinated me, and I saw in them a key with which I could unlock a boundless world.
    The CORRECT answer is:
       A. IV, I, III, V, II   B. I, V, III, IV, II   C. II, I, V, III, IV   D. V, IV, II, III, I

10. I. Gary King of Harvard University says that one main reason null results are not published is because there were many ways to produce them by messing up.
    II. Oddly enough, there is little hard data on how often or why null results are squelched.
    III. The various errors make the null reports almost impossible to predict, Mr. King believes.
    IV. In recent years, the debate has spread to social and behavioral science, which help sway public and social policy.
    V. The question of what to do with null results in research has long been hotly debated among those conducting medical trials.
    The CORRECT answer is:
       A. I, III, IV, V, II   B. V, I, II, IV, III   C. III, II, I, V, IV   D. V, IV, II, I, III

11.
   I. In a recent study, Stanford political economist Neil Malholtra and two of his graduate students examined all studies funded by TESS (Time-sharing Experiments for Social Sciences).
   II. Scientists of these experiments cited deeper problems within their studies but also believed many journalists wouldn't be interested in their findings.
   III. TESS allows scientists to order up internet-based surveys of a representative sample of U.S. adults to test a particular hypothesis.
   IV. One scientist went on record as saying, "The reality is that null effects do not tell a clear story."
   V. Well, Malholtra's team tracked down working papers from most of the experiments that weren't published to find out what had happened to their results.

   The CORRECT answer is:
   A. IV, II, V, III, I   B. I, III, V, II, IV   C. III, V, I, IV, II   D. I, III, IV, II, V

11.____

12.
   I. The work also suggests that these ultra-tiny salt wires may already exist in sea spray and large underground salt deposits.
   II. Scientists expect for metals such as gold or lead to stretch out at temperatures well below their melting points, but they never expected this superplasticity in a rigid, crystalline material like salt.
   III. Inflexible old salt becomes a softy in the nanoworld, stretching like taffy to more than twice its length, researchers report.
   IV. The findings may lead to new approaches for making nanowires that could end up in solar cells or electronic circuits.
   V. According to Nathan Moore of Sandia National Laboratories, these nanowires are special and much more common than we may think.

   The CORRECT answer is:
   A. IV, III, V, II, I   B. I, V, III, IV, II   C. III, IV, I, V, II   D. V, II, III, I, IV

12.____

13.
   I. The Venus flytrap (Dionaea muscipula) needs to know when an ideal meal is crawling across its leaves.
   II. The large black hairs on their lobes allow the Venus flytraps to literally feel their prey, and they act as triggers that spring the trap closed.
   III. To be clear, if an insect touches just one hair, the trap will not spring shut; but a large enough bug will likely touch two hairs within twenty seconds which is the signal the Venus flytrap waits for.
   IV. Closing its trap requires a huge expense of energy, and reopening can take several hours.
   V. When the proper prey makes its way across the trap, the Dionaea launches into action.

   The CORRECT answer is:
   A. IV, I, V, II, III   B. II, V, I, III, IV   C. I, II, V, IV, III   D. I, IV, II, V, III

13.____

5 (#2)

14. I. These books usually contain collections of stories, many of which are much older than the books themselves.
    II. Where other early European authors wrote their literary works in Latin, the Irish began writing down their stories in their own language as early as 6th century B.C.E.
    III. Ireland has the oldest vernacular literature in Europe.
    IV. One of the most famous of these collections is the epic cycle, *The Táin Bó Culainge*, which translates to "The Cattle Raid of Cooley."
    V. While much of the earliest Irish writing has been lost or destroyed, several manuscripts survive from the late medieval period.
    The CORRECT answer is:
    A. V, IV, I, II, III   B. III, II, V, I, IV   C. III, I, IV, V, II   D. IV, II, III, I, V

15. I. Obviously the plot is thin, but it works better as a thematic peace, exploring several great issues that plagued authors and people during that era.
    II. The story begins during a raid when Meb's forces are joined by Frederick and his men.
    III. In the end, many warriors on both sides perish, the prize is lost, and peace is somehow re-established between the opposing sides.
    IV. The middle of the story tells of how Chulu fends off Meb's army by herself while Concho's men struggle against witchcraft.
    V. The prize is defended by the current king, Concho, and the young warrior, Chulu.
    The CORRECT answer is:
    A. II, V, IV, III, I   B. V, I, IV, III, II   C. I, III, V, IV, II   D. III, II, I, V, IV

16. I. However, sometimes the flowers that are treated with the pesticides are not as vibrant as those that did not receive the treatment.
    II. The first phase featured no pesticides and the second featured a pesticide that varied in doses.
    III. In the cultivation of roses, certain pesticides are often applied when the presence of aphids is detected.
    IV. Recently, researchers conducted two phases of an experiment to study the effects of certain pesticides on rose bushes.
    V. To start, aphids are small plant-eating insects known to feed on rose bushes.
    The CORRECT answer is:
    A. IV, III, II, I, V   B. I, II, V, III, IV   C. V, III, I, IV, II   D. II, V, IV, I, III

17. I. My passion for it took hold many years ago when I happened to cross paths with a hiker in a national park.
    II. The wilderness has a way of cleansing the spirit.
    III. His excitement was infectious as he quoted various poetic verses pertaining to the wild; I was hooked.
    IV. For some, backpacking is the ultimate vacation.
    V. While it once felt tedious and tiring, backpacking is now an essential part of my summer recreation.
    The CORRECT answer is:
    A. IV, II, V, I, III   B. II, III, I, IV, V   C. I, IV, II, V, III   D. V, I, III, II, IV

18.
   I. When I was preparing for my two-week vacation to southern Africa, I realized that the continent would be like nothing I have ever seen.
   II. I wanted to explore the continent's urban streets as well as the savannah; it's always been my dream to have "off the grid" experiences as well as touristy ones.
   III. The largest gap in understanding came from an unlikely source; it was the way I played with my host family's dog.
   IV. Upon my arrival to Africa, the people I met welcomed me with open arms.
   V. Aside from the pleasant welcome, it was obvious that our cultural differences were stark, which led to plenty of laughter and confusion.
   The CORRECT answer is:
   A. IV, I, II, III, V   B. III, V, IV, II, I   C. I, IV, II, III, V   D. I, II, IV, V, III

18.____

19.
   I. There, I signed up for a full-contact, downhill ice-skating race that looked like a bobsled run.
   II. It wasn't until I took a trip to Montreal that I realized how wrong I was.
   III. As an avid skier and inline skater, I figured I had cornered the market on downhill speeds.
   IV. After avoiding hip and body checks, both of which were perfectly legal, I was able to reach a top speed of forty-five miles per hour!
   V. It was Carnaval season, the time when people from across the province flock to the city for two weeks of food, drink and winter sports.
   The CORRECT answer is:
   A. II, I, III, IV, V   B. III, II, V, I, IV   C. IV, V, I, III, II   D. I, IV, II, V, III

19.____

20.
   I. It is a spell that sets upon one's soul and a sense of euphoria is felt by all who experience it.
   II. Pictures and postcards of the Caribbean do not lie; the water there shines with every shade of aquamarine, from pastel to emerald.
   III. As I imagine these sights, I recall one trip in particular that neatly captures the allure of the Caribbean.
   IV. The ocean hypnotizes with its glassy vastness.
   V. On that beautiful day, I was incredibly happy to sail with my family and friends.
   The CORRECT answer is:
   A. I, V, IV, III, II   B. V, I, II, IV, III   C. II, IV, I, III, V   D. I, II, IV, III, V

20.____

21.
   I. It wasn't until the early 1700s that it began to resemble the masterpiece museum it is today.
   II. The Louvre contains some of the most famous works of art in the history of the world including the *Mona Lisa* and the *Venus de Milo*.
   III. Before it was a world famous museum, The Louvre was a fort built by King Philip sometime around 1200 A.D.
   IV. The Louvre, in Paris, France, is one of the largest museums in the world.
   V. It has almost 275,000 works of art, which are displayed in over 140 exhibition rooms.
   The CORRECT answer is:
   A. V, I, III, IV, II   B. II, IV, I, V, III   C. V, III, I, IV, II   D. IV, V, II, III, I

21.____

22. I. It danced on the glossy hair and bright eyes of two girls, who sat together hemming ruffles for a white muslin dress.
    II. The September sun was glinting cheerfully into a pretty bedroom furnished with blue.
    III. These girls were Clover and Elsie Carr, and it was Clover's first evening dress for which they were hemming ruffles.
    IV. The half-finished skirt of the dress lay on the bed, and as each crisp ruffle was completed, the girls added it to the snowy heap, which looked like a drift of transparent clouds.
    V. It was nearly two years since a certain visit made by Johnnie to Inches Mills and more than three since Clover and Katy had returned home from the boarding school at Hillsover.
    The CORRECT answer is:
    A. III, V, IV, I, II   B. II, I, IV, III, V   C. V, II, I, IV, III   D. II, IV, III, I, V

23. I. The "invisible hand" theory is harshly criticized by parties who argue that untampered self-interest is immoral and that charity is the superior vehicle for community improvement.
    II. Standing as a testament to his benevolence, Smith bequeathed much of his wealth to charity.
    III. Second, Smith was not arguing that all self-interest is positive for society; he simply did not agree that it was necessarily bad.
    IV. First, he was not declaring that people should adopt a pattern of overt self-interest, but rather that people already act in such a way.
    V. Some of these people, though, fail to recognize several important aspects of Adam Smith's the Scottish economist who championed this theory, concept.
    The CORRECT answer is:
    A. I, V, IV, III, II   B. III, IV, II, I, V   C. II, III, V, IV, I   D. IV, III, I, V, II

24. I. Though they rarely are awarded for their many accomplishments, composers and performers continue to innovate and represent a substantial reason for classical music's persistent popularity.
    II. It is often the subject of experimentation on the part of composers and performers.
    III. Even more restrictive is the mainstream definition of "classical," which only includes the music of generations past that has seemingly been pushed aside by such contemporary forms of music as jazz, rock, and rap.
    IV. In spite of its waning limelight, however, classical music occupies an enduring niche in Western culture.
    V. Many people take classical music to be the realm of the symphony orchestra or smaller ensembles of orchestral instruments.
    The CORRECT answer is:
    A. IV, I, III, II, V   B. II, IV, V, I, III   C. V, III, IV, II, I   D. I, V, III, IV, II

25.
  I. The Great Pyramid at Giza is arguably one of the most fascinating and contentious pieces of architecture in the world.
  II. Instead of clarifying or expunging older theories about its age, the results of the study left the researchers mystified.
  III. In the 1980s, researchers began focusing on studying the mortar from the pyramid, hoping it would reveal important clues about the pyramid's age and construction.
  IV. This discovery was controversial because these dates claimed that the structure was built over 400 years earlier than most archaeologists originally believed it had been constructed.
  V. Carbon dating revealed that the pyramid had been built between 3100 BCE and 2850 BCE with an average date of 2977 BCE.

  The CORRECT answer is:
   A. I, III, II, V, IV   B. II, III, IV, V, I   C. V, I, III, IV, II   D. III, IV, V, I, II

25.____

KEY (CORRECT ANSWERS)

1.	C	11.	B
2.	A	12.	C
3.	D	13.	D
4.	B	14.	B
5.	B	15.	A
6.	C	16.	C
7.	A	17.	A
8.	D	18.	D
9.	A	19.	B
10.	D	20.	C

21. D
22. B
23. A
24. C
25. A

PREPARING WRITTEN MATERIAL
EXAMINATION SECTION
TEST 1

DIRECTIONS: Each question or incomplete statement is followed by several suggested answers or completions. Select the one that BEST answers the question or completes the statement. *PRINT THE LETTER OF THE CORRECT ANSWER IN THE SPACE AT THE RIGHT.*

Questions 1-4.

DIRECTIONS: Questions 1 through 4 each consist of a sentence which may or may not be an example of good English. The underlined parts of each sentence may be correct or incorrect. Examine each sentence, considering grammar, punctuation, spelling, and capitalization. If the English usage in the underlined parts of the sentence given is better than any of the changes in the underlined words suggested in options B, C, or D, choose option A. If the changes in the underlined words suggested in options B, C, or D would make the sentence correct, choose the correct option. Do not choose an option that will change the meaning of the sentence.

1. This Fall, the office will be closed on Columbus Day, October 9th. 1.____
   A. Correct as is
   B. fall...Columbus Day; October
   C. Fall...columbus day, October
   D. fall...Columbus Day – October

2. There weren't no paper in the supply closet. 2.____
   A. Correct as is
   B. weren't any
   C. wasn't any
   D. wasn't no

3. The alphabet, or A to Z sequence are the basis of most filing systems. 3.____
   A. Correct as is
   B. alphabet, or A to Z sequence, is
   C. alphabet, or A to Z sequence, are
   D. alphabet, or A too Z sequence, is

4. The Office Aide checked the register and finding the date of the meeting. 4.____
   A. Correct as is
   B. regaster and finding
   C. register and found
   D. regaster and found

Questions 5-10.

DIRECTIONS: Questions 5 through 10 consist of sentences which contain examples of correct or incorrect English usage. Examine each sentence with reference to grammar, spelling, punctuation, and capitalization. Chooses one of the following options that would be BEST for correct English usage:

175

A. The sentence is correct
B. There is one mistake
C. There are two mistakes
D. There are three mistakes

5. Mrs. Fitzgerald came to the 59th Precinct to retreive her property which were stolen earlier in the week.

6. The two officer's responded to the call, only to find that the perpatrator and the victim have left the scene.

7. Mr. Coleman called the 61st Precinct to report that, upon arriving at his store, he discovered that there was a large hole in the wall and that three boxes of radios were missing.

8. The Administrative Leiutenant of the 62nd Precinct held a meeting which was attended by all the civilians, assigned to the Precinct.

9. Three days after the robbery occurred the detective apprahended two suspects and recovered the stolen items.

10. The Community Affairs Officer of the 64th Precinct is the liaison between the Precinct and the community; he works closely with various community organizations, and elected officials,

Questions 11-18.

DIRECTIONS: Questions 11 through 18 are to be answered on the basis of the following paragraph, which contains some deliberate errors in spelling and/or grammar and/or punctuation. Each line of the paragraph is preceded by a number. There are 9 lines and 9 numbers.

Line No.	Paragraph Line
1	The protection of life and proprety are, one of
2	the oldest and most important functions of a city.
3	New York City has it's own full-time police Agency.
4	The police Department has the power an it shall
5	be there duty to preserve the Public piece,
6	prevent crime detect and arrest offenders, supress
7	riots, protect the rites of persons and property, etc.
8	The maintainance of sound relations with the community they
9	serve is an important function of law enforcement officers

11. How many errors are contained in line one?

12. How many errors are contained in line two?

13. How many errors are contained in line three?

14. How many errors are contained in line four? 14._____

15. How many errors are contained in line five? 15._____

16. How many errors are contained in line six? 16._____

17. How many errors are contained in line seven? 17._____

18. How many errors are contained in line eight? 18._____

19. In the sentence, *The candidate wants to file his application for preference before it is too late*, the word *before* is used as a(n) 19._____
    A. preposition
    B. subordinating conjunction
    C. pronoun
    D. adverb

20. The one of the following sentences which is grammatically PREFERABLE to the others is: 20._____
    A. Our engineers will go over your blueprints so that you may have no problems in construction.
    B. For a long time he had been arguing that we, not he, are to blame for the confusion.
    C. I worked on this automobile for two hours and still cannot find out what is wrong with it.
    D. Accustomed to all kinds of hardships, fatigue seldom bothers veteran policemen.

KEY (CORRECT ANSWERS)

1.	A	11.	C
2.	C	12.	D
3.	B	13.	C
4.	C	14.	B
5.	C	15.	C
6.	D	16.	B
7.	A	17.	A
8.	C	18.	A
9.	C	19.	B
10.	B	20.	A

TEST 2

DIRECTIONS: Each question or incomplete statement is followed by several suggested answers or completions. Select the one that BEST answers the question or completes the statement. *PRINT THE LETTER OF THE CORRECT ANSWER IN THE SPACE AT THE RIGHT.*

1. The plural of
   A. turkey is turkies
   B. cargo is cargoes
   C. bankruptcy is bankruptcys
   D. son-in-law is son-in-laws

2. The abbreviation *viz.* means MOST NEARLY
   A. namely   B. for example   C. the following   D. see

3. In the sentence, *A man in a light-grey suit waited thirty-five minutes in the ante-room for the all-important document,* the word IMPROPERLY hyphenated is
   A. light-grey   B. thirty-five   C. ante-room   D. all-important

4. The MOST accurate of the following sentences is:
   A. The commissioner, as well as his deputy and various bureau heads, were present.
   B. A new organization of employers and employees have been formed.
   C. One or the other of these men have been selected.
   D. The number of pages in the book is enough to discourage a reader.

5. The MOST accurate of the following sentences is:
   A. Between you and me, I think he is the better man.
   B. He was believed to be me.
   C. Is it us that you wish to see?
   D. The winners are him and her.

Questions 6-13.

DIRECTIONS: The sentences numbered 6 through 13 deal with some phase of police activity. They may be classified most appropriately under one of the following four categories.

   A. Faulty because of incorrect grammar
   B. Faulty because of incorrect punctuation
   C. Faulty because of incorrect use of a word
   D. Correct

Examine each sentence carefully. Then, in the space at the right, print the capital letter preceding the option which is the BEST of the four suggested above. All incorrect sentences contain only one type of error. Consider a sentence correct if it contains none of the types of errors mentioned, even though there may be other correct ways of expressing the same thought.

2 (#2)

6. The Department Medal of Honor is awarded to a member of the Police Force who distinguishes himself inconspicuously in the line of police duty by the performance of an act of gallantry.

6.____

7. Members of the Detective Division are charged with the prevention of crime, the detection and arrest of criminals and the recovery of lost or stolen property,

7.____

8. Detectives are selected from the uniformed patrol forces after they have indicated by conduct, aptitude and performance that they are qualified for the more intricate duties of a detective.

8.____

9. The patrolman, pursuing his assailant, exchanged shots with the gunman and immortally wounded him as he fled into a nearby building.

9.____

10. The members of the Traffic Division has to enforce the Vehicle and Traffic Law, the Traffic Regulations and ordinances relating to vehicular and pedestrian traffic.

10.____

11. After firing a shot at the gunman, the crowd dispersed from the patrolman's line of fire.

11.____

12. The efficiency of the Missing Persons Bureau is maintained with a maximum of public personnel due to the specialized training given to its members.

12.____

13. Records of persons arrested for violations of Vehicle and Traffic Regulations are transmitted upon request to precincts, courts and other authorized agencies.

13.____

14. Following are two sentences which may or may not be written in correct English:
   I. Two clients assaulted the officer.
   II. The van is illegally parked.
   Which one of the following statements is CORRECT?
   A. Only Sentence I is written in correct English.
   B. Only Sentence II is written in correct English.
   C. Sentences I and II are both written in correct English.
   D. Neither Sentence I nor Sentence II is written in correct English.

14.____

15. Following are two sentences which may or may not be written in correct English:
   I. Security Officer Rollo escorted the visitor to the patrolroom.
   II. Two entry were made in the facility logbook.
   Which one of the following statements is CORRECT?
   A. Only Sentence I is written in correct English.
   B. Only Sentence II is written in correct English.
   C. Sentences I and II are both written in correct English.
   D. Neither Sentence I nor Sentence II is written in correct English.

15.____

16. Following are two sentences which may or may not be written in correct English:
    I. Officer McElroy putted out a small fire in the wastepaper basket.
    II. Special Officer Janssen told the visitor where he could obtained a pass.
    Which one of the following statements is CORRECT?
    A. Only Sentence I is written in correct English.
    B. Only Sentence II is written in correct English.
    C. Sentences I and II are both written in correct English.
    D. Neither Sentence I nor Sentence II is written in correct English.

16._____

17. Following are two sentences which may or may not be written in correct English:
    I. Security Officer Warren observed a broken window while he was on his post in Hallway C.
    II. The worker reported that two typewriters had been stolen from the office,
    Which one of the following statements is CORRECT?
    A. Only Sentence I is written in correct English.
    B. Only Sentence II is written in correct English.
    C. Sentences I and II are both written in correct English.
    D. Neither Sentence I nor Sentence II is written in correct English,

17._____

18. Following are two sentences which may or may not be written in correct English:
    I. Special Officer Cleveland was attempting to calm an emotionally disturbed visitor.
    II. The visitor did not stop crying and calling for his wife.
    Which one of the following statements is CORRECT?
    A. Only Sentence I is written in correct English.
    B. Only Sentence II is written in correct English.
    C. Sentences I and II are both written in correct English.
    D. Neither Sentence I nor Sentence II is written in correct English.

18._____

19. Following are two sentences that may or may not be written in correct English:
    I. While on patrol, I observes a vagrant loitering near the drug dispensary.
    II. I escorted the vagrant out of the building and off the premises.
    Which one of the following statements is CORRECT?
    A. Only Sentence I is written in correct English.
    B. Only Sentence II is written in correct English.
    C. Sentences I and II are both written in correct English.
    D. Neither Sentence I nor Sentence II is written in correct English.

19._____

20. Following are two sentences which may or may not be written in correct English:
    I. At 4:00 P.M., Sergeant Raymond told me to evacuate the waiting area immediately due to a bomb threat.
    II. Some of the clients did not want to leave the building.
    Which one of the following statements is CORRECT?
    A. Only Sentence I is written in correct English.
    B. Only Sentence II is written in correct English.
    C. Sentences I and II are both written in correct English.
    D. Neither Sentence I nor Sentence II is written in correct English.

20._____

KEY (CORRECT ANSWERS)

1.	B	11.	A
2.	A	12.	C
3.	C	13.	D
4.	D	14.	C
5.	A	15.	A
6.	C	16.	D
7.	B	17.	A
8.	D	18.	A
9.	C	19.	B
10.	A	20.	C

PREPARING WRITTEN MATERIAL
EXAMINATION SECTION
TEST 1

DIRECTIONS: Each question or incomplete statement is followed by several suggested answers or completions. Select the one that BEST answers the question or completes the statement. *PRINT THE LETTER OF THE CORRECT ANSWER IN THE SPACE AT THE RIGHT.*

1. The one of the following sentences which is LEAST acceptable from the viewpoint of correct usage is:
   A. The police thought the fugitive to be him.
   B. The criminals set a trap for whoever would fall into it.
   C. It is ten years ago since the fugitive fled from the city.
   D. The lecturer argued that criminals are usually cowards.
   E. The police removed four bucketfuls of earth from the scene of the crime.

1.____

2. The one of the following sentences which is LEAST acceptable from the viewpoint of correct usage is:
   A. The patrolman scrutinized the report with great care.
   B. Approaching the victim of the assault, two bruises were noticed by the patrolman.
   C. As soon as I had broken down the door, I stepped into the room.
   D. I observed the accused loitering near the building, which was closed at the time.
   E. The storekeeper complained that his neighbor was guilty of violating a local ordinance.

2.____

3. The one of the following sentences which is LEAST acceptable from the viewpoint of correct usage is:
   A. I realized immediately that he intended to assault the woman, so I disarmed him.
   B. It was apparent that Mr. Smith's explanation contained many inconsistencies.
   C. Despite the slippery condition of the street, he managed to stop the vehicle before injuring the child.
   D. Not a single one of them wish, despite the damage to property, to make a formal complaint.
   E. The body was found lying on the floor.

3.____

4. The one of the following sentences which contains NO error in usage is:
   A. After the robbers left, the proprietor stood tied in his chair for about two hours before help arrived.
   B. In the cellar I found the watchman's hat and coat.
   C. The persons living in adjacent apartments stated that they had heard no unusual noises.

4.____

D. Neither a knife or any firearms were found in the room.
E. Walking down the street, the shouting of the crowd indicated that something was wrong.

5. The one of the following sentences which contains NO error in usage is:
   A. The policeman lay a firm hand on the suspect's shoulder.
   B. It is true that neither strength nor agility are the most important requirement for a good patrolman.
   C. Good citizens constantly strive to do more than merely comply the restraints imposed by society.
   D. No decision was made as to whom the prize should be awarded.
   E. Twenty years is considered a severe sentence for a felony.

6. Which of the following sentences is NOT expressed in standard English usage?
   A. The victim reached a pay-phone booth and manages to call police headquarters.
   B. By the time the call was received, the assailant had left the scene.
   C. The victim has been a respected member of the community for the past eleven years.
   D. Although the lighting was bad and the shadows were deep, the storekeeper caught sight of the attacker.
   E. Additional street lights have since been installed, and the patrols have been strengthened.

7. Which of the following sentences is NOT expressed in standard English usage?
   A. The judge upheld the attorney's right to question the witness about the missing glove.
   B. To be absolutely fair to all parties is the jury's chief responsibility.
   C. Having finished the report, a loud noise in the next room startled the sergeant.
   D. The witness obviously enjoyed having played a part in the proceedings.
   E. The sergeant planned to assign the case to whoever arrived first.

8. In which of the following sentences is a word misused?
   A. As a matter of principle, the captain insisted that the suspect's partner be brought for questioning.
   B. The principle suspect had been detained at the station house for most of the day.
   C. The principal in the crime had no previous criminal record, but his closest associate had been convicted of felonies on two occasions.
   D. The interest payments had been made promptly, but the firm had been drawing upon the principal for these payments.
   E. The accused insisted that his high school principal would furnish him a character reference.

9. Which of the following statements is ambiguous?
   A. Mr. Sullivan explained why Mr. Johnson had been dismissed from his job.
   B. The storekeeper told the patrolman he had made a mistake.
   C. After waiting three hours, the patients in the doctor's office were sent home.
   D. The janitor's duties were to maintain the building in good shape and to answer tenants' complaints.
   E. The speed limit should, in my opinion, be raised to sixty miles an hour on that stretch of road.

9.____

10. In which of the following is the punctuation or capitalization faulty?
   A. The accident occurred at an intersection in the Kew Gardens section of Queens, near the bus stop.
   B. The sedan, not the convertible, was struck in the side.
   C. Before any of the patrolmen had left the police car received an important message from headquarters.
   D. The dog that had been stolen was returned to his master, John Dempsey, who lived in East Village.
   E. The letter had been sent to 12 Hillside Terrace, Rutland, Vermont 05702.

10.____

Questions 11-25.

DIRECTIONS: Questions 11 through 25 are to be answered in accordance with correct English usage; that is, standard English rather than nonstandard or substandard. Nonstandard and substandard English includes words or expressions usually classified as slang, dialect, illiterate, etc., which are not generally accepted as correct in current written communication. Standard English also requires clarity, proper punctuation and capitalization and appropriate use of words. Write the letter of the sentence NOT expressed in standard English usage in the space at the right.

11. A. There were three witnesses to the accident.
    B. At least three witnesses were found to testify for the plaintiff.
    C. Three of the witnesses who took the stand was uncertain about the defendant's competence to drive.
    D. Only three witnesses came forward to testify for the plaintiff.
    E. The three witnesses to the accident were pedestrians.

11.____

12. A. The driver had obviously drunk too many martinis before leaving for home.
    B. The boy who drowned had swum in these same waters many times before.
    C. The petty thief had stolen a bicycle from a private driveway before he was apprehended.
    D. The detectives had brung in the heroin shipment they intercepted.
    E. The passengers had never ridden in a converted bus before.

12.____

13. A. Between you and me, the new platoon plan sounds like a good idea.
    B. Money from an aunt's estate was left to his wife and he.
    C. He and I were assigned to the same patrol for the first time in two months.
    D. Either you or he should check the front door of that store.
    E. The captain himself was not sure of the witness's reliability.

14. A. The alarm had scarcely begun to ring when the explosion occurred.
    B. Before the firemen arrived at the scene, the second story had been destroyed.
    C. Because of the dense smoke and heat, the firemen could hardly approach the now-blazing structure.
    D. According to the patrolman's report, there wasn't nobody in the store when the explosion occurred.
    E. The sergeant's suggestion was not at all unsound, but no one agreed with him.

15. A. The driver and the passenger they were both found to be intoxicated.
    B. The driver and the passenger talked slowly and not too clearly.
    C. Neither the driver nor his passengers were able to give a coherent account of the accident.
    D. In a corner of the room sat the passenger, quietly dozing.
    E. the driver finally told a strange and unbelievable story, which the passenger contradicted.

16. A. Under the circumstances I decided not to continue my examination of the premises.
    B. There are many difficulties now not comparable with those existing in 1960.
    C. Friends of the accused were heard to announce that the witness had better been away on the day of the trial.
    D. The two criminals escaped in the confusion that followed the explosion.
    E. The aged man was struck by the considerateness of the patrolman's offer.

17. A. An assemblage of miscellaneous weapons lay on the table.
    B. Ample opportunities were given to the defendant to obtain counsel.
    C. The speaker often alluded to his past experience with youthful offenders in the armed forces.
    D. The sudden appearance of the truck aroused my suspicions.
    E. Her studying had a good affect on her grades in high school.

18. A. He sat down in the theater and began to watch the movie.
    B. The girl had ridden horses since she was four years old.
    C. Application was made on behalf of the prosecutor to cite the witness for contempt.
    D. The bank robber, with his two accomplices, were caught in the act.
    E. His story is simply not credible.

19.
- A. The angry boy said that he did not like those kind of friends.
- B. The merchant's financial condition was so precarious that he felt he must avail himself of any offer of assistance.
- C. He is apt to promise more than he can perform.
- D. Looking at the messy kitchen, the housewife felt like crying.
- E. A clerk was left in charge of the stolen property.

20.
- A. His wounds were aggravated by prolonged exposure to sub-freezing temperatures.
- B. The prosecutor remarked that the witness was not averse to changing his story each time he was interviewed.
- C. The crime pattern indicated that the burglars were adapt in the handling of explosives.
- D. His rigid adherence to a fixed plan brought him into renewed conflict with his subordinates.
- E. He had anticipated that the sentence would be delivered by noon.

21.
- A. The whole arraignment procedure is badly in need of revision.
- B. After his glasses were broken in the fight, he would of gone to the optometrist if he could.
- C. Neither Tom nor Jack brought his lunch to work.
- D. He stood aside until the quarrel was over.
- E. A statement in the psychiatrist's report disclosed that the probationer vowed to have his revenge.

22.
- A. His fiery and intemperate speech to the striking employees fatally affected any chance of a future reconciliation.
- B. The wording of the statute has been variously construed.
- C. The defendant's attorney, speaking in the courtroom, called the official a demagogue who contempuously disregarded the judge's orders.
- D. The baseball game is likely to be the most exciting one this year.
- E. The mother divided the cookies among her two children.

23.
- A. There was only a bed and a dresser in the dingy room.
- B. John was one of the few students that have protested the new rule.
- C. It cannot be argued that the child's testimony is negligible; it is, on the contrary, of the greatest importance.
- D. The basic criterion for clearance was so general that officials resolved any doubts in favor of dismissal.
- E. Having just returned from a long vacation, the officer found the city unbearably hot.

24.
- A. The librarian ought to give more help to small children.
- B. The small boy was criticized by the teacher because he often wrote careless.
- C. It was generally doubted whether the women would permit the use of her apartment for intelligence operations.
- D. The probationer acts differently every time the officer visits him.
- E. Each of the newly appointed officers has 12 years of service.

25.	A.	The North is the most industrialized region in the country.
	B.	L. Patrick Gray 3d, the bureau's acting director, stated that, while "rehabilitation is fine" for some convicted criminals, "it is a useless gesture for those who resist every such effort."
	C.	Careless driving, faulty mechanism, narrow or badly kept roads all play their part in causing accidents.
	D.	The childrens' books were left in the bus.
	E.	It was a matter of internal security; consequently, he felt no inclination to rescind his previous order.

KEY (CORRECT ANSWERS)

1.	C		11.	C
2.	B		12.	D
3.	D		13.	B
4.	C		14.	D
5.	E		15.	A
6.	A		16.	C
7.	C		17.	E
8.	B		18.	D
9.	B		19.	A
10.	C		20.	C

21.	B
22.	E
23.	B
24.	B
25.	D

TEST 2

DIRECTIONS: Each question or incomplete statement is followed by several suggested answers or completions. Select the one that BEST answers the question or completes the statement. *PRINT THE LETTER OF THE CORRECT ANSWER IN THE SPACE AT THE RIGHT.*

Questions 1-6.

DIRECTIONS: Each of Questions 1 through 6 consists of a statement which contains a word (one of those underlined) that is either incorrectly used because it is not in keeping with the meaning the quotation is evidently intended to convey, or is misspelled. There is only one INCORRECT word in each quotation. Of the four underlined words, determine if the first one should be replaced by the word lettered A, the second replaced by the word lettered B, the third replaced by the word lettered C, or the fourth replaced by the word lettered D.

1. Whether one depends on fluorescent or artificial light or both, adequate standards should be maintained by means of systematic tests.
   A. natural   B. safeguards   C. established   D. routine

   1.____

2. A police officer has to be prepared to assume his knowledge as a social scientist in the community.
   A. forced   B. role   C. philosopher   D. street

   2.____

3. It is practically impossible to indicate whether a sentence is too long simply by measuring its length.
   A. almost   B. tell   C. very   D. guessing

   3.____

4. Strong leaders are required to organize a community for delinquency prevention and for dissemination of organized crime and drug addiction.
   A. tactics   B. important   C. control   D. meetings

   4.____

5. The demonstrators who were taken to the Criminal Courts building in Manhattan (because it was large enough to accommodate them), contended that the arrests were unwarranted.
   A. demonstraters   B. Manhatten
   C. accomodate   D. unwarranted

   5.____

6. They were guaranteed a calm atmosphere, free from harassment, which would be conducive to quiet consideration of the indictments.
   A. guarenteed   B. atmspher
   C. harassment   D. inditements

   6.____

Questions 7-11.

DIRECTIONS: Each of Questions 7 through 11 consists of a statement containing four words in capital letters. One of these words in capital letters is not in keeping with the meaning which the statement is evidently intended to carry. The four words in capital letters in each statement are reprinted after the statement. Print the capital letter preceding the one of the four words which does MOST to spoil the true meaning of the statement in the space at the right.

7. Retirement and pension systems are essential not only to provide employees with with a means of support in the future, but also to prevent longevity and CHARITABLE considerations from UPSETTING the PROMOTIONAL opportunities RETIRED members of the career service.
   A. charitable   B. upsetting   C. promotional   D. retired

8. Within each major DIVISION in a properly set up public or private organization, provision is made so that each NECESSARY activity is CARED for and lines of authority and responsibility are clear-cut and INFINITE.
   A. division   B. necessary   C. cared   D. infinite

9. In public service, the scale of salaries paid must be INCIDENTAL to the services rendered, with due CONSIDERATION for the attraction of the desired MANPOWER and for the maintenance of a standard of living COMMENSURATE with the work to be performed.
   A. incidental   B. consideration
   C. manpower   D. commensurate

10. An understanding of the AIMS of an organization by the staff will AID greatly in increasing the DEMAND of the correspondence work of the office, and will to a large extent DETERMINE the nature of the correspondence.
    A. aims   B. aid   C. demand   D. determine

11. BECAUSE the Civil Service Commission strongly feels that the MERIT system is a key factor in the MAINTENANCE of democratic government, it has adopted as one of its major DEFENSES the progressive democratization of its own procedures in dealing with candidates for positions in the public service.
    A. Because   B. merit   C. maintenance   D. defenses

Questions 12-14.

DIRECTIONS: Questions 12 through 14 consist of one sentence each. Each sentence contains an incorrectly used word. First, decide which is the incorrectly used word. Then, from among the options given, decide which word, when substituted for the incorrectly used word, makes the meaning of the sentence clear.
EXAMPLE:
The U.S. national income exhibits a pattern of long term deflection.
   A. reflection   B. subjection   C. rejoicing   D. growth

The word *deflection* in the sentence does not convey the meaning the sentence evidently intended to convey. The word *growth* (Answer D), when substituted for the word *deflection*, makes the meaning of the sentence clear. Accordingly, the answer to the question is D.

12. The study commissioned by the joint committee fell compassionately short of the mark and would have to be redone.
    A. successfully   B. insignificantly
    C. experimentally   D. woefully

13. He will not idly exploit any violation of the provisions of the order.
    A. tolerate   B. refuse   C. construe   D. guard

14. The defendant refused to be virile and bitterly protested service.
    A. irked   B. feasible   C. docile   D. credible

Questions 15-25.

DIRECTIONS: Questions 15 through 25 consist of short paragraphs. Each paragraph contains one word which is INCORRECTLY used because it is NOT in keeping with the meaning of the paragraph. Find the word in each paragraph which is INCORRECTLY used and then select as the answer the suggested word which should be substituted for the incorrectly used word.

SAMPLE QUESTION:
In determining who is to do the work in your unit, you will have to decide just who does what from day to day. One of your lowest responsibilities is to assign work so that everybody gets a fair share and that everyone can do his part well.
    A. new   B. old   C. important   D. performance

EXPLANATION:
The word which is NOT in keeping with the meaning of the paragraph is *lowest*. This is the INCORRECTLY used word. The suggested word *important* would be in keeping with the meaning of the paragraph and should be substituted for *lowest*. Therefore, the CORRECT answer is choice C.

15. If really good practice in the elimination of preventable injuries is to be achieved and held in any establishment, top management must refuse full and definite responsibility and must apply a good share of its attention to the task.
    A. accept   B. avoidable   C. duties   D. problem

16. Recording the human face for identification is by no means the only service performed by the camera in the field of investigation. When the trial of any issue takes place, a word picture is sought to be distorted to the court of incidents, occurrences, or events which are in dispute.
    A. appeals   B. description   C. portrayed   D. deranged

17. In the collection of physical evidence, it cannot be emphasized too strongly that a haphazard systematic search at the scene of the crime is vital. Nothing must be overlooked. Often the only leads in a case will come from the results of this search.
    A. important B. investigation C. proof D. thorough

18. If an investigator has reason to suspect that the witness is mentally stable, or a habitual drunkard, he should leave no stone unturned in his investigation to determine if the witness was under the influence of liquor or drugs, or was mentally unbalanced either at the time of the occurrence to which he testified or at the time of the trial.
    A. accused B. clue C. deranged D. question

19. The use of records is a valuable step in crime investigation and is the main reason every department should maintain accurate reports. Crimes are not committed through the use of departmental records alone but from the use of all records, of almost every type, wherever they may be found and whenever they give any incidental information regarding the criminal.
    A. accidental B. necessary C. reported D. solved

20. In the years since passage of the Harrison Narcotic Act of 1914, making the possession of opium amphetamines illegal in most circumstances, drug use has become a subject of considerable scientific interest and investigation. There is at present a voluminous literature on drug use of various kinds.
    A. ingestion B. derivatives C. addiction D. opiates

21. Of course, the fact that criminal laws are extremely patterned in definition does not mean that the majority of persons who violate them are dealt with as criminals. Quite the contrary, for a great many forbidden acts are voluntarily engaged in within situations of privacy and go unobserved and unreported.
    A. symbolic B. casual C. scientific D. broad-gauged

22. The most punitive way to study punishment is to focus attention on the pattern of punitive action: to study how a penalty is applied, too study what is done to or taken from an offender.
    A. characteristic B. degrading C. objective D. distinguished

23. The most common forms of punishment in times past have been death, physical torture, mutilation, branding, public humiliation, fines, forfeits of property, banishment, transportation, and imprisonment. Although this list is by no means differentiated, practically every form of punishment has had several variations and applications.
    A. specific B. simple C. exhaustive D. characteristic

24. There is another important line of inference between ordinary and professional criminals, and that is the source from which they are recruited. The professional criminal seems to be drawn from legitimate employment and, in many instances, from parallel vocations or pursuits. 24.____
    A. demarcation   B. justification   C. superiority   D. reference

25. He took the position that the success of the program was insidious on getting additional revenue. 25.____
    A. reputed   B. contingent   C. failure   D. indeterminate

KEY (CORRECT ANSWERS)

1.	A	11.	D
2.	B	12.	D
3.	B	13.	A
4.	C	14.	C
5.	D	15.	A
6.	C	16.	C
7.	D	17.	D
8.	D	18.	C
9.	A	19.	D
10.	C	20.	B

21. D
22. C
23. C
24. A
25. B

TEST 3

DIRECTIONS: Each question or incomplete statement is followed by several suggested answers or completions. Select the one that BEST answers the question or completes the statement. *PRINT THE LETTER OF THE CORRECT ANSWER IN THE SPACE AT THE RIGHT.*

Questions 1-5.

DIRECTIONS: Questions 1 through 5 are to be answered on the basis of the following.

You are a supervising officer in an investigative unit. Earlier in the day, you directed Detectives Tom Dixon and Sal Mayo to investigate a reported assault and robbery in a liquor store within your area of jurisdiction.

Detective Dixon has submitted to you a preliminary investigative report containing the following information:

- At 1630 hours on 2/20, arrived at Joe's Liquor Store at 350 SW Avenue with Detective Mayo to investigate A & R.
- At store interviewed Rob Ladd, store manager, who stated that he and Joe Brown (store owner) had been stuck up about ten minutes prior to our arrival.
- Ladd described the robbers as male whites in their late teens or early twenties. Further stated that one of the robbers displayed what appeared to be an automatic pistol as he entered the store, and said, *Give us the money or we'll kill you.* Ladd stated that Brown then reached under the counter where he kept a loaded .38 caliber pistol. Several shots followed, and Ladd threw himself to the floor.
- The robbers fled, and Ladd didn't know if any money had been taken.
- At this point, Ladd realized that Brown was unconscious on the floor and bleeding from a head wound.
- Ambulance called by Ladd, and Brown was removed by same to General Hospital.
- Personally interviewed John White, 382 Dartmouth Place, who stated he was inside store at the time of occurrence. White states that he hid behind a wine display upon hearing someone say, *Give us the money.* He then heard shots and saw two young men run from the store to a yellow car parked at the curb. White was unable to further describe auto. States the taller of the two men drove the car away while the other sat on passenger side in front.
- Recovered three spent .38 caliber bullets from premises and delivered them to Crime Lab.
- To General Hospital at 1800 hours but unable to interview Brown, who was under sedation and suffering from shock and a laceration of the head.
- Alarm #12487 transmitted for car and occupants.
- Case Active.

Based solely on the contents of the preliminary investigation submitted by Detective Dixon, select one sentence from the following groups of sentences which is MOST accurate and is grammatically correct.

2 (#3)

1.
   A. Both robbers were armed.
   B. Each of the robbers were described as a male white.
   C. Neither robber was armed.
   D. Mr. Ladd stated that one of the robbers was armed.

   1._____

2.
   A. Mr. Brown fired three shots from his revolver.
   B. Mr. Brown was shot in the head by one of the robbers.
   C. Mr. Brown suffered a gunshot wound of the head during the course of the robbery.
   D. Mr. Brown was taken to General Hospital by ambulance.

   2._____

3.
   A. Shots were fired after one of the robbers said, *Give us the money or we'll kill you.*
   B. After one of the robbers demanded the money from Mr. Brown, he fired a shot.
   C. The preliminary investigation indicated that although Mr. Brown did not have a license for the gun, he was justified in using deadly physical force.
   D. Mr. Brown was interviewed at General Hospital.

   3._____

4.
   A. Each of the witnesses were customers in the store at the time of occurrence.
   B. Neither of the witnesses interviewed was the owner of the liquor store.
   C. Neither of the witnesses interviewed were the owner of the store.
   D. Neither of the witnesses was employed by Mr. Brown.

   4._____

5.
   A. Mr. Brown arrived at General Hospital at about 5:00 P.M.
   B. Neither of the robbers was injured during the robbery.
   C. The robbery occurred at 3:30 P.M. on February 10.
   D. One of the witnesses called the ambulance.

   5._____

Questions 6-10.

DIRECTIONS: Each of Questions 6 through 10 consists of information given in outline form and four sentences labeled A, B, C, and D. For each question, choose the one sentence which CORRECTLY expresses the information given in outline form and which also displays PROPER English usage.

6. Client's Name: Joanna Jones
   Number of Children: 3
   Client's Income: None
   Client's Marital Status: Single

   A. Joanna Jones is an unmarried client with three children who have no income.
   B. Joanna Jones, who is single and has no income, a client she has three children.
   C. Joanna Jones, whose three children are clients, is single and has no income.
   D. Joanna Jones, who has three children, is an unmarried client with no income.

   6._____

7. Client's Name: Bertha Smith
   Number of Children: 2
   Client's Rent: $1050 per month
   Number of Rooms: 4

   A. Bertha Smith, a client, pays $1050 per month for her four rooms with two children.
   B. Client Bertha Smith has two children and pays $1050 per month for four rooms.
   C. Client Bertha Smith is paying $1050 per month for two children with four rooms.
   D. For four rooms and two children client Bertha Smith pays $1050 per month.

7._____

8. Name of Employee: Cynthia Dawes
   Number of Cases Assigned: 9
   Date Cases were Assigned: 12/16
   Number of Assigned Cases Completed: 8

   A. On December 16, employee Cynthia Dawes was assigned nine cases; she has completed eight of these cases.
   B. Cynthia Dawes, employee on December 16, assigned nine cases, completed eight.
   C. Being employed on December 16, Cynthia Dawes completed eight of nine assigned cases.
   D. Employee Cynthia Dawes, she was assigned nine cases and completed eight, on December 16.

8._____

9. Place of Audit: Broadway Center
   Names of Auditors: Paul Cahn, Raymond Perez
   Date of Audit: 11/20
   Number of Cases Audited: 41

   A. On November 20, at the Broadway Center 41 cases was audited by auditors Paul Cahn and Raymond Perez.
   B. Auditors Raymond Perez and Paul Cahn has audited 41 cases at the Broadway Center on November 20.
   C. At the Broadway Center, on November 20, auditors Paul Cahn and Raymond Perez audited 41 cases.
   D. Auditors Paul Cahn and Raymond Perez at the Broadway Center, on November 20, is auditing 41 cases.

9._____

10. Name of Client: Barbra Levine
    Client's Monthly Income: $2100
    Client's Monthly Expenses: $4520

    A. Barbra Levine is a client, her monthly income is $2100 and her monthly expenses is $4520.
    B. Barbra Levine's monthly income is $2100 and she is a client, with whose monthly expenses are $4520.

10._____

C. Barbra Levine is a client whose monthly income is $2100 and whose monthly expenses are $4520.
D. Barbra Levine, a client, is with a monthly income which is $2100 and monthly expenses which are $4520.

Questions 11-13.

DIRECTIONS: Questions 11 through 13 involve several statements of fact presented in a very simple way. These statements of fact are followed by 4 choices which attempt to incorporate all of the facts into one logical statement which is properly constructed and grammatically correct.

11. I. Mr. Brown was sweeping the sidewalk in front of his house.
    II. He was sweeping it because it was dirty.
    III. He swept the refuse into the street.
    IV. Police Officer gave him a ticket.

    Which one of the following BEST presents the information given above?
    A. Because his sidewalk was dirty, Mr. Brown received a ticket from Officer Green when he swept the refuse into the street.
    B. Police Officer Green gave Mr. Brown a ticket because his sidewalk was dirty and he swept the refuse into the street.
    C. Police Officer Green gave Mr. Brown a ticket for sweeping refuse into the street because his sidewalk was dirty.
    D. Mr. Brown, who was sweeping refuse from his dirty sidewalk into the street, was given a ticket by Police Officer Green.

11.____

12. I. Sergeant Smith radioed for help.
    II. The sergeant did so because the crowd was getting larger.
    III. It was 10:00 A.M. when he made his call.
    IV. Sergeant Smith was not in uniform at the time of occurrence.

    Which one of the following BEST presents the information given above?
    A. Sergeant Smith, although not on duty at the time, radioed for help at 10 o'clock because the crowd was getting uglier.
    B. Although not in uniform, Sergeant Smith called for help at 10:00 A.M. because the crowd was getting uglier.
    C. Sergeant Smith radioed for help at 10:00 A.M. because the crowd was getting larger.
    D. Although he was not in uniform, Sergeant Smith radioed for help at 10:00 A.M. because the crowd was getting larger.

12.____

13. I. The payroll office is open on Fridays.
    II. Paychecks are distributed from 9:00 A.M. to 12 Noon.
    III. The office is open on Fridays because that's the only day the payroll staff is available.
    IV. It is open for the specified hours in order to permit employees to cash checks at the bank during lunch hour.

13.____

The choice below which MOST clearly and accurately presents the above idea is:
A. Because the payroll office is open on Fridays from 9:00 A.M. to 12 Noon, employees can cash their checks when the payroll staff is available.
B. Because the payroll staff is only available on Fridays until noon, employees can cash their checks during their lunch hour.
C. Because the payroll staff is available only on Fridays, the office is open from 9:00 A.M. to 12 Noon to allow employees to cash their checks.
D. Because of payroll staff availability, the payroll office is open on Fridays. It is open from 9:00 A.M. to 12 Noon so that distributed paychecks can be cashed at the bank while employees are on their lunch hour.

Questions 14-16.

DIRECTIONS: In each of Questions 14 through 6, the four sentences are from a paragraph in a report. They are not in the right order. Which of the following arrangements is the BEST one?

14. I. An executive may answer a letter by writing his reply on the face of the letter itself instead of having a return letter typed.
    II. This procedure is efficient because it saves the executive's time, the typist's time, and saves office file space.
    III. Copying machines are used in small offices as well as large offices to save time and money in making brief replies to business letters.
    IV. A copy is made on a copy machine to go into the company files, while the original is mailed back to the sender.

    The CORRECT answer is:
    A. I, II, IV, III   B. I, IV, II, III   C. III, I, IV, II   D. III, IV, II, I

15. I. Most organizations favor one of the types but always include the others to a lesser degree.
    II. However, we can detect a definite trend toward greater use of symbolic control.
    III. We suggest that our local police agencies are today primarily utilizing material control.
    IV. Control can be classified into three types: physical, material, and symbolic.

    The CORRECT answer is:
    A. IV, II, III, I   B. II, I, IV, III   C. III, IV, II, I   D. IV, I, III, II

16. I. They can and do take advantage of ancient political and geographical boundaries, which often give them sanctuary from effective policy activity.
    II. This country is essentially a country of small police forces, each operating independently within the limits of its jurisdiction.
    III. The boundaries that define and limit police operations do not hinder the movement of criminals, of course.
    IV. The machinery of law enforcement in America is fragmented, complicated, and frequently overlapping.

The CORRECT answer is:
A. III, I, IV   B. II, IV, I, III   C. IV, II, III, I   D. IV, III, II, I

17. Examine the following sentence, and then choose from below the words which should be inserted in the blank spaces to produce the best sentence.
The unit has exceeded _____ goals and the employees are satisfied with _____ accomplishments.
A. their, it's   B. it's; it's   C. its, there   D. its, their

17.____

18. Examine the following sentence, and then choose from below the words which should be inserted in the blank spaces to produce the best sentence.
Research indicates that employees who _____ no opportunity for close social relationships often find their work unsatisfying, and this _____ of satisfaction often reflects itself in low production.
A. have; lack   B. have; excess   C. has; lack   D. has; excess

18.____

19. Words in a sentence must be arranged properly to make sure that the intended meaning of the sentence is clear.
The sentence below that does NOT make sense because a clause has been separated from the word on which its meaning depends is:
A. To be a good writer, clarity is necessary.
B. To be a good writer, you must write clearly.
C. You must write clearly to be a good writer.
D. Clarity is necessary to good writing.

19.____

Questions 20-21.

DIRECTIONS: Each of Questions 20 and 21 consists of a statement which contains a word (one of those underlined) that is either incorrectly used because it is not in keeping with the meaning the quotation is evidently intended to convey, or is misspelled. There is only one INCORRECT word in each quotation. Of the four underlined words, determine if the first one should be replaced by the word lettered A, the second one replaced by the word lettered B, the third one replaced by the word lettered C, or the fourth one replaced by the word lettered D.

20. The alleged killer was occasionally permitted to excercise in the corridor.
A. alledged   B. ocasionally   C. permited   D. exercise

20.____

21. Defense counsel stated, in affect, that their conduct was permissible under the First Amendment.
A. council   B. effect   C. there   D. permissable

21.____

Question 22.

DIRECTIONS: Question 22 consists of one sentence. This sentence contains an incorrectly used word. First, decide which is the incorrectly used word. Then, from among the options given, decide which word, when substituted for the incorrectly used word, makes the meaning of the sentence clear.

22. As today's violence has no single cause, so its causes have no single scheme. 22.____
    A. deference   B. cure   C. flaw   D. relevance

23. In the sentence, *A man in a light-grey suit waited thirty-five minutes in the ante-room for the all-important document*, the word IMPROPERLY hyphenated is 23.____
    A. light-grey   B. thirty-five
    C. ante-room   D. all-important

24. In the sentence, *The candidate wants to file his application for preference before it is too late*, the word *before* is used as a(n) 24.____
    A. preposition   B. subordinating conjunction
    C. pronoun   D. adverb

25. In the sentence, *The perpetrators ran from the scene*, the word *from* is a 25.____
    A. preposition   B. pronoun   C. verb   D. conjunction

KEY (CORRECT ANSWERS)

1.	D		11.	D
2.	D		12.	D
3.	A		13.	D
4.	B		14.	C
5.	D		15.	D
6.	D		16.	C
7.	B		17.	D
8.	A		18.	A
9.	C		19.	A
10.	C		20.	D

21. B
22. B
23. C
24. B
25. A

ARITHMETIC

EXAMINATION SECTION
TEST 1

DIRECTIONS: Each question or incomplete statement is followed by several suggested answers or completions. Select the one that BEST answers the question or completes the statement. *PRINT THE LETTER OF THE CORRECT ANSWER IN THE SPACE AT THE RIGHT.*

1. The sum of 76342 + 49050 + 21206 + 59989 is 1._____
   A. 196586   B. 206087   C. 206587   D. 234487

2. The sum of $452.13 + $963.83 + $621.25 is 2._____
   A. $1936.83   B. $2037.21   C. $2095.73   D. $2135.73

3. The sum of 36392 + 42156 + 98765 is 3._____
   A. 167214   B. 177203   C. 177313   D. 178213

4. The sum of 40125 + 87123 + 24689 is 4._____
   A. 141827   B. 151827   C. 151937   D. 161947

5. The sum of 2379 + 4015 + 6521 + 9986 is 5._____
   A. 22901   B. 22819   C. 21801   D. 21791

6. From 50962 subtract 36197. The answer should be 6._____
   A. 14675   B. 14765   C. 14865   D. 24765

7. From 90000 subtract 31928. The answer should be 7._____
   A. 58072   B. 59062   C. 68172   D. 69182

8. From 63764 subtract 21548. The answer should be 8._____
   A. 42216   B. 43122   C. 45126   D. 85312

9. From $9605.13 subtract $2715.96. The answer should be 9._____
   A. $12,321.09   B. $8,690.16
   C. $6,990.07   D. $6,889.17

10. From 76421 subtract 73101. The answer should be 10._____
    A. 3642   B. 3540   C. 3320   D. 3242

11. From $8.25 subtract $6.50. The answer should be 11._____
    A. $1.25   B. $1.50   C. $1.75   D. $2.25

12. Multiply 563 by 0.50. The answer should be 12._____
    A. 281.50   B. 28.15   C. 2.815   D. 0.2815

201

13. Multiply 0.35 by 1045. The answer should be   13._____
    A. 0.36575   B. 3.6575   C. 36.575   D. 365.75

14. Multiply 25 by 2513. The answer should be   14._____
    A. 62825   B. 62725   C. 60825   D. 52825

15. Multiply 423 by 0.01. The answer should be   15._____
    A. 0.0423   B. 0.423   C. 4.23   D. 42.3

16. Multiply 6.70 by 3.2. The answer should be   16._____
    A. 2.1440   B. 21.440   C. 214.40   D. 2144.0

17. Multiply 630 by 517. The answer should be   17._____
    A. 325,710   B. 345,720   C. 362,425   D. 385,660

18. Multiply 35 by 846. The answer should be   18._____
    A. 4050   B. 9450   C. 18740   D. 29610

19. Multiply 823 by 0.05. The answer should be   19._____
    A. 0.4115   B. 4.115   C. 41.15   D. 411.50

20. Multiply 1690 by 0.10. The answer should be   20._____
    A. 0.169   B. 1.69   C. 16.90   D. 169.0

21. Divide 2765 by 35. The answer should be   21._____
    A. 71   B. 79   C. 87   D. 93

22. From $18.55 subtract $6.80. The answer should be   22._____
    A. $9.75   B. $10.95   C. $11.75   D. $25.35

23. The sum of 2.75 + 4.50 + 3.60 is   23._____
    A. 9.75   B. 10.85   C. 11.15   D. 11.95

24. The sum of 9.63 + 11.21 + 17.25 is   24._____
    A. 36.09   B. 38.09   C. 39.92   D. 41.22

25. The sum of 112.0 + 16.9 + 3.84 is   25._____
    A. 129.3   B. 132.74   C. 136.48   D. 167.3

KEY (CORRECT ANSWERS)

1.	C	11.	C
2.	B	12.	A
3.	C	13.	D
4.	C	14.	A
5.	A	15.	C
6.	B	16.	B
7.	A	17.	A
8.	A	18.	D
9.	D	19.	C
10.	C	20.	D

21. B
22. C
23. B
24. B
25. B

4 (#1)

SOLUTIONS TO PROBLEMS

1. 76,342 + 49,050 + 21,206 + 59,989 = 206,587

2. $452.13 + $963.83 + $621.25 = $2037.21

3. 36,392 + 42,156 + 98,765 = 177,313

4. 40,125 + 87,123 + 24,689 = 151,937

5. 2379 + 4015 + 6521 + 9986 = 22901

6. 50,962 - 36,197 = 14,765

7. 90,000 - 31,928 = 58,072

8. 63,764 - 21,548 = 42,216

9. $9605.13 - $2715.96 = $6889.17

10. 76,421 - 73,101 = 3320

11. $8.25 - $6.50 = $1.75

12. (563)(.50) = 281.50

13. (.35)(1045) = 365.75

14. (25)(2513) = 62,825

15. (423)(.01) = 4.23

16. (6.70)(3.2) = 21.44

17. (630)(517) = 325,710

18. (35)(846) = 29,610

19. (823)(.05) = 41.15

20. (1690)(.10) = 169

21. 2765 ÷ 35 = 79

22. $18.55 - $6.80 = $11.75

23. 2.75 + 4.50 + 3.60 = 10.85

24. 9.63 + 11.21 + 17.25 = 38.09

25. 112.0 + 16.9 + 3.84 = 132.74

TEST 2

Questions 1-10.

DIRECTIONS: Questions 1 through 10 refer to the arithmetic examples shown in the boxes below. Be sure to refer to the proper box when answering each question.

23.3 - 5.72	$491.26 -127.47	$7.95 ÷ $0.15	4758 1639 2075 864 23	27.6 179.47 8.73 46.5
BOX 1	BOX 2	BOX 3	BOX 4	BOX 5
243 x57	57697 -9748	23.65 x 9.7	3/4 260	25/1975
BOX 6	BOX 7	BOX 8	BOX 9	BOX 10

1. The difference between the two numbers in Box 1 is
   A. 17.42   B. 17.58   C. 23.35   D. 29.02

2. The difference between the two numbers in Box 2 is
   A. $274.73   B. $363.79   C. $374.89   D. $618.73

3. The result of the division indicated in Box 3 is
   A. $0.53   B. $5.30   C. 5.3   D. 53

4. The sum of the five numbers in Box 4 is
   A. 8355   B. 9359   C. 9534   D. 10359

5. The sum of the four numbers in Box 5 is
   A. 262.30   B. 272.03   C. 372.23   D. 372.30

6. The product of the two numbers in Box 6 is
   A. 138.51   B. 1385.1   C. 13851   D. 138510

7. The difference between the two numbers in Box 7 is
   A. 67445   B. 48949   C. 47949   D. 40945

8. The product of the two numbers in Box 8 is
   A. 22.9405   B. 229.405   C. 2294.05   D. 229405

9. The product of the two numbers in Box 9 is
   A. 65   B. 120   C. 195   D. 240

205

10. The result of the division indicated in Box 10 is 10.____

    A. 790   B. 379   C. 179   D. 79

Questions 11-20.

DIRECTIONS: Questions 11 through 20 refer to the arithmetic examples shown in the boxes below. Be sure to refer to the proper box when answering each question.

3849 728 3164 773 32 BOX 1	18.70 268.38 17.64 9.40 BOX 2	66788 -8639 BOX 3	154 x48 BOX 4	32.56 x 8.6 BOX 5
34/2890 BOX 6	32.49 - 8.7 BOX 7	$582.17 -38.58 BOX 8	$6.72 ÷ $0.24 BOX 9	3/8 x 264 BOX 10

11. The sum of the five numbers in Box 1 is 11.____

    A. 7465   B. 7566   C. 8465   D. 8546

12. The sum of the four numbers in Box 2 is 12.____

    A. 341.21   B. 341.12   C. 314.21   D. 314.12

13. The difference between the two numbers in Box 3 is 13.____

    A. 75427   B. 74527   C. 58149   D. 57149

14. The product of the two numbers in Box 4 is 14.____

    A. 1232   B. 6160   C. 7392   D. 8392

15. The product of the two numbers in Box 5 is 15.____

    A. 28.016   B. 280.016   C. 280.16   D. 2800.16

16. The result of the division indicated in Box 6 is 16.____

    A. 85   B. 850   C. 8.5   D. 185

17. The difference between the two numbers in Box 7 is 17.____

    A. 23.79   B. 21.53   C. 19.97   D. 18.79

18. The difference between the two numbers in Box 8 is 18.____

    A. $620.75   B. $602.59   C. $554.75   D. $543.59

19. The result of the division indicated in Box 9 is 19.____

    A. .0357   B. 28.0   C. 280   D. 35.7

20. The product of the two numbers in Box 10 is   20._____
    A. 9.90   B. 89.0   C. 99.0   D. 199.

21. When 2597 is added to the result of 257 multiplied by 65, the answer is   21._____
    A. 16705   B. 19302   C. 19392   D. 19402

22. When 948 is subtracted from the sum of 6527 + 324, the answer is   22._____
    A. 5255   B. 5903   C. 7151   D. 7799

23. When 736 is subtracted from the sum of 3191 + 1253, the answer is   23._____
    A. 2674   B. 3708   C. 4444   D. 5180

24. Divide 6 2/3 by 2 1/2.   24._____
    A. 2 2/3   B. 16 2/3   C. 3 1/3   D. 2 1/2

25. Add: 1/2 + 2 1/4 + 2/3   25._____
    A. 3 1/4   B. 2 7/8   C. 4 1/4   D. 3 5/12

KEY (CORRECT ANSWERS)

1.	B	11.	D
2.	B	12.	D
3.	D	13.	C
4.	B	14.	C
5.	A	15.	B
6.	C	16.	A
7.	C	17.	A
8.	B	18.	D
9.	C	19.	B
10.	D	20.	C

21. B
22. B
23. B
24. A
25. D

SOLUTIONS TO PROBLEMS

1. 23.3 - 5.72 = 17.58

2. $491.26 - $127.47 = $363.79

3. $7.95 $.15 = 53

4. 4758 + 1639 + 2075 + 864 + 23 = 9359

5. 27.6 + 179.47 + 8.73 + 46.5 = 262.3

6. (243)(57) = 13,851

7. 57,697 - 9748 = 47,949

8. (23.65X9.7) = 229.405

9. $(\frac{3}{4})(260) = 195$

10. 1975 ÷ 25 = 79

11. 3849 + 728 + 3164 + 773 + 32 = 8546

12. 18.70 + 268.38 + 17.64 + 9.40 = 314.12

13. 66,788 - 8639 = 58,149

14. (154)(48) = 7392

15. (32.56)(8.6) = 280.016

16. 2890 34 = 85

17. 32.49 - 8.7 = 23.79

18. $582.17 - $38.58 = $543.59

19. $6.72 ÷ $.24 = 28

20. $(\frac{3}{8})(264) = 99$

21. 2597 + (257)(65) = 2597 + 16,705 = 19,302

22. (6527 + 324) - 948 = 6851 - 948 = 5903

23. (3191 + 1253) - 736 = 4444 - 736 = 3708

24. $6\frac{2}{3} \div 2\frac{1}{2} = (\frac{20}{3})(\frac{2}{5}) = \frac{40}{15} = 2\frac{2}{3}$

25. $\frac{1}{2} + 2\frac{1}{4} + \frac{2}{3} = \frac{6}{12} + 2\frac{3}{12} + \frac{8}{12} = 2\frac{17}{12} = 3\frac{5}{12}$

TEST 3

Questions 1-10.

DIRECTIONS: Questions 1 through 10 refer to the arithmetic examples shown in the boxes below. Be sure to refer to the proper box when answering each item.

8462 2974 5109 763 47	14/1890	182 x63	27412 -8426	$275.15 -162.28
BOX 1	BOX 2	BOX 3	BOX 4	BOX 5
2/3 x 246	14.36 x 7.2	14.6 9.22 143.18 27.1	$6.45 ÷ $0.15	16.6 - 7.91
BOX 6	BOX 7	BOX 8	BOX 9	BOX 10

1. The sum of the five numbers in Box 1 is
   A. 16245   B. 16355   C. 17245   D. 17355

2. The result of the division indicated in Box 2 is
   A. 140   B. 135   C. 127 6/7   D. 125

3. The product of the two numbers in Box 3 is
   A. 55692   B. 16552   C. 11466   D. 1638

4. The difference between the two numbers in Box 4 is
   A. 18986   B. 19096   C. 35838   D. 38986

5. The difference between the two numbers in Box 5 is
   A. $103.87   B. $112.87   C. $113.97   D. $212.87

6. The product of the two numbers in Box 6 is
   A. 82   B. 123   C. 164   D. 369

7. The product of the two numbers in Box 7 is
   A. 103.492   B. 103.392   C. 102.392   D. 102.292

8. The sum of the four numbers in Box 8 is
   A. 183.00   B. 183.10   C. 194.10   D. 204.00

9. The result of the division indicated in Box 9 is
   A. $0.43   B. 4.3   C. 43   D. $4.30

10. The difference between the two numbers in Box 10 is

    A. 8.69   B. 8.11   C. 6.25   D. 3.75

11. Add $4.34, $34.50, $6.00, $101.76, and $90.67. From the result, subtract $60.54 and $10.56.

    A. $76.17   B. $156.37   C. $166.17   D. $300.37

12. Add 2,200, 2,600, 252, and 47.96. From the result, subtract 202.70, 1,200, 2,150, and 434.43.

    A. 1,112.83   B. 1,213.46   C. 1,341.51   D. 1,348.91

13. Multiply 1850 by .05 and multiply 3300 by .08. Then, add both results.

    A. 242.50   B. 264.00   C. 333.25   D. 356.50

14. Multiply 312.77 by .04. Round off the result to the nearest hundredth.

    A. 12.52   B. 12.511   C. 12.518   D. 12.51

15. Add 362.05, 91.13, 347.81, and 17.46. Then, divide the result by 6. The answer rounded off to the nearest hundredth is

    A. 138.409   B. 137.409   C. 136.41   D. 136.40

16. Add 66.25 and 15.06. Then, multiply the result by 2 1/6. The answer is MOST NEARLY

    A. 176.18   B. 176.17   C. 162.66   D. 162.62

17. Each of the following options contains three decimals. In which case do all three decimals have the same value?

    A. .3; .30; .03
    B. .25; .250; .2500
    C. 1.9; 1.90; 1.09
    D. .35; .350; .035

18. Add 1/2 the sum of (539.84 and 479.26) to 1/3 the sum of (1461.93 and 927.27). Round off the result to the nearest whole number.

    A. 3408   B. 2899   C. 1816   D. 1306

19. Multiply $5,906.09 by 15%. Then, divide the result by 3.

    A. $295.30   B. $885.91   C. $8,859.14   D. $29,530.45

20. A team has won 10 games, lost 4, and has 6 games yet to play. How many of these remaining games MUST be won if the team is to win 65% of its games for the season?

    A. One
    B. Two
    C. Four
    D. None of the above

21. If a certain candy sells at the rate of $1 for 2 1/2 ounces, what is the price per pound? (Do not include tax.)

    A. $2.50   B. $6.40   C. $8.50   D. $4.00

22. Which is the SMALLEST of the following numbers? 22.____

    A. .3980 B. .3976 C. .39752 D. .399

23. A tank can be filled by one pipe in 10 minutes and by another in 15 minutes. 23.____
    How long will it take to fill the tank if both pipes are opened?
    _____ min.

    A. 4 B. 5 C. 6 D. 7.5

24. If $17.60 is to be divided between two people so that one person receives one and three- 24.____
    fourths as much as the other, how much should each receive?

    A. $6.40 and $11.20
    B. $5.50 and $12.10
    C. $6.60 and $11.20
    D. $6.00 and $11.60

25. Mr. Burns owns a block of land which is exactly 320 ft. long and 140 ft. wide. 25.____
    At 40¢ per square foot, how much will it cost to build a 4 foot cement walk around this
    land, bound by its outer edge?

    A. $1420.80 B. $1472 C. $368 D. $1446.40

KEY (CORRECT ANSWERS)

1. D		11. C	
2. B		12. A	
3. C		13. D	
4. A		14. D	
5. B		15. C	
6. C		16. B	
7. B		17. B	
8. C		18. D	
9. C		19. A	
10. A		20. D	

21. B
22. C
23. C
24. A
25. D

SOLUTIONS TO PROBLEMS

1. $8462 + 2974 + 5109 + 763 + 47 = 17{,}355$

2. $1890 \div 14 = 135$

3. $(182)(63) = 11{,}466$

4. $27{,}412 - 8426 = 18{,}986$

5. $\$275.15 - \$162.28 = \$112.87$

6. $(\frac{2}{3})(246) = 164$

7. $(14.36)(7.2) = 103.392$

8. $14.6 + 9.22 + 143.18 + 27.1 = 194.1$

9. $\$6.45\ \$.15 = 43$

10. $16.6 - 7.91 = 8.69$

11. $(\$4.34 + \$34.50 + \$6.00 + \$101.76 + \$90.67) - (\$60.54 + \$10.56) = \$237.27 - \$71.10 = \$166.17$

12. $(2200 + 2600 + 252 + 47.96) - (202.70 + 1200 + 2150 + 434.43) = 5099.96 - 3987.13 = 1112.83$

13. $(1850)(.05) + (3300 \text{X} .08) = 92.5 + 264 = 356.5$

14. $(312.77)(.04) = 12.5108 = 12.51$ rounded off to nearest hundredth

15. $(362.05 + 91.13 + 347.81 + 17.46)\ 6 = 818.45\ 6 = 136.4083" = 136.41$ rounded off to nearest hundredth

16. $(66.25 + 15.06)(2\frac{1}{6}) = (81.31)(2\frac{1}{6}) \approx 176.17$

17. $.25 = .250 = .2500$

18. $1/2(539.84 + 479.26) + 1/3(1461.93 + 927.27) = 509.55 + 796.4 = 1305.95 = 1306$ rounaed off to nearest whole number

19. $(\$5906.09)(.15)(\frac{1}{3}) = \$295.3045 = \$295.30$ rounded off to 2 places

213

5 (#3)

20. $(.65)(20) = 13$ games won. Thus, the team must win 3 more games.

21. Let x = price per pound. Then, $\dfrac{1.00}{x} = \dfrac{2\frac{1}{2}}{16}$. Solving, x = 6.40

22. .39752 is the smallest of the numbers.

23. Let x = required minutes. Then, $\dfrac{x}{10} + \dfrac{x}{15} = 1$. So, $3x + 2x = 30$. Solving, x = 6.

24. Let x, 1.75x represent the two amounts. Then, x + 1.75x = $17.60. Solving, x = $6.40 and 1.75x = $11.20.

25. Area of cement walk = $(320)(140) - (312)(132) = 3616$ sq.ft. Then, $(3616)(.40) = \$1446.40$.

TEST 4

DIRECTIONS: Each question or incomplete statement is followed by several suggested answers or completions. Select the one that BEST answers the question or completes the statement. *PRINT THE LETTER OF THE CORRECT ANSWER IN THE SPACE AT THE RIGHT.*

1. Subtract: 10,376
   -8,492

   A. 1834   B. 1884   C. 1924   D. 2084

   1.____

2. Subtract: $155.22
   - 93.75

   A. $61.47   B. $59.33   C. $59.17   D. $58.53

   2.____

3. Subtract: $22.50
   -13.78

   A. $9.32   B. $9.18   C. $8.92   D. $8.72

   3.____

4. Multiply: 485
   x32

   A. 13,350   B. 15,520   C. 16,510   D. 17,630

   4.____

5. Multiply: $3.29
   x 14

   A. $41.16   B. $42.46   C. $44.76   D. $46.06

   5.____

6. Multiply: 106
   x318

   A. 33,708   B. 33,632   C. 33,614   D. 33,548

   6.____

7. Multiply: 119
   x1.15

   A. 136.85   B. 136.94   C. 137.15   D. 137.34

   7.____

8. Divide: 432 by 16

   A. 37   B. 32   C. 27   D. 24

   8.____

9. Divide: $115.65 by 5

   A. $24.25   B. $23.13   C. $22.83   D. $22.55

   9.____

10. Divide: 18,711 by 63

    A. 267   B. 273   C. 283   D. 297

    10.____

11. Divide: 327.45 by .15

    A. 1,218   B. 2,183   C. 2,243   D. 2,285

    11.____

12. The sum of 637.894, 8352.16, 4.8673, and 301.5 is MOST NEARLY

    A. 8989.5   B. 9021.35   C. 9294.9   D. 9296.4

13. If 30 is divided by .06, the result is

    A. 5   B. 50   C. 500   D. 5000

14. The sum of the fractions 1/3, 4/6, 3/4, 1/2, and 1/12 is

    A. 3 1/4   B. 2 1/3   C. 2 1/6   D. 1 11/12

15. If 96934.42 is divided by 53.496, the result is MOST NEARLY

    A. 181   B. 552   C. 1812   D. 5520

16. If 25% of a number is 48, the number is

    A. 12   B. 60   C. 144   D. 192

17. The average number of reports filed per day by a clerk during a five-day week was 720. He filed 610 reports the first day, 720 reports the second day, 740 reports the third day, and 755 reports the fourth day.
    The number of reports he filed the fifth day was

    A. 748   B. 165   C. 775   D. 565

18. The number 88 is 2/5 of

    A. 123   B. 141   C. 220   D. 440

19. If the product of 8.3 multiplied by .42 is subtracted from the product of 156 multiplied by .09, the result is MOST NEARLY

    A. 10.6   B. 13.7   C. 17.5   D. 20.8

20. The sum of 284.5, 3016.24, 8.9736, and 94.15 is MOST NEARLY

    A. 3402.9   B. 3403.0   C. 3403.9   D. 4036.1

21. If 8394.6 is divided by 29.17, the result is MOST NEARLY

    A. 288   B. 347   C. 2880   D. 3470

22. If two numbers are multiplied together, the result is 3752. If one of the two numbers is 56, the other number is

    A. 41   B. 15   C. 109   D. 67

23. The sum of the fractions 1/4, 2/3, 3/8, 5/6, and 3/4 is

    A. 20/33   B. 1 19/24   C. 2 1/4   D. 2 7/8

24. The fraction 7/16 expressed as a decimal is

    A. .1120   B. .2286   C. .4375   D. .4850

25. If .10 is divided by 50, the result is

    A. .002   B. .02   C. .2   D. 2

KEY (CORRECT ANSWERS)

1.	B	11.	B
2.	A	12.	D
3.	D	13.	C
4.	B	14.	B
5.	D	15.	C
6.	A	16.	D
7.	A	17.	C
8.	C	18.	C
9.	B	19.	A
10.	D	20.	C

21. A
22. D
23. D
24. C
25. A

SOLUTIONS TO PROBLEMS

1. 10,376 - 8492 = 1884

2. $155.22 - $93.75 = $61.47

3. $22.50 - $13.78 = $8.72

4. (485)(32) = 15,520

5. ($3.29)(14) = $46.06

6. (106)(318) = 33,708

7. (119)(1.15) = 136.85

8. 432 ÷ 16 = 27

9. $115.65 ÷ 5 = $23.13

10. 18,711 ÷ 63 = 297

11. 327.45 ÷ .15 = 2183

12. 637.894 + 8352.16 + 4.8673 + 301.5 = 9296.4213 ≈ 9296.4

13. 30 ÷ .06 = 500

14. $\frac{1}{3}+\frac{4}{6}+\frac{3}{4}+\frac{1}{2}+\frac{1}{12}=\frac{4}{12}+\frac{8}{12}+\frac{9}{12}+\frac{6}{12}+\frac{1}{12}=\frac{28}{12}=2\frac{1}{3}$

15. 96,934.42 ÷ 53.496 ≈ 1811.99 ≈ 1812

16. Let x = number. Then, .25x = 48. Solving, x = 192.

17. Let x = number of reports on 5th day. Then, (610 + 720 + 740 + 755 + x)/5 = 720. Simplifying, 2825 + x = 3600, so x = 775.

18. $88 \div \frac{2}{5} = 220$

19. (156)(.09) - (8.3)(.42) = 10.554 ≈ 10.6

20. 284.5 + 3016.24 + 8.9736 + 94.15 = 3403.8636 ≈ 3403.9

5 (#4)

21. 8394.6 ÷ 29.17 ≈ 287.78 ≈ 288

22. The other number = 3752 ÷ 56 = 67

23. $\frac{1}{4}+\frac{2}{3}+\frac{3}{8}+\frac{5}{6}+\frac{3}{4}=\frac{6}{24}+\frac{16}{24}+\frac{9}{24}+\frac{20}{24}+\frac{18}{24}=\frac{69}{24}=2\frac{7}{8}$

24. $\frac{7}{16}=.4375$

25. .10 ÷ 50 = .002

COURTROOM TERMS

A/K/A: Acronym that stands for "also known as" and introduces any alternative or assumed names or aliases of an individual. A term to indicate another name by which a person is known.

Arraignment: The bringing of a defendant before the court to answer the matters charged against him in an indictment or information. The defendant is read the charges and must respond with his plea.

Arrest: Deprivation of one's liberty by legal authority.

Bail: An amount of money set by the court to procure the release of a person from legal custody; this money is to be forfeited if the defendant fails to appear for trial.

Beyond a Reasonable Doubt: The standard of proof required for a finding of guilty in a criminal matter. Satisfied to a moral certainty. This is a higher standard of proof than that required in a civil matter (preponderance of the evidence).

Co-Defendant: Any additional defendant or respondent in the same case.

Confession: A voluntary statement made by a person charged with a crime wherein said person acknowledges his/her guilt of the offense charged and discloses participation in the act.

Controlled Dangerous Substance: That group of legally designated drugs, which, by statute, it is illegal to possess or distribute.

Criminal complaint: The initial written notice to a defendant that he/she is being charged with a public offense.

Due Process of Law: The exercise of the powers of the government with the safeguards for the protection of individual rights as set forth in the constitution, statutes, and common case law.

Felony: A crime of a more serious nature than a misdemeanor, the exact nature of which is defined by state statute and which is punishable by a term of imprisonment exceeding one year or by death.

Grand Jury: A jury of inquiry whose duty is to receive complaints and accusations in criminal cases, hear the evidence presented on the part of the state, and determine whether to indict (see "indictment" below).

Impeach: As used in the Law of Evidence, to call into question the truthfulness of a witness, by means of introducing evidence to discredit him or her.

Indictment: A written accusation presented by a grand jury after having been presented with evidence, charging that a person named therein has done some act, or has been guilty of some omission that by law is a public offense.

Miranda Warnings: The compulsory advisement of a person's rights prior to any custodial interrogation; these include: a) the right to remain silent; b) that any statement made may be used against him/her; c) the right to an attorney; d) the appointment of counsel if the accused cannot afford his or her own attorney. Unless these rights are given, any evidence obtained in an interrogation cannot be used in the individual's trial against him/her.

Misdemeanor: Offense lower than felony and generally punishable by a fine or imprisonment other than in a penitentiary.

Motion to Quash: Application to the court to set aside the complaint, indictment or subpoena due to a lack of probable cause to arrest the defendant, or in matters heard by a grand jury, due to evidence not properly presented to the grand jury.

Motion to Sever: Application to the court made when there are two defendants charged with the same crimes or who acted jointly in the commission of a crime, when their attorneys feel it would be in their best interest if they had separate trials.

Motion to Suppress Evidence: Application to the court to prevent evidence from being presented at trial when said evidence has been obtained by illegal means. It applies to physical evidence, statements made by defendant when not advised by counsel or through wiretapping, prior convictions, etc..

Parole: A conditional release from custody at the discretion of the paroling authority prior to his or her completing the prison sentence imposed. During said release the offender is required to observe conditions of this status under the supervision of a parole agency.

Plea: A defendant's formal answer in court to the charges contained in a charging document.

Guilty: A plea by the defendant in which he acknowledges guilt either of the offense charged or of a less serious offense pursuant to an agreement with the prosecuting attorney. It should be understood, however, that the court may not be obliged to recognize this.

Nolo Contendere: A plea that is admissible in some jurisdictions, in which the defendant states that he does not contest the charges against him. Also called "no contest", this plea has the same effect as a guilty plea, except that it cannot be used against the defendant in civil actions arising out of the same incident which gave rise to the criminal charges.

Not Guilty: A plea of innocence by the defendant.

Not Guilty by Reason of Insanity: A plea that is sometimes entered in conjunction with the "not guilty" plea.

Double Jeopardy: A plea entered by a defendant who has been tried for an offense wherein he asserts that he cannot be tried a second time for said offense, unless he successfully secured a new trial after an appeal, or after a motion for a new trial was granted by the trial court.

Police Report: The official report made by any police officer involved with the incident or appearing after the incident, setting forth the officer's observations and statements of parties and witnesses. It can be used as evidence in a trial.

Pre-Trial Intervention: Utilized in some states when a defendant is accused of a first offense, to divert the defendant from the criminal justice system.

Probation: To allow a person convicted of a minor offense to go at large, under a suspension of sentence, during good behavior, and generally under the supervision of a probation officer.

Prosecutor: The attorney who prosecutes defendants for crimes, in the name of the government.

Search Warrant: A written order, issued by the court, directing the police to search a specified location for particular personal property (stolen or illegally possessed).

Speedy Trial: Mandate by the government that all criminal trials must take place within a specified time after arrest.

Writ of Habeas Corpus: A mandate issued from a court requiring that an individual be brought before the court.

GLOSSARY OF LEGAL TERMS

TABLE OF CONTENTS

	Page
Action ... Affiant	1
Affidavit ... At Bar	2
At Issue ... Burden of Proof	3
Business ... Commute	4
Complainant ... Conviction	5
Cooperative ... Demur (v.)	6
Demurrage ... Endorsement	7
Enjoin ... Facsimile	8
Factor ... Guilty	9
Habeas Corpus ... Incumbrance	10
Indemnify ... Laches	11
Landlord and Tenant ... Malice	12
Mandamus ... Obiter Dictum	13
Object (v.) ... Perjury	14
Perpetuity ... Proclamation	15
Proffered Evidence ... Referee	16
Referendum ... Stare Decisis	17
State ... Term	18
Testamentary ... Warrant (Warranty) (v.)	19
Warrant (n.) ... Zoning	20

GLOSSARY OF LEGAL TERMS

A

ACTION - "Action" includes a civil action and a criminal action.

A FORTIORI - A term meaning you can reason one thing from the existence of certain facts.

A POSTERIORI - From what goes after; from effect to cause.

A PRIORI - From what goes before; from cause to effect.

AB INITIO - From the beginning.

ABATE - To diminish or put an end to.

ABET - To encourage the commission of a crime.

ABEYANCE - Suspension, temporary suppression.

ABIDE - To accept the consequences of.

ABJURE - To renounce; give up.

ABRIDGE - To reduce; contract; diminish.

ABROGATE - To annul, repeal, or destroy.

ABSCOND - To hide or absent oneself to avoid legal action.

ABSTRACT - A summary.

ABUT - To border on, to touch.

ACCESS - Approach; in real property law it means the right of the owner of property to the use of the highway or road next to his land, without obstruction by intervening property owners.

ACCESSORY - In criminal law, it means the person who contributes or aids in the commission of a crime.

ACCOMMODATED PARTY - One to whom credit is extended on the strength of another person signing a commercial paper.

ACCOMMODATION PAPER - A commercial paper to which the accommodating party has put his name.

ACCOMPLICE - In criminal law, it means a person who together with the principal offender commits a crime.

ACCORD - An agreement to accept something different or less than that to which one is entitled, which extinguishes the entire obligation.

ACCOUNT - A statement of mutual demands in the nature of debt and credit between parties.

ACCRETION - The act of adding to a thing; in real property law, it means gradual accumulation of land by natural causes.

ACCRUE - To grow to; to be added to.

ACKNOWLEDGMENT - The act of going before an official authorized to take acknowledgments, and acknowledging an act as one's own.

ACQUIESCENCE - A silent appearance of consent.

ACQUIT - To legally determine the innocence of one charged with a crime.

AD INFINITUM - Indefinitely.

AD LITEM - For the suit.

AD VALOREM - According to value.

ADJECTIVE LAW - Rules of procedure.

ADJUDICATION - The judgment given in a case.

ADMIRALTY - Court having jurisdiction over maritime cases.

ADULT - Sixteen years old or over (in criminal law).

ADVANCE - In commercial law, it means to pay money or render other value before it is due.

ADVERSE - Opposed; contrary.

ADVOCATE - (v.) To speak in favor of;
(n.) One who assists, defends, or pleads for another.

AFFIANT - A person who makes and signs an affidavit.

AFFIDAVIT - A written and sworn to declaration of facts, voluntarily made.
AFFINITY - The relationship between persons through marriage with the kindred of each other; distinguished from consanguinity, which is the relationship by blood.
AFFIRM - To ratify; also when an appellate court affirms a judgment, decree, or order, it means that it is valid and right and must stand as rendered in the lower court.
AFOREMENTIONED; AFORESAID - Before or already said.
AGENT - One who represents and acts for another.
AID AND COMFORT - To help; encourage.
ALIAS - A name not one's true name.
ALIBI - A claim of not being present at a certain place at a certain time.
ALLEGE - To assert.
ALLOTMENT - A share or portion.
AMBIGUITY - Uncertainty; capable of being understood in more than one way.
AMENDMENT - Any language made or proposed as a change in some principal writing.
AMICUS CURIAE - A friend of the court; one who has an interest in a case, although not a party in the case, who volunteers advice upon matters of law to the judge. For example, a brief amicus curiae.
AMORTIZATION - To provide for a gradual extinction of (a future obligation) in advance of maturity, especially, by periodical contributions to a sinking fund which will be adequate to discharge a debt or make a replacement when it becomes necessary.
ANCILLARY - Aiding, auxiliary.
ANNOTATION - A note added by way of comment or explanation.
ANSWER - A written statement made by a defendant setting forth the grounds of his defense.
ANTE - Before.
ANTE MORTEM - Before death.
APPEAL - The removal of a case from a lower court to one of superior jurisdiction for the purpose of obtaining a review.
APPEARANCE - Coming into court as a party to a suit.
APPELLANT - The party who takes an appeal from one court or jurisdiction to another (appellate) court for review.
APPELLEE - The party against whom an appeal is taken.
APPROPRIATE - To make a thing one's own.
APPROPRIATION - Prescribing the destination of a thing; the act of the legislature designating a particular fund, to be applied to some object of government expenditure.
APPURTENANT - Belonging to; accessory or incident to.
ARBITER - One who decides a dispute; a referee.
ARBITRARY - Unreasoned; not governed by any fixed rules or standard.
ARGUENDO - By way of argument.
ARRAIGN - To call the prisoner before the court to answer to a charge.
ASSENT - A declaration of willingness to do something in compliance with a request.
ASSERT - Declare.
ASSESS - To fix the rate or amount.
ASSIGN - To transfer; to appoint; to select for a particular purpose.
ASSIGNEE - One who receives an assignment.
ASSIGNOR - One who makes an assignment.
AT BAR - Before the court.

AT ISSUE - When parties in an action come to a point where one asserts something and the other denies it.
ATTACH - Seize property by court order and sometimes arrest a person.
ATTEST - To witness a will, etc.; act of attestation.
AVERMENT - A positive statement of facts.

B

BAIL - To obtain the release of a person from legal custody by giving security and promising that he shall appear in court; to deliver (goods, etc.) in trust to a person for a special purpose.
BAILEE - One to whom personal property is delivered under a contract of bailment.
BAILMENT - Delivery of personal property to another to be held for a certain purpose and to be returned when the purpose is accomplished.
BAILOR - The party who delivers goods to another, under a contract of bailment.
BANC (OR BANK) - Bench; the place where a court sits permanently or regularly; also the assembly of all the judges of a court.
BANKRUPT - An insolvent person, technically, one declared to be bankrupt after a bankruptcy proceeding.
BAR - The legal profession.
BARRATRY - Exciting groundless judicial proceedings.
BARTER - A contract by which parties exchange goods for other goods.
BATTERY - Illegal interfering with another's person.
BEARER - In commercial law, it means the person in possession of a commercial paper which is payable to the bearer.
BENCH - The court itself or the judge.
BENEFICIARY - A person benefiting under a will, trust, or agreement.
BEST EVIDENCE RULE, THE - Except as otherwise provided by statute, no evidence other than the writing itself is admissible to prove the content of a writing. This section shall be known and may be cited as the best evidence rule.
BEQUEST - A gift of personal property under a will.
BILL - A formal written statement of complaint to a court of justice; also, a draft of an act of the legislature before it becomes a law; also, accounts for goods sold, services rendered, or work done.
BONA FIDE - In or with good faith; honestly.
BOND - An instrument by which the maker promises to pay a sum of money to another, usually providing that upon performances of a certain condition the obligation shall be void.
BOYCOTT - A plan to prevent the carrying on of a business by wrongful means.
BREACH - The breaking or violating of a law, or the failure to carry out a duty.
BRIEF - A written document, prepared by a lawyer to serve as the basis of an argument upon a case in court, usually an appellate court.
BURDEN OF PRODUCING EVIDENCE - The obligation of a party to introduce evidence sufficient to avoid a ruling against him on the issue.
BURDEN OF PROOF - The obligation of a party to establish by evidence a requisite degree of belief concerning a fact in the mind of the trier of fact or the court. The burden of proof may require a party to raise a reasonable doubt concerning the existence of nonexistence of a fact or that he establish the existence or nonexistence of a fact by a preponderance of the evidence, by clear and convincing proof, or by proof beyond a reasonable doubt.

Except as otherwise provided by law, the burden of proof requires proof by a preponderance of the evidence.

BUSINESS, A - Shall include every kind of business, profession, occupation, calling or operation of institutions, whether carried on for profit or not.

BY-LAWS - Regulations, ordinances, or rules enacted by a corporation, association, etc., for its own government.

C

CANON - A doctrine; also, a law or rule, of a church or association in particular.

CAPIAS - An order to arrest.

CAPTION - In a pleading, deposition or other paper connected with a case in court, it is the heading or introductory clause which shows the names of the parties, name of the court, number of the case on the docket or calendar, etc.

CARRIER - A person or corporation undertaking to transport persons or property.

CASE - A general term for an action, cause, suit, or controversy before a judicial body.

CAUSE - A suit, litigation or action before a court.

CAVEAT EMPTOR - Let the buyer beware. This term expresses the rule that the purchaser of an article must examine, judge, and test it for himself, being bound to discover any obvious defects or imperfections.

CERTIFICATE - A written representation that some legal formality has been complied with.

CERTIORARI - To be informed of; the name of a writ issued by a superior court directing the lower court to send up to the former the record and proceedings of a case.

CHANGE OF VENUE - To remove place of trial from one place to another.

CHARGE - An obligation or duty; a formal complaint; an instruction of the court to the jury upon a case.

CHARTER - (n.) The authority by virtue of which an organized body acts;

    (v.) in mercantile law, it means to hire or lease a vehicle or vessel for transportation.

CHATTEL - An article of personal property.

CHATTEL MORTGAGE - A mortgage on personal property.

CIRCUIT - A division of the country, for the administration of justice; a geographical area served by a court.

CITATION - The act of the court by which a person is summoned or cited; also, a reference to legal authority.

CIVIL (ACTIONS) - It indicates the private rights and remedies of individuals in contrast to the word "criminal" (actions) which relates to prosecution for violation of laws.

CLAIM (n.) - Any demand held or asserted as of right.

CODICIL - An addition to a will.

CODIFY - To arrange the laws of a country into a code.

COGNIZANCE - Notice or knowledge.

COLLATERAL - By the side; accompanying; an article or thing given to secure performance of a promise.

COMITY - Courtesy; the practice by which one court follows the decision of another court on the same question.

COMMIT - To perform, as an act; to perpetrate, as a crime; to send a person to prison.

COMMON LAW - As distinguished from law created by the enactment of the legislature (called statutory law), it relates to those principles and rules of action which derive their authority solely from usages and customs of immemorial antiquity, particularly with reference to the ancient unwritten law of England. The written pronouncements of the common law are found in court decisions.

COMMUTE - Change punishment to one less severe.

COMPLAINANT - One who applies to the court for legal redress.
COMPLAINT - The pleading of a plaintiff in a civil action; or a charge that a person has committed a specified offense.
COMPROMISE - An arrangement for settling a dispute by agreement.
CONCUR - To agree, consent.
CONCURRENT - Running together, at the same time.
CONDEMNATION - Taking private property for public use on payment therefor.
CONDITION - Mode or state of being; a qualification or restriction.
CONDUCT - Active and passive behavior; both verbal and nonverbal.
CONFESSION - Voluntary statement of guilt of crime.
CONFIDENTIAL COMMUNICATION BETWEEN CLIENT AND LAWYER - Information transmitted between a client and his lawyer in the course of that relationship and in confidence by a means which, so far as the client is aware, discloses the information to no third persons other than those who are present to further the interest of the client in the consultation or those to whom disclosure is reasonably necessary for the transmission of the information or the accomplishment of the purpose for which the lawyer is consulted, and includes a legal opinion formed and the advice given by the lawyer in the course of that relationship.
CONFRONTATION - Witness testifying in presence of defendant.
CONSANGUINITY - Blood relationship.
CONSIGN - To give in charge; commit; entrust; to send or transmit goods to a merchant, factor, or agent for sale.
CONSIGNEE - One to whom a consignment is made.
CONSIGNOR - One who sends or makes a consignment.
CONSPIRACY - In criminal law, it means an agreement between two or more persons to commit an unlawful act.
CONSPIRATORS - Persons involved in a conspiracy.
CONSTITUTION - The fundamental law of a nation or state.
CONSTRUCTION OF GENDERS - The masculine gender includes the feminine and neuter.
CONSTRUCTION OF SINGULAR AND PLURAL - The singular number includes the plural; and the plural, the singular.
CONSTRUCTION OF TENSES - The present tense includes the past and future tenses; and the future, the present.
CONSTRUCTIVE - An act or condition assumed from other parts or conditions.
CONSTRUE - To ascertain the meaning of language.
CONSUMMATE - To complete.
CONTIGUOUS - Adjoining; touching; bounded by.
CONTINGENT - Possible, but not assured; dependent upon some condition.
CONTINUANCE - The adjournment or postponement of an action pending in a court.
CONTRA - Against, opposed to; contrary.
CONTRACT - An agreement between two or more persons to do or not to do a particular thing.
CONTROVERT - To dispute, deny.
CONVERSION - Dealing with the personal property of another as if it were one's own, without right.
CONVEYANCE - An instrument transferring title to land.
CONVICTION - Generally, the result of a criminal trial which ends in a judgment or sentence that the defendant is guilty as charged.

COOPERATIVE - A cooperative is a voluntary organization of persons with a common interest, formed and operated along democratic lines for the purpose of supplying services at cost to its members and other patrons, who contribute both capital and business.
CORPUS DELICTI - The body of a crime; the crime itself.
CORROBORATE - To strengthen; to add weight by additional evidence.
COUNTERCLAIM - A claim presented by a defendant in opposition to or deduction from the claim of the plaintiff.
COUNTY - Political subdivision of a state.
COVENANT - Agreement.
CREDIBLE - Worthy of belief.
CREDITOR - A person to whom a debt is owing by another person, called the "debtor."
CRIMINAL ACTION - Includes criminal proceedings.
CRIMINAL INFORMATION - Same as complaint.
CRITERION (sing.)
CRITERIA (plural) - A means or tests for judging; a standard or standards.
CROSS-EXAMINATION - Examination of a witness by a party other than the direct examiner upon a matter that is within the scope of the direct examination of the witness.
CULPABLE - Blamable.
CY-PRES - As near as (possible). The rule of *cy-pres* is a rule for the construction of instruments in equity by which the intention of the party is carried out *as near as may be*, when it would be impossible or illegal to give it literal effect.

D

DAMAGES - A monetary compensation, which may be recovered in the courts by any person who has suffered loss, or injury, whether to his person, property or rights through the unlawful act or omission or negligence of another.
DECLARANT - A person who makes a statement.
DE FACTO - In fact; actually but without legal authority.
DE JURE - Of right; legitimate; lawful.
DE MINIMIS - Very small or trifling.
DE NOVO - Anew; afresh; a second time.
DEBT - A specified sum of money owing to one person from another, including not only the obligation of the debtor to pay, but the right of the creditor to receive and enforce payment.
DECEDENT - A dead person.
DECISION - A judgment or decree pronounced by a court in determination of a case.
DECREE - An order of the court, determining the rights of all parties to a suit.
DEED - A writing containing a contract sealed and delivered; particularly to convey real property.
DEFALCATION - Misappropriation of funds.
DEFAMATION - Injuring one's reputation by false statements.
DEFAULT - The failure to fulfill a duty, observe a promise, discharge an obligation, or perform an agreement.
DEFENDANT - The person defending or denying; the party against whom relief or recovery is sought in an action or suit.
DEFRAUD - To practice fraud; to cheat or trick.
DELEGATE (v.)- To entrust to the care or management of another.
DELICTUS - A crime.
DEMUR (v.) - To dispute the sufficiency in law of the pleading of the other side.

DEMURRAGE - In maritime law, it means, the sum fixed or allowed as remuneration to the owners of a ship for the detention of their vessel beyond the number of days allowed for loading and unloading or for sailing; also used in railroad terminology.
DENIAL - A form of pleading; refusing to admit the truth of a statement, charge, etc.
DEPONENT - One who gives testimony under oath reduced to writing.
DEPOSITION - Testimony given under oath outside of court for use in court or for the purpose of obtaining information in preparation for trial of a case.
DETERIORATION - A degeneration such as from decay, corrosion or disintegration.
DETRIMENT - Any loss or harm to person or property.
DEVIATION - A turning aside.
DEVISE - A gift of real property by the last will and testament of the donor.
DICTUM (sing.)
DICTA (plural) - Any statements made by the court in an opinion concerning some rule of law not necessarily involved nor essential to the determination of the case.
DIRECT EVIDENCE - Evidence that directly proves a fact, without an inference or presumption, and which in itself if true, conclusively establishes that fact.
DIRECT EXAMINATION - The first examination of a witness upon a matter that is not within the scope of a previous examination of the witness.
DISAFFIRM - To repudiate.
DISMISS - In an action or suit, it means to dispose of the case without any further consideration or hearing.
DISSENT - To denote disagreement of one or more judges of a court with the decision passed by the majority upon a case before them.
DOCKET (n.) - A formal record, entered in brief, of the proceedings in a court.
DOCTRINE - A rule, principle, theory of law.
DOMICILE - That place where a man has his true, fixed and permanent home to which whenever he is absent he has the intention of returning.
DRAFT (n.) - A commercial paper ordering payment of money drawn by one person on another.
DRAWEE - The person who is requested to pay the money.
DRAWER - The person who draws the commercial paper and addresses it to the drawee.
DUPLICATE - A counterpart produced by the same impression as the original enlargements and miniatures, or by mechanical or electronic re-recording, or by chemical reproduction, or by other equivalent technique which accurately reproduces the original.
DURESS - Use of force to compel performance or non-performance of an act.

E

EASEMENT - A liberty, privilege, or advantage without profit, in the lands of another.
EGRESS - Act or right of going out or leaving; emergence.
EIUSDEM GENERIS - Of the same kind, class or nature. A rule used in the construction of language in a legal document.
EMBEZZLEMENT - To steal; to appropriate fraudulently to one's own use property entrusted to one's care.
EMBRACERY - Unlawful attempt to influence jurors, etc., but not by offering value.
EMINENT DOMAIN - The right of a state to take private property for public use.
ENACT - To make into a law.
ENDORSEMENT - Act of writing one's name on the back of a note, bill or similar written instrument.

ENJOIN - To require a person, by writ of injunction from a court of equity, to perform or to abstain or desist from some act.
ENTIRETY - The whole; that which the law considers as one whole, and not capable of being divided into parts.
ENTRAPMENT - Inducing one to commit a crime so as to arrest him.
ENUMERATED - Mentioned specifically; designated.
ENURE - To operate or take effect.
EQUITY - In its broadest sense, this term denotes the spirit and the habit of fairness, justness, and right dealing which regulate the conduct of men.
ERROR - A mistake of law, or the false or irregular application of law as will nullify the judicial proceedings.
ESCROW - A deed, bond or other written engagement, delivered to a third person, to be delivered by him only upon the performance or fulfillment of some condition.
ESTATE - The interest which any one has in lands, or in any other subject of property.
ESTOP - To stop, bar, or impede.
ESTOPPEL - A rule of law which prevents a man from alleging or denying a fact, because of his own previous act.
ET AL. (alii) - And others.
ET SEQ. (sequential) - And the following.
ET UX. (uxor) - And wife.
EVIDENCE - Testimony, writings, material objects, or other things presented to the senses that are offered to prove the existence or non-existence of a fact.
   Means from which inferences may be drawn as a basis of proof in duly constituted judicial or fact finding tribunals, and includes testimony in the form of opinion and hearsay.
EX CONTRACTU
EX DELICTO - In law, rights and causes of action are divided into two classes, those arising *ex contractu* (from a contract) and those arising *ex delicto* (from a delict or tort).
EX OFFICIO - From office; by virtue of the office.
EX PARTE - On one side only; by or for one.
EX POST FACTO - After the fact.
EX POST FACTO LAW - A law passed after an act was done which retroactively makes such act a crime.
EX REL. (relations) - Upon relation or information.
EXCEPTION - An objection upon a matter of law to a decision made, either before or after judgment by a court.
EXECUTOR (male)
EXECUTRIX (female) - A person who has been appointed by will to execute the will.
EXECUTORY - That which is yet to be executed or performed.
EXEMPT - To release from some liability to which others are subject.
EXONERATION - The removal of a burden, charge or duty.
EXTRADITION - Surrender of a fugitive from one nation to another.

F

F.A.S.- "Free alongside ship"; delivery at dock for ship named.
F.O.B.- "Free on board"; seller will deliver to car, truck, vessel, or other conveyance by which goods are to be transported, without expense or risk of loss to the buyer or consignee.
FABRICATE - To construct; to invent a false story.
FACSIMILE - An exact or accurate copy of an original instrument.

FACTOR - A commercial agent.
FEASANCE - The doing of an act.
FELONIOUS - Criminal, malicious.
FELONY - Generally, a criminal offense that may be punished by death or imprisonment for more than one year as differentiated from a misdemeanor.
FEME SOLE - A single woman.
FIDUCIARY - A person who is invested with rights and powers to be exercised for the benefit of another person.
FIERI FACIAS - A writ of execution commanding the sheriff to levy and collect the amount of a judgment from the goods and chattels of the judgment debtor.
FINDING OF FACT - Determination from proof or judicial notice of the existence of a fact. A ruling implies a supporting finding of fact; no separate or formal finding is required unless required by a statute of this state.
FISCAL - Relating to accounts or the management of revenue.
FORECLOSURE (sale) - A sale of mortgaged property to obtain satisfaction of the mortgage out of the sale proceeds.
FORFEITURE - A penalty, a fine.
FORGERY - Fabricating or producing falsely, counterfeited.
FORTUITOUS - Accidental.
FORUM - A court of justice; a place of jurisdiction.
FRAUD - Deception; trickery.
FREEHOLDER - One who owns real property.
FUNGIBLE - Of such kind or nature that one specimen or part may be used in the place of another.

G

GARNISHEE - Person garnished.
GARNISHMENT - A legal process to reach the money or effects of a defendant, in the possession or control of a third person.
GRAND JURY - Not less than 16, not more than 23 citizens of a county sworn to inquire into crimes committed or triable in the county.
GRANT - To agree to; convey, especially real property.
GRANTEE - The person to whom a grant is made.
GRANTOR - The person by whom a grant is made.
GRATUITOUS - Given without a return, compensation or consideration.
GRAVAMEN - The grievance complained of or the substantial cause of a criminal action.
GUARANTY (n.) - A promise to answer for the payment of some debt, or the performance of some duty, in case of the failure of another person, who, in the first instance, is liable for such payment or performance.
GUARDIAN - The person, committee, or other representative authorized by law to protect the person or estate or both of an incompetent (or of a *sui juris* person having a guardian) and to act for him in matters affecting his person or property or both. An incompetent is a person under disability imposed by law.
GUILTY - Establishment of the fact that one has committed a breach of conduct; especially, a violation of law.

H

HABEAS CORPUS - You have the body; the name given to a variety of writs, having for their object to bring a party before a court or judge for decision as to whether such person is being lawfully held prisoner.
HABENDUM - In conveyancing; it is the clause in a deed conveying land which defines the extent of ownership to be held by the grantee.
HEARING - A proceeding whereby the arguments of the interested parties are heared.
HEARSAY - A type of testimony given by a witness who relates, not what he knows personally, but what others have told hi, or what he has heard said by others.
HEARSAY RULE, THE - (a) "Hearsay evidence" is evidence of a statement that was made other than by a witness while testifying at the hearing and that is offered to prove the truth of the matter stated; (b) Except as provided by law, hearsay evidence is inadmissible; (c) This section shall be known and may be cited as the hearsay rule.
HEIR - Generally, one who inherits property, real or personal.
HOLDER OF THE PRIVILEGE - (a) The client when he has no guardian or conservator; (b) A guardian or conservator of the client when the client has a guardian or conservator; (c) The personal representative of the client if the client is dead; (d) A successor, assign, trustee in dissolution, or any similar representative of a firm, association, organization, partnership, business trust, corporation, or public entity that is no longer in existence.
HUNG JURY - One so divided that they can't agree on a verdict.
HUSBAND-WIFE PRIVILEGE - An accused in a criminal proceeding has a privilege to prevent his spouse from testifying against him.
HYPOTHECATE - To pledge a thing without delivering it to the pledgee.
HYPOTHESIS - A supposition, assumption, or toehry.

I

I.E. (id est) - That is.
IB., OR IBID.(ibidem) - In the same place; used to refer to a legal reference previously cited to avoid repeating the entire citation.
ILLICIT - Prohibited; unlawful.
ILLUSORY - Deceiving by false appearance.
IMMUNITY - Exemption.
IMPEACH - To accuse, to dispute.
IMPEDIMENTS - Disabilities, or hindrances.
IMPLEAD - To sue or prosecute by due course of law.
IMPUTED - Attributed or charged to.
IN LOCO PARENTIS - In place of parent, a guardian.
IN TOTO - In the whole; completely.
INCHOATE - Imperfect; unfinished.
INCOMMUNICADO - Denial of the right of a prisoner to communicate with friends or relatives.
INCOMPETENT - One who is incapable of caring for his own affairs because he is mentally deficient or undeveloped.
INCRIMINATION - A matter will incriminate a person if it constitutes, or forms an essential part of, or, taken in connection with other matters disclosed, is a basis for a reasonable inference of such a violation of the laws of this State as to subject him to liability to punishment therefor, unless he has become for any reason permanently immune from punishment for such violation.
INCUMBRANCE - Generally a claim, lien, charge or liability attached to and binding real property.

INDEMNIFY - To secure against loss or damage; also, to make reimbursement to one for a loss already incurred by him.
INDEMNITY - An agreement to reimburse another person in case of an anticipated loss falling upon him.
INDICIA - Signs; indications.
INDICTMENT - An accusation in writing found and presented by a grand jury charging that a person has committed a crime.
INDORSE - To write a name on the back of a legal paper or document, generally, a negotiable instrument
INDUCEMENT - Cause or reason why a thing is done or that which incites the person to do the act or commit a crime; the motive for the criminal act.
INFANT - In civil cases one under 21 years of age.
INFORMATION - A formal accusation of crime made by a prosecuting attorney.
INFRA - Below, under; this word occurring by itself in a publication refers the reader to a future part of the publication.
INGRESS - The act of going into.
INJUNCTION - A writ or order by the court requiring a person, generally, to do or to refrain from doing an act.
INSOLVENT - The condition of a person who is unable to pay his debts.
INSTRUCTION - A direction given by the judge to the jury concerning the law of the case.
INTERIM - In the meantime; time intervening.
INTERLOCUTORY - Temporary, not final; something intervening between the commencement and the end of a suit which decides some point or matter, but is not a final decision of the whole controversy.
INTERROGATORIES - A series of formal written questions used in the examination of a party or a witness usually prior to a trial.
INTESTATE - A person who dies without a will.
INURE - To result, to take effect.
IPSO FACTO - By the fact iself; by the mere fact.
ISSUE (n.) The disputed point or question in a case,

J

JEOPARDY - Danger, hazard, peril.
JOINDER - Joining; uniting with another person in some legal steps or proceeding.
JOINT - United; combined.
JUDGE - Member or members or representative or representatives of a court conducting a trial or hearing at which evidence is introduced.
JUDGMENT - The official decision of a court of justice.
JUDICIAL OR JUDICIARY - Relating to or connected with the administration of justice.
JURAT - The clause written at the foot of an affidavit, stating when, where and before whom such affidavit was sworn.
JURISDICTION - The authority to hear and determine controversies between parties.
JURISPRUDENCE - The philosophy of law.
JURY - A body of persons legally selected to inquire into any matter of fact, and to render their verdict according to the evidence.

L

LACHES - The failure to diligently assert a right, which results in a refusal to allow relief.

LANDLORD AND TENANT - A phrase used to denote the legal relation existing between the owner and occupant of real estate.
LARCENY - Stealing personal property belonging to another.
LATENT - Hidden; that which does not appear on the face of a thing.
LAW - Includes constitutional, statutory, and decisional law.
LAWYER-CLIENT PRIVILEGE - (1) A "client" is a person, public officer, or corporation, association, or other organization or entity, either public or private, who is rendered professional legal services by a lawyer, or who consults a lawyer with a view to obtaining professional legal services from him; (2) A "lawyer" is a person authorized, or reasonably believed by the client to be authorized, to practice law in any state or nation; (3) A "representative of the lawyer" is one employed to assist the lawyer in the rendition of professional legal services; (4) A communication is "confidential" if not intended to be disclosed to third persons other than those to whom disclosure is in furtherance of the rendition of professional legal services to the client or those reasonably necessary for the transmission of the communication.

General rule of privilege - A client has a privilege to refuse to disclose and to prevent any other person from disclosing confidential communications made for the purpose of facilitating the rendition of professional legal services to the client, (1) between himself or his representative and his lawyer or his lawyer's representative, or (2) between his lawyer and the lawyer's representative, or (3) by him or his lawyer to a lawyer representing another in a matter of common interest, or (4) between representatives of the client or between the client and a representative of the client, or (5) between lawyers representing the client.
LEADING QUESTION - Question that suggests to the witness the answer that the examining party desires.
LEASE - A contract by which one conveys real estate for a limited time usually for a specified rent; personal property also may be leased.
LEGISLATION - The act of enacting laws.
LEGITIMATE - Lawful.
LESSEE - One to whom a lease is given.
LESSOR - One who grants a lease
LEVY - A collecting or exacting by authority.
LIABLE - Responsible; bound or obligated in law or equity.
LIBEL (v.) - To defame or injure a person's reputation by a published writing.
    (n.) - The initial pleading on the part of the plaintiff in an admiralty proceeding.
LIEN - A hold or claim which one person has upon the property of another as a security for some debt or charge.
LIQUIDATED - Fixed; settled.
LIS PENDENS - A pending civil or criminal action.
LITERAL - According to the language.
LITIGANT - A party to a lawsuit.
LITATION - A judicial controversy.
LOCUS - A place.
LOCUS DELICTI - Place of the crime.
LOCUS POENITENTIAE - The abandoning or giving up of one's intention to commit some crime before it is fully completed or abandoning a conspiracy before its purpose is accomplished.

M

MALFEASANCE - To do a wrongful act.
MALICE - The doing of a wrongful act Intentionally without just cause or excuse.

MANDAMUS - The name of a writ issued by a court to enforce the performance of some public duty.
MANDATORY (adj.) Containing a command.
MARITIME - Pertaining to the sea or to commerce thereon.
MARSHALING - Arranging or disposing of in order.
MAXIM - An established principle or proposition.
MINISTERIAL - That which involves obedience to instruction, but demands no special discretion, judgment or skill.
MISAPPROPRIATE - Dealing fraudulently with property entrusted to one.
MISDEMEANOR - A crime less than a felony and punishable by a fine or imprisonment for less than one year.
MISFEASANCE - Improper performance of a lawful act.
MISREPRESENTATION - An untrue representation of facts.
MITIGATE - To make or become less severe, harsh.
MITTIMUS - A warrant of commitment to prison.
MOOT (adj.) Unsettled, undecided, not necessary to be decided.
MORTGAGE - A conveyance of property upon condition, as security for the payment of a debt or the performance of a duty, and to become void upon payment or performance according to the stipulated terms.
MORTGAGEE - A person to whom property is mortgaged.
MORTGAGOR - One who gives a mortgage.
MOTION - In legal proceedings, a "motion" is an application, either written or oral, addressed to the court by a party to an action or a suit requesting the ruling of the court on a matter of law.
MUTUALITY - Reciprocation.

N

NEGLIGENCE - The failure to exercise that degree of care which an ordinarily prudent person would exercise under like circumstances.
NEGOTIABLE (instrument) - Any instrument obligating the payment of money which is transferable from one person to another by endorsement and delivery or by delivery only.
NEGOTIATE - To transact business; to transfer a negotiable instrument; to seek agreement for the amicable disposition of a controversy or case.
NOLLE PROSEQUI - A formal entry upon the record, by the plaintiff in a civil suit or the prosecuting officer in a criminal action, by which he declares that he "will no further prosecute" the case.
NOLO CONTENDERE - The name of a plea in a criminal action, having the same effect as a plea of guilty; but not constituting a direct admission of guilt.
NOMINAL - Not real or substantial.
NOMINAL DAMAGES - Award of a trifling sum where no substantial injury is proved to have been sustained.
NONFEASANCE - Neglect of duty.
NOVATION - The substitution of a new debt or obligation for an existing one.
NUNC PRO TUNC - A phrase applied to acts allowed to be done after the time when they should be done, with a retroactive effect.("Now for then.")

O

OATH - Oath includes affirmation or declaration under penalty of perjury.
OBITER DICTUM - Opinion expressed by a court on a matter not essentially involved in a case and hence not a decision; also called dicta, if plural.

OBJECT (v.) - To oppose as improper or illegal and referring the question of its propriety or legality to the court.
OBLIGATION - A legal duty, by which a person is bound to do or not to do a certain thing.
OBLIGEE - The person to whom an obligation is owed.
OBLIGOR - The person who is to perform the obligation.
OFFER (v.) - To present for acceptance or rejection.
    (n.) - A proposal to do a thing, usually a proposal to make a contract.
OFFICIAL INFORMATION - Information within the custody or control of a department or agency of the government the disclosure of which is shown to be contrary to the public interest.
OFFSET - A deduction.
ONUS PROBANDI - Burden of proof.
OPINION - The statement by a judge of the decision reached in a case, giving the law as applied to the case and giving reasons for the judgment; also a belief or view.
OPTION - The exercise of the power of choice; also a privilege existing in one person, for which he has paid money, which gives him the right to buy or sell real or personal property at a given price within a specified time.
ORDER - A rule or regulation; every direction of a court or judge made or entered in writing but not including a judgment.
ORDINANCE - Generally, a rule established by authority; also commonly used to designate the legislative acts of a municipal corporation.
ORIGINAL - Writing or recording itself or any counterpart intended to have the same effect by a person executing or issuing it. An "original" of a photograph includes the negative or any print therefrom. If data are stored in a computer or similar device, any printout or other output readable by sight, shown to reflect the data accurately, is an "original."
OVERT - Open, manifest.

P

PANEL - A group of jurors selected to serve during a term of the court.
PARENS PATRIAE - Sovereign power of a state to protect or be a guardian over children and incompetents.
PAROL - Oral or verbal.
PAROLE - To release one in prison before the expiration of his sentence, conditionally.
PARITY - Equality in purchasing power between the farmer and other segments of the economy.
PARTITION - A legal division of real or personal property between one or more owners.
PARTNERSHIP - An association of two or more persons to carry on as co-owners a business for profit.
PATENT (adj.) - Evident.
    (n.) - A grant of some privilege, property, or authority, made by the government or sovereign of a country to one or more individuals.
PECULATION - Stealing.
PECUNIARY - Monetary.
PENULTIMATE - Next to the last.
PER CURIAM - A phrase used in the report of a decision to distinguish an opinion of the whole court from an opinion written by any one judge.
PER SE - In itself; taken alone.
PERCEIVE - To acquire knowledge through one's senses.
PEREMPTORY - Imperative; absolute.
PERJURY - To lie or state falsely under oath.

PERPETUITY - Perpetual existence; also the quality or condition of an estate limited so that it will not take effect or vest within the period fixed by law.
PERSON - Includes a natural person, firm, association, organization, partnership, business trust, corporation, or public entity.
PERSONAL PROPERTY - Includes money, goods, chattels, things in action, and evidences of debt.
PERSONALTY - Short term for personal property.
PETITION - An application in writing for an order of the court, stating the circumstances upon which it is founded and requesting any order or other relief from a court.
PLAINTIFF - A person who brings a court action.
PLEA - A pleading in a suit or action.
PLEADINGS - Formal allegations made by the parties of their respective claims and defenses, for the judgment of the court.
PLEDGE - A deposit of personal property as a security for the performance of an act.
PLEDGEE - The party to whom goods are delivered in pledge.
PLEDGOR - The party delivering goods in pledge.
PLENARY - Full; complete.
POLICE POWER - Inherent power of the state or its political subdivisions to enact laws within constitutional limits to promote the general welfare of society or the community.
POLLING THE JURY - Call the names of persons on a jury and requiring each juror to declare what his verdict is before it is legally recorded.
POST MORTEM - After death.
POWER OF ATTORNEY - A writing authorizing one to act for another.
PRECEPT - An order, warrant, or writ issued to an officer or body of officers, commanding him or them to do some act within the scope of his or their powers.
PRELIMINARY FACT - Fact upon the existence or nonexistence of which depends the admissibility or inadmissibility of evidence. The phrase "the admissibility or inadmissibility of evidence" includes the qualification or disqualification of a person to be a witness and the existence or nonexistence of a privilege.
PREPONDERANCE - Outweighing.
PRESENTMENT - A report by a grand jury on something they have investigated on their own knowledge.
PRESUMPTION - An assumption of fact resulting from a rule of law which requires such fact to be assumed from another fact or group of facts found or otherwise established in the action.
PRIMA FACUE - At first sight.
PRIMA FACIE CASE - A case where the evidence is very patent against the defendant.
PRINCIPAL - The source of authority or rights; a person primarily liable as differentiated from "principle" as a primary or basic doctrine.
PRO AND CON - For and against.
PRO RATA - Proportionally.
PROBATE - Relating to proof, especially to the proof of wills.
PROBATIVE - Tending to prove.
PROCEDURE - In law, this term generally denotes rules which are established by the Federal, State, or local Governments regarding the types of pleading and courtroom practice which must be followed by the parties involved in a criminal or civil case.
PROCLAMATION - A public notice by an official of some order, intended action, or state of facts.

PROFFERED EVIDENCE - The admissibility or inadmissibility of which is dependent upon the existence or nonexistence of a preliminary fact.
PROMISSORY (NOTE) - A promise in writing to pay a specified sum at an expressed time, or on demand, or at sight, to a named person, or to his order, or bearer.
PROOF - The establishment by evidence of a requisite degree of belief concerning a fact in the mind of the trier of fact or the court.
PROPERTY - Includes both real and personal property.
PROPRIETARY (adj.) - Relating or pertaining to ownership; usually a single owner.
PROSECUTE - To carry on an action or other judicial proceeding; to proceed against a person criminally.
PROVISO - A limitation or condition in a legal instrument.
PROXIMATE - Immediate; nearest
PUBLIC EMPLOYEE - An officer, agent, or employee of a public entity.
PUBLIC ENTITY - Includes a national, state, county, city and county, city, district, public authority, public agency, or any other political subdivision or public corporation, whether foreign or domestic.
PUBLIC OFFICIAL - Includes an official of a political dubdivision of such state or territory and of a municipality.
PUNITIVE - Relating to punishment.

Q

QUASH - To make void.
QUASI - As if; as it were.
QUID PRO QUO - Something for something; the giving of one valuable thing for another.
QUITCLAIM (v.) - To release or relinquish claim or title to, especially in deeds to realty.
QUO WARRANTO - A legal procedure to test an official's right to a public office or the right to hold a franchise, or to hold an office in a domestic corporation.

R

RATIFY - To approve and sanction.
REAL PROPERTY - Includes lands, tenements, and hereditaments.
REALTY - A brief term for real property.
REBUT - To contradict; to refute, especially by evidence and arguments.
RECEIVER - A person who is appointed by the court to receive, and hold in trust property in litigation.
RECIDIVIST - Habitual criminal.
RECIPROCAL - Mutual.
RECOUPMENT - To keep back or get something which is due; also, it is the right of a defendant to have a deduction from the amount of the plaintiff's damages because the plaintiff has not fulfilled his part of the same contract.
RECROSS EXAMINATION - Examination of a witness by a cross-examiner subsequent to a redirect examination of the witness.
REDEEM - To release an estate or article from mortgage or pledge by paying the debt for which it stood as security.
REDIRECT EXAMINATION - Examination of a witness by the direct examiner subsequent to the cross-examination of the witness.
REFEREE - A person to whom a cause pending in a court is referred by the court, to take testimony, hear the parties, and report thereon to the court.

REFERENDUM - A method of submitting an important legislative or administrative matter to a direct vote of the people.
RELEVANT EVIDENCE - Evidence including evidence relevant to the credulity of a witness or hearsay declarant, having any tendency in reason to prove or disprove any disputed fact that is of consequence to the determination of the action.
REMAND - To send a case back to the lower court from which it came, for further proceedings.
REPLEVIN - An action to recover goods or chattels wrongfully taken or detained.
REPLY (REPLICATION) - Generally, a reply is what the plaintiff or other person who has instituted proceedings says in answer to the defendant's case.
RE JUDICATA - A thing judicially acted upon or decided.
RES ADJUDICATA - Doctrine that an issue or dispute litigated and determined in a case between the opposing parties is deemed permanently decided between these parties.
RESCIND (RECISSION) - To avoid or cancel a contract.
RESPONDENT - A defendant in a proceeding in chancery or admiralty; also, the person who contends against the appeal in a case.
RESTITUTION - In equity, it is the restoration of both parties to their original condition (when practicable), upon the rescission of a contract for fraud or similar cause.
RETROACTIVE (RETROSPECTIVE) - Looking back; effective as of a prior time.
REVERSED - A term used by appellate courts to indicate that the decision of the lower court in the case before it has been set aside.
REVOKE - To recall or cancel.
RIPARIAN (RIGHTS) - The rights of a person owning land containing or bordering on a water course or other body of water, such as lakes and rivers.

S

SALE - A contract whereby the ownership of property is transferred from one person to another for a sum of money or for any consideration.
SANCTION - A penalty or punishment provided as a means of enforcing obedience to a law; also, an authorization.
SATISFACTION - The discharge of an obligation by paying a party what is due to him; or what is awarded to him by the judgment of a court or otherwise.
SCIENTER - Knowingly; also, it is used in pleading to denote the defendant's guilty knowledge.
SCINTILLA - A spark; also the least particle.
SECRET OF STATE - Governmental secret relating to the national defense or the international relations of the United States.
SECURITY - Indemnification; the term is applied to an obligation, such as a mortgage or deed of trust, given by a debtor to insure the payment or performance of his debt, by furnishing the creditor with a resource to be used in case of the debtor's failure to fulfill the principal obligation.
SENTENCE - The judgment formally pronounced by the court or judge upon the defendant after his conviction in a criminal prosecution.
SET-OFF - A claim or demand which one party in an action credits against the claim of the opposing party.
SHALL and MAY - "Shall" is mandatory and "may" is permissive.
SITUS - Location.
SOVEREIGN - A person, body or state in which independent and supreme authority is vested.
STARE DECISIS - To follow decided cases.

STATE - "State" means this State, unless applied to the different parts of the United States. In the latter case, it includes any state, district, commonwealth, territory or insular possession of the United States, including the District of Columbia.

STATEMENT - (a) Oral or written verbal expression or (b) nonverbal conduct of a person intended by him as a substitute for oral or written verbal expression.

STATUTE - An act of the legislature. Includes a treaty.

STATUTE OF LIMITATION - A statute limiting the time to bring an action after the right of action has arisen.

STAY - To hold in abeyance an order of a court.

STIPULATION - Any agreement made by opposing attorneys regulating any matter incidental to the proceedings or trial.

SUBORDINATION (AGREEMENT) - An agreement making one's rights inferior to or of a lower rank than another's.

SUBORNATION - The crime of procuring a person to lie or to make false statements to a court.

SUBPOENA - A writ or order directed to a person, and requiring his attendance at a particular time and place to testify as a witness.

SUBPOENA DUCES TECUM - A subpoena used, not only for the purpose of compelling witnesses to attend in court, but also requiring them to bring with them books or documents which may be in their possession, and which may tend to elucidate the subject matter of the trial.

SUBROGATION - The substituting of one for another as a creditor, the new creditor succeeding to the former's rights.

SUBSIDY - A government grant to assist a private enterprise deemed advantageous to the public.

SUI GENERIS - Of the same kind.

SUIT - Any civil proceeding by a person or persons against another or others in a court of justice by which the plaintiff pursues the remedies afforded him by law.

SUMMONS - A notice to a defendant that an action against him has been commenced and requiring him to appear in court and answer the complaint.

SUPRA - Above; this word occurring by itself in a book refers the reader to a previous part of the book.

SURETY - A person who binds himself for the payment of a sum of money, or for the performance of something else, for another.

SURPLUSAGE - Extraneous or unnecessary matter.

SURVIVORSHIP - A term used when a person becomes entitled to property by reason of his having survived another person who had an interest in the property.

SUSPEND SENTENCE - Hold back a sentence pending good behavior of prisoner.

SYLLABUS - A note prefixed to a report, especially a case, giving a brief statement of the court's ruling on different issues of the case.

T

TALESMAN - Person summoned to fill a panel of jurors.

TENANT - One who holds or possesses lands by any kind of right or title; also, one who has the temporary use and occupation of real property owned by another person (landlord), the duration and terms of his tenancy being usually fixed by an instrument called "a lease."

TENDER - An offer of money; an expression of willingness to perform a contract according to its terms.

TERM - When used with reference to a court, it signifies the period of time during which the court holds a session, usually of several weeks or months duration.

TESTAMENTARY - Pertaining to a will or the administration of a will.
TESTATOR (male)
TESTATRIX (female) - One who makes or has made a testament or will.
TESTIFY (TESTIMONY) - To give evidence under oath as a witness.
TO WIT - That is to say; namely.
TORT - Wrong; injury to the person.
TRANSITORY - Passing from place to place.
TRESPASS - Entry into another's ground, illegally.
TRIAL - The examination of a cause, civil or criminal, before a judge who has jurisdiction over it, according to the laws of the land.
TRIER OF FACT - Includes (a) the jury and (b) the court when the court is trying an issue of fact other than one relating to the admissibility of evidence.
TRUST - A right of property, real or personal, held by one party for the benefit of another.
TRUSTEE - One who lawfully holds property in custody for the benefit of another.

U

UNAVAILABLE AS A WITNESS - The declarant is (1) Exempted or precluded on the ground of privilege from testifying concerning the matter to which his statement is relevant; (2) Disqualified from testifying to the matter; (3) Dead or unable to attend or to testify at the hearing because of then existing physical or mental illness or infirmity; (4) Absent from the hearing and the court is unable to compel his attendance by its process; or (5) Absent from the hearing and the proponent of his statement has exercised reasonable diligence but has been unable to procure his attendance by the court's process.
ULTRA VIRES - Acts beyond the scope and power of a corporation, association, etc.
UNILATERAL - One-sided; obligation upon, or act of one party.
USURY - Unlawful interest on a loan.

V

VACATE - To set aside; to move out.
VARIANCE - A discrepancy or disagreement between two instruments or two aspects of the same case, which by law should be consistent.
VENDEE - A purchaser or buyer.
VENDOR - The person who transfers property by sale, particularly real estate; the term "seller" is used more commonly for one who sells personal property.
VENIREMEN - Persons ordered to appear to serve on a jury or composing a panel of jurors.
VENUE - The place at which an action is tried, generally based on locality or judicial district in which an injury occurred or a material fact happened.
VERDICT - The formal decision or finding of a jury.
VERIFY - To confirm or substantiate by oath.
VEST - To accrue to.
VOID - Having no legal force or binding effect.
VOIR DIRE - Preliminary examination of a witness or a juror to test competence, interest, prejudice, etc.

W

WAIVE - To give up a right.
WAIVER - The intentional or voluntary relinquishment of a known right.
WARRANT (WARRANTY) (v.) - To promise that a certain fact or state of facts, in relation to the subject matter, is, or shall be, as it is represented to be.

WARRANT (n.) - A writ issued by a judge, or other competent authority, addressed to a sheriff, or other officer, requiring him to arrest the person therein named, and bring him before the judge or court to answer or be examined regarding the offense with which he is charged.

WRIT - An order or process issued in the name of the sovereign or in the name of a court or judicial officer, commanding the performance or nonperformance of some act.

WRITING - Handwriting, typewriting, printing, photostating, photographing and every other means of recording upon any tangible thing any form of communication or representation, including letters, words, pictures, sounds, or symbols, or combinations thereof.

WRITINGS AND RECORDINGS - Consists of letters, words, or numbers, or their equivalent, set down by handwriting, typewriting, printing, photostating, photographing, magnetic impulse, mechanical or electronic recording, or other form of data compilation.

Y

YEA AND NAY - Yes and no.

YELLOW DOG CONTRACT - A contract by which employer requires employee to sign an instrument promising as condition that he will not join a union during its continuance, and will be discharged if he does join.

Z

ZONING - The division of a city by legislative regulation into districts and the prescription and application in each district of regulations having to do with structural and architectural designs of buildings and of regulations prescribing use to which buildings within designated districts may be put.

Printed in the USA
CPSIA information can be obtained
at www.ICGtesting.com
CBHW080606070924
14234CB00014B/680

9 781799 349785